D0071792

What's Wrong with Me?

The Frustrated Patient's Guide to Getting an Accurate Diagnosis

LYNN M. DANNHEISSER

AND

JERRY M. ROSENBAUM, M.D.

610.696
D 188

LIBRARY
MILWAUKEE AREA
TECHNICAL COLLEGE
NORTH CAMPUS
5555 W. Highland Road
Mequon, WI 53092

McGraw·Hill

New York   Chicago   San Francisco   Lisbon   London   Madrid   Mexico City
Milan   New Delhi   San Juan   Seoul   Singapore   Sydney   Toronto

The McGraw·Hill Companies

Library of Congress Cataloging-in-Publication Data

Dannheisser, Lynn M.
    What's wrong with me? : the frustrated patient's guide to getting an accurate
diagnosis / Lynn M. Dannheisser, Jerry M. Rosenbaum.—1st ed.
        p.   cm.
    Includes bibliographical references and index.
    ISBN 0-07-143506-9
        1. Medicine, Popular.   2. Medical personnel and patient.   3. Self-care,
Health.   I. Rosenbaum, Jerry M.   II. Title.

    RC81.D25   2005
    610.69′6—dc22   2004029983

Copyright © 2005 by Lynn Dannheisser and Jerry Rosenbaum. All rights reserved. Printed
in the United States of America. Except as permitted under the United States Copyright Act
of 1976, no part of this publication may be reproduced or distributed in any form or by any
means, or stored in a database or retrieval system, without the prior written permission of
the publisher.

1 2 3 4 5 6 7 8 9 0   FGR/FGR   0 9 8 7 6 5

ISBN 0-07-143506-9

McGraw-Hill books are available at special quantity discounts to use as premiums and
sales promotions, or for use in corporate training programs. For more information, please
write to the Director of Special Sales, Professional Publishing, McGraw-Hill, Two Penn
Plaza, New York, NY 10121-2298. Or contact your local bookstore.

This book is printed on acid-free paper.

Contents

Part 1 Becoming Your Own Medical Detective

Part 2 Diagnosing Your Mystery Malady

Part 3 Living with Your Mystery Malady

Acknowledgments

I HAVE ALWAYS felt a deep sense of gratitude to the many teachers and healers who have been sent into my life—especially Twila Grandchamp; Marlene Potter; Marsha Cohen; Rene Geada, M.D.; Diana Lee; Chesterfield Smith; Sister Jean; and Shirley B., wherever you are. My medical healers are individually and collectively acknowledged in Chapter 8 (except Philip R. Glade, M.D., who began my medical healing many years ago and taught me so much about both medicine and patient empowerment). However, I want to specifically acknowledge my coauthor, Jerry Rosenbaum, M.D., who was and continues to be one of the best doctors I know and the embodiment of the practice of medicine as both an art and a science. I can't thank all of you enough.

With respect to this book, special thanks go to our agent, Natasha Kern, who "got it" from the moment she saw the proposal and was precisely the right agent for this project. Many thanks are also due to the editor she recommended, Laura Conner, who taught me how to make this a better book and worked me to the bone! I also want to acknowledge Barbara Nichols, our first editor, without whom this book would have never gotten off the ground in the early days. And of course, thanks to Michele Pezzuti, our delightful editor at McGraw-Hill, for her good humor, support, and assistance throughout the process.

On a personal note, I am indebted to a man who does not like public acknowledgment but who has shown me a love so heavenly it could shush the stars and has provided unwavering patience, support, and faith in my abilities to heal and to write. And finally, my love and gratitude to the perennial keepers of my heart, my children: Matthew Reininger, my absolute soul child, and Samantha Reininger, who, as she frequently reminds me, "made me who I am today."

—LYNN M. DANNHEISSER

First, I am indebted to Lynn Dannheisser, my coauthor, who had the inspiration for this book and put her heart and soul into it. I am in awe of her skill with words. She has worked long, hard, and selflessly in the pursuit of recognition and support for sufferers of undiagnosed conditions.

Second, I am indebted to Dr. Warren Katz of Philadelphia, my mentor and role model, who taught me what caring for patients is all about. He was and continues to be a paragon of good medicine and good doctoring.

I wish to thank my wife, Barbara, who makes my life complete. Barbara is my partner in marriage, business, and life. Without her, I would be lost. To my children, Erica, Debra, and Josh: you remain my greatest source of pride and inspiration.

I wish to thank my mother, Ruth, for her endless bounty of love and support, and my siblings, Bonny, Fredda, and Sandy Wax, for always being there.

Lastly, I wish to thank all the mystery malady sufferers who have led me to a better understanding of their plight by sharing their lives and stories with me, both as patients and as friends. This book is about them and for them and for all others like them who struggle to cope with illness and adversity. Health is a gift never to be taken for granted.

—Jerry M. Rosenbaum, M.D.

Introduction

IF YOU OR someone you love has a disease that the doctors can't cure, a recurring condition that can't be diagnosed, or a medical problem that has meant seeing one specialist after another without finding any relief, this book is for you.

• Perhaps you have pain in your back, muscles, or joints for which you have undergone every available medical test and procedure to no avail.

• Maybe you've seen several doctors and have had a number of tests or procedures only to be given an incorrect diagnosis, a contradictory diagnosis, or worse still, no diagnosis at all.

• Possibly your doctor, family, or friends think that your illness is psychosomatic and have told you, "It's all in your head and you should see a therapist." Yet you know intuitively that there is something truly wrong with your body. Their comments have frustrated or even angered you, and as a result you are feeling lonely, isolated, or depressed.

If you have an undiagnosed or a misdiagnosed illness, you are not alone. Millions of patients suffer from mysterious symptoms and cannot obtain a correct diagnosis or relief. If you or someone you love is unable to find solutions from the medical establishment, you'll find hope and help in this book.

I have been a practicing lawyer for more than twenty-five years, a writer, and a mother. I know firsthand the frustration of living with doubt, the endless search for answers, and the disruption that can result from having symptoms that physicians can't diagnose. From time to time, I have had conditions that defied diagnosis. Most recently, I had a neuropathic condition of seven years' duration which, until last year, caused chronic urinary tract infections and unrelenting pain. Even now, though the infections are gone and my pain has lessened, I still cannot sit for any great length of time without some discomfort. (Imagine practicing law and writing this book having to stand rather than sit!)

After years without a correct diagnosis, I did my own "medical detective" work and used the Eight Steps to Self-Diagnosis to find a diagnosis and secure significant relief. I share the details of my personal story in Chapter 8.

When I first discussed my symptoms with my friend Jerry Rosenbaum, M.D., a board-certified rheumatologist, I described my condition as a "mystery malady." He liked the term, and it has stuck.

As a highly regarded physician and diagnostician with more than twenty-six years of medical experience, Dr. Rosenbaum has seen, and often helped, thousands of patients with such conditions. Even though he is a doctor, he too has suffered his share of mystery maladies. In fact, before we started writing this book, he was struck with a new one: an eye disease that ranking specialists in the nation have been unable to accurately diagnose or cure. You'll find Dr. Rosenbaum's personal story in Chapter 16.

Plato once said, "Good doctors themselves ought to have the diseases they want to cure, and been subject themselves to the misfortunes and circumstances they have to diagnose. Let them catch the pox, if they want to know how to cure it. Then, and only then, I'd trust such a doctor." We are fortunate to have such a physician in Dr. Rosenbaum.

What's Wrong with Me? The Frustrated Patient's Guide to Getting an Accurate Diagnosis represents the culmination of our personal experiences in learning to become "medical detectives" from the perspective of both patient and physician. Using my deductive reasoning abilities as an attorney and Dr. Rosenbaum's clinical skills and medical knowledge, we have developed this revolutionary self-diagnosis model that has helped not only us but many others as well. The real beauty of this model is that it so simple to learn. You don't have to be a doctor. *Anyone* can use it.

Our intention is to help others help themselves, just as we have done. We offer information and ideas to stimulate new ways of thinking about undiagnosed and misdiagnosed ailments. And given the current state of health care and its diagnostic crisis, we believe that patients *must* assume responsibility for their own health.

In Part 1, we will show you how to approach your condition much like any other mystery you are trying to solve and invite you to become your own "medical detective." We'll guide you through the simple, easy-to-use Eight Steps to Self-Diagnosis and show you how to develop your own clues and follow them to a correct diagnosis.

We'll also show you how to choose the right physicians and generate the most effective ways to communicate with them to obtain the maximum cooperation. This is particularly important if your symptoms cross over several areas of medical specialization, because physicians tend to focus exclusively on their own area while the patient as a "whole" is often not addressed. We'll also give you some do's and don'ts of using the Internet for doing medical research. This is a program designed for getting to the bottom of what's wrong with you.

In Part 2, you will have an opportunity to apply what you have learned about medical detective work. Case studies of real patients (men, women, and children) involving a wide array of frequently undiagnosed and misdiagnosed conditions are presented. Each story contains all the "clues" you need to work out a diagnosis and illustrates how the Eight Steps were used to get to a diagnosis. We hope that by observing the diagnostic process you will be able to apply what you've learned to your own condition. We intend to make you a real medical detective and enlist the aid of your physician in this goal.

In Part 3, we share practical advice for living with a mystery illness. We offer suggestions for improving your emotional and physical health until a diagnosis and cure is found, including information on chronic pain and the stresses that accompany it. We will also look at many ways to take care of yourself and your relationships and emphasize that "health" is a much broader concept than the absence of physical disease. We offer supportive guidance and ideas on how to find health in your mind and spirit.

The advice we give is intended to enhance your relationship with your physicians, not to replace it. But there is no reason you cannot solve your own mystery malady with a physician's assistance. I did, and we know you can too! We are right beside you.

Authors' Note

THE INFORMATION CONTAINED in this book is meant to help you identify the cause of your mystery malady and put you on a path to finding solutions because your doctor has been unable to do so up to this point. However, this book is not intended to replace your physician; it is designed to be used in partnership with him or her (or them). So even if you believe you have found your diagnosis, by working through these steps and following the advice in this book, you must confirm that diagnosis with your doctor. We strongly urge you not to act on any information you have uncovered *without* first obtaining a physician's advice.

Part 1

BECOMING YOUR OWN MEDICAL DETECTIVE

I

The Diagnosis Dilemma

As long as diagnosis is in doubt, cause and treatment are guesswork.
—MELVIN GRAY, M.D.

MODERN MEDICINE HAS extended our life span and protects us from the epidemics that once wiped out millions of people. High-tech medical facilities dot the national landscape, billions of dollars are spent on research, and the constant advances in diagnostic equipment and testing continue to reveal hidden secrets of the human body. Our doctors are trained in medical schools that are indisputably the best in the world.

To some of you, the idea that doctors can make diagnostic mistakes when they have all this research and technology at their disposal may be inconceivable. Perhaps like millions of Americans you believe that you're getting good medical care from your own physician, and we would generally agree. But if you are reading this book, chances are you or someone you love is suffering from unexplained medical symptoms.

So if you think doctors can accurately diagnose every patient each time one walks into their offices, think again. We are about to share some tragic stories and startling statistics in this chapter. They are not meant to scare you. Rather, we hope that once you understand the extent of the diagnosis dilemma facing doctors and patients today, you will be encouraged to take charge of your health and become more proactive in your search for the correct diagnosis and treatment.

In her book, *Cancer Schmancer*, television star Fran Drescher writes about her frustrating two-year search for a diagnosis that took her to eight physicians, all of them highly reputable. They gave her erroneous diagnoses and failed to check her for cancer because she did not "fit the profile." It was only through her own persistence that she finally received the correct diagnosis and treatment.

Unfortunately, this celebrity case is not a rare or isolated instance. Consider the case of Laverne, an older, intelligent, and highly respected nurse. She visited the doctors at her health maintenance organization (HMO) repeatedly for more than a year with symptoms that made her concerned about the possibility of cancer. She shared her "intuitions" that something was wrong, but her doctors didn't think any special testing was indicated, so her HMO wouldn't pay for it. The fact that her own medical colleagues didn't take her seriously caused tremendous psychological distress.

Laverne, like so many undiagnosed patients, succumbed to the belief that it must be "all in her head." It was only when she reached the advanced stages of her cancer that her doctors finally realized their mistake. By then it was too late; Laverne passed away within months. The local nursing community mourned her death both as a personal tragedy and as a failure of the medical system they all worked for.

If you're still not convinced about how often these kinds of tragedies can happen, consider the shocking findings from an article in the *Journal of the American Medical Association* (*JAMA*). A study of autopsy reports covering a ten-year period found that doctors failed to diagnose serious cases of cancer in *one of every ten patients*. In half of these cases, the untreated cancer caused the patient's death.

Unfortunately, the huge margin of diagnostic error in medicine is not limited to cancer. Research studies, for example, reveal that at least a quarter of a million deaths are medically induced every year; that is, four times as many people die from misdiagnosis and other medical mishaps than died in the entire Vietnam War.

The Critical Proportions of the Diagnosis Dilemma

A survey conducted by the Harvard School of Public Health and the Henry J. Kaiser Foundation examined the views of eight hundred American doctors and twelve hundred adult patients. Fully 35 percent of the physicians said that either they or members of their family had experienced medical errors in the course of being treated. Most said the errors had "serious consequences" such as death, long-term disability, or severe pain. Three in ten of these doctors had seen an error that caused serious harm to patients (outside of their families) within the past year.[1]

A recent study published in *Chest*, the journal of the American College of Chest Physicians, showed that one out of every five patients who died in medical intensive care units (ICUs) was misdiagnosed. An accurate diagnosis would have resulted in different treatment that might have saved patients' lives. This study was conducted at the prestigious Cleveland Clinic Foundation in Ohio, whose state-of-the-art diagnostic facilities are considered among the best in the world. Other research indicates that this misdiagnosis rate is typical of ICUs nationwide.

In another *JAMA* issue, the largest study ever conducted on peripheral artery disease (which is believed to affect eight to ten million Americans and Western Europeans) revealed that almost 30 percent of people with this condition are undiagnosed, underdiagnosed, or undertreated.

In a random study of medical practices conducted by two HMOs, 14 percent of patients labeled with hypertension (high blood pressure) did not have this condition. Other error rates were 44 percent for coronary artery disease, 50 percent for congestive heart failure, and 33 percent for arterial fibrillation. The nineteen-physician practice receiving this "report card" is among the most reputable in Philadelphia.

The National Library of Science reported a 1989 case study of 1,000 patients followed in an internal medicine clinic in Maryland over a three-year period. Eighty-four percent of those patients (840 out of 1,000) could not be diagnosed—a staggering statistic.

In another study at the University of Iowa Medical College, half of the more than four hundred patients interviewed reported having unexplained physical symptoms "usually" or "always."

Older patients often experience diagnostic nightmares. For example, the asthma death rate in those over sixty-five is ten times the death rate for the same condition in younger adults. According to researcher Paul L. Enright, M.D., of Tucson, "Diagnosis in these patients is only half as good as it should be. Fifty percent of elderly asthmatics have not been diagnosed."

In his bestselling book *Head First*, Norman Cousins discussed a study of the medical records of elderly cardiac pacemaker recipients at Albert Einstein Medical Center in Philadelphia which revealed "twenty percent of implantations to have been completely unjustified and done on a misdiagnosis of information."

If we generalize from these alarming statistics to the U.S. population as a whole, it would not be unreasonable to assume that literally millions of patients are undiagnosable, misdiagnosed, or diagnosable but not yet identified. And while the plight of undiagnosed patients is bad enough, the misdiagnosed patient may be a walking time bomb. Medications and procedures meant to cure the misdiagnosed condition can backfire and will often cause further damage, while the real (undiagnosed) condition is left untreated.

Case Study: Penny

It took six years and visits to multiple doctors for Penny, a woman in her forties, to finally receive the correct diagnosis and treatment. She suffered from numerous symptoms that appeared at different times over a six-year period, including dry eyes, pleurisy, aches and pains, flashing lights in the periphery of her vision, and rashes that looked like small bruises. The problem was that Penny's doctors never treated her array of symptoms as a whole. Instead, each symptom was treated individually: artificial tears for her eyes, ibuprofen for her aches, dermatological creams for her rash, and medications to treat migraines.

Because she was not properly diagnosed, her condition steadily declined. It was not until her symptoms became so severe that she had become bedridden, receiving massive doses of intravenous steroids, that her doctors finally connected her diverse symptoms to make the correct diagnosis of Sjögren's syndrome, an autoimmune disease in which the body's immune system mistakenly attacks its own moisture-producing glands.

Why Doctors Can't Always Make the Correct Diagnosis

In his article "Mystery Maladies Pose Challenge for Doctors and Patients," Arthur Hartz, M.D., candidly explains, "Doctors have more of a medical model for treating strep throat or heart disease . . . but when it comes to unexplained illnesses or symptoms, they don't really have an approach that is established."

As illustrated by Penny's story, even diagnosable diseases are often difficult for doctors to identify, and this is especially true for many immune and autoimmune disorders. According to the American Autoimmune and Related Diseases Foundation (AARD), as many as fifty million Americans (75 percent of them women) may suffer from autoimmune disorders, which are notoriously difficult to diagnose in spite of advances in medical technology. "Women have to see five or six doctors before they find someone who can tell them what they have," the AARD report states. Clearly, ". . . the biggest obstacle that patients with autoimmune disease face is *just getting a diagnosis.*"

Well-documented diseases such as lupus are elusive and difficult to diagnose, so patients with these conditions are often dismissed out of hand, with doctors telling them "it's all in your head" (in the same way that multiple sclerosis sufferers used to be referred to as "fakers" before the advent of the technology that could prove the existence of this disease). Part of the problem with such diseases, as Jeff Baggish, M.D., explains, is that "almost half of all persons afflicted with an autoimmune disease experience periods of spontaneous remission and exacerbation as opposed to a continuous worsening of symptoms." Unless a doctor is particularly knowledgeable or can take the time to follow a patient closely, it is difficult to find the correct diagnosis.

Doctors themselves will admit that medical technology doesn't necessarily guarantee diagnosis. For example, Dr. Kurt Kroenke, M.D., senior scientist at the prestigious Regenstrief Institute for Health Care, warns, "Only half of all symptoms evaluated by a doctor have a discrete physical cause and at least one-third are medically unexplained."

What's the Answer?

Dr. Rosenbaum and I are two of the staggering number of patients who have been trapped in the diagnosis dilemma. We know that if you're reading this book, you've experienced the frustration of having medically unexplained symptoms. You've probably been to more than one physician complaining of your symptoms. You've received no diagnosis at all or (worse yet) contradictory diagnoses. The medications you've been prescribed don't seem to help, and some of them may make you feel worse. As hard as you try, your symptoms make it difficult to keep functioning and meet all your responsibilities; perhaps your family life is being affected or your job is in jeopardy. We have written this book to offer you hope, and the best part is that you can help yourself!

Making a correct diagnosis is like solving a crime. Physical exams and laboratory tests can eliminate some of the suspects, but the culprit is still at large. The evidence must be tracked down and documented with precision. In some cases, it might literally be a life-and-death matter to find it. And you cannot be totally reliant on your doctors to do it. Among other reasons, they simply may not have the time to help you in the way you need. *You* must learn to become your own medical detective and follow that evidence trail in order to find your answers.

This book is in no way intended to replace your physician. Rather, your doctor will become your consultant much in the way Dr. Rosenbaum has become mine (Lynn's). But you will have to assume the main responsibility for your own health care. Dr. Pamela Gallin, one of the world's leading pediatric surgeons, writes in her book *How to Survive Your Doctor's Care* (Lifeline Press, 2003), "Now, more than ever, the onus is on the patient to ensure proper medical treatment." In the following chapters, we'll discuss all the aspects of good medical detective work, including how to do some of your own medical research and sift through that information in order to consider all the possibilities while keeping an open mind. We will reveal our revolutionary Eight Steps to Self-Diagnosis, the centerpiece of this program, and explain how to choose the right physicians and create productive partnerships with them as you go through the process. If you're willing to put in the time and effort, we'll show you how to improve your chances of quickly getting to an accurate diagnosis.

Now let's take a look at some of the pitfalls that contribute to the existing diagnosis dilemma.

Factors That Can Affect the Diagnostic Process

We believe there are many elements that contribute to the diagnosis dilemma, including the following:

- Numerous conditions may look alike on casual inspection.

- You might not fit the profile of a typical patient with your condition.

- Your physician may not have the expertise to diagnose your condition.

- Physicians sometimes treat symptoms without examining underlying causes.

- You might have forgotten to mention a symptom or a medication you are taking that would provide a significant diagnostic clue to your doctor because you think it's inconsequential or irrelevant. Or perhaps you have withheld an embarrassing symptom or circumstance.

- Sometimes medical tests are compromised by a variety of factors and can yield erroneous results that can mislead physicians.

- The way medical care is delivered—by a wide variety of specialists—sometimes hinders diagnosis, particularly if your condition crosses several areas of specialty and no one is looking at the whole picture.

- You may have an "iatrogenic" condition, meaning that it is caused by the testing, medications, or treatments prescribed by your physicians.

- Microbes and viruses can mutate, causing new forms of disease.

- Old diseases that may have been presumed to be extinct or confined to certain areas are reemerging as the planet's ecosystems are altered and as people travel globally.

- Diseases caused by environmental factors are not yet widely recognized or well understood. There are also potential dangers from genetically modified foods.

- The quest to find genetic links to diseases is still in its infancy.

In the following pages, we'll discuss these factors in more detail.

Diagnosing the Medical System

Until recently, family doctors were an institution. They were the first to welcome us into the world, treat our childhood illnesses, care for us into adulthood, and then deliver our children and our children's children. They knew us intimately—our bodies and minds, our lives and family histories—and we knew them. The delivery of medical care was a personal and special matter to patient and doctor alike. Medicine was not just a profession; it was a calling, both an art and a science.

Today, such close doctor-patient relationships rarely exist. The practice of medicine as an intuitive art has been muddled by the requirements of insurance companies and their often incomprehensible coverage plans. In the managed-care environment, patients are simply authorization numbers and their doctors are "providers" and "gatekeepers." Accountants and actuaries rather than physicians now make life-and-death decisions as to whether treatment will be allowed.

Patients may wait weeks to get appointments and then endure long hours in waiting rooms merely to be given five minutes of their physician's time. Then they are quickly handed off to assistants who set up tests—assuming their insurance plan allows the doctor to order them.

In an incredibly honest indictment of the medical system as it exists today, John Lantos, M.D., spends approximately two hundred pages of his book *Do We Still Need Doctors?* (Routledge, 1997) asking himself whether he can still be a good doctor under our health care system. One of the many instances he cites is a case in which he was treating a "thin" and "in pain" sixteen-year-old girl named Jane who had been diagnosed with sickle cell anemia. Because her symptoms were not totally typical of that ailment, Dr. Lantos believed she was also suffering from an undiagnosed disease—anorexia nervosa. He brought this to her family's attention and requested that they follow up with their primary care physician.

When nothing was done, Dr. Lantos wondered if he should have done more. But he pointed out, ". . . I had lots of other patients. Nobody would pay me for what I was doing for [Jane]. Just the opposite. If I kept bugging the HMO, it wouldn't send too many more patients my way. It was a big one, too, and our hospital was desperate to fill beds, eager for the HMO's business. . . . If Jane lost too much weight, we could give her hyperalimentation and charge the HMO for that. My impulses about what was needed seemed to run counter to every obvious notion of what was good for me . . . [and] my hospital. . . ." Here was a physician who clearly cared but was discouraged by the system from acting in the patient's best interests; that is simply reality.[2]

Dr. Lantos was a hospital physician, but private office practitioners are also stressed by what has become "assembly-line medicine." To keep their medical practices alive in the managed-care environment, many work eighteen-hour days during which they see two or three times as many patients as before insurers' requirements dictated time limits. As hard as they try, many doctors have little time to call another physician on our behalf, research our case, or give thoughtful consideration to our condition and its treatment. One of the finest neurologists in Miami admitted in an off-the-cuff conversation that his time is so limited that he often cannot return telephone calls. An appointment, which may take weeks to get, is the only way to communicate with him.

The American Medical Association reports that Medicare payments to physicians have been reduced, whereas malpractice insurance premiums have increased. This may result in rushed doctors trying to see more patients to support their practice and spending less time taking detailed medical histories, which are so critical to the diagnostic process.

A 2003 *New York Times* editorial on teaching hospitals complained that in the very institutions where doctors learn their craft, they are too busy to engage in medical analysis: "Residents today are preoccupied with getting their work done. Anything that gets in the way—even a bona fide medical mystery—is more often seen as a bother rather than a learning opportunity."

The Trend Toward Medical Specialization

Another factor contributing to the diagnosis dilemma is the failure to take a holistic view of the body as an integrated unit. In the medical profession, there's been a trend toward specialization for many years. As more medical students opt to become specialists rather than general practitioners, fewer general diagnosticians are trained. The task of taking comprehensive medical histories, which are often good predictors of diagnostic outcomes, may be missed or skipped. Specialists who may not view or consider any body systems or parts other than the ones they are trained to treat may prescribe medications or interventions that create additional problems elsewhere in the body.

Complications from Medications and Supplements

Patients who are taking harmful combinations of drugs can easily be overlooked. Pharmacists should be alert to such combinations, but it can't be tracked if patients don't pay for their prescriptions with insurance. If patients take over-the-counter medications or nutritional supplements that are not in the pharmacist's database or if they fail to report the use of such products to their pharmacist, the patients themselves may be facilitating serious drug interactions, which may in turn bring about undiagnosable symptoms.

Another medication-related problem that contributes to the diagnosis dilemma is drug dosages. Several drug studies have revealed that dosages recommended by drug companies are often far higher than what many patients need. One example is Prozac, a widely prescribed and popular antidepressant. Its manufacturer recommends a dose of 20 milligrams per day, but early research showed that many patients needed only one-half or one-quarter that amount. Nevertheless, most physicians prescribe the dose recommended by the manufacturer. They may fail to recognize, report, or even correlate the onset of certain reactions or symptoms, especially if their patients' reactions are different than those reported by the manufacturer in its literature.

Problems can also arise when medications are prescribed for a condition other than the approved one, known as "off-label" use.

According to a six-month nationwide investigation by Knight-Ridder, three-quarters of antiseizure medications are prescribed for off-label purposes, as are nearly two-thirds of antipsychotics and one-fourth of antidepressants. Using the FDA's own data, Knight-Ridder estimates that in 2003 at least eight thousand people became seriously ill after taking some of the nation's most frequently prescribed drugs. The true number is likely many times higher since there is no formal reporting system for such incidents.

In May 2004, Pfizer Pharmaceuticals pled guilty and agreed to pay $430 million to resolve criminal and civil charges that it paid doctors to prescribe an antiseizure medication to patients with ailments which the drug was not federally approved to treat.

Case Study: Harold

Harold, an eighty-two-year-old Alzheimer's patient, was declining quickly. His family pressured the doctor to "do something." So the doctor tried a number of medications in an effort to improve Harold's symptoms. Harold did show marked improvements for about two months, and then he suddenly experienced the first in a series of "strokelike" events.

The next to last of these episodes rendered him an invalid. He was unable to walk, his face drooped, and his speech was slurred. Several months later, Harold died of another stroke. Had his family done some research immediately after the first stroke, they might have made the connection to the powerful drug he had been taking. His doctor had prescribed an antipsychotic for the off-label purpose of treating Alzheimer's disease. A potential side effect of this drug is an increased risk of stroke. Public warnings about the increase in strokes from this off-label use came out in Canada, and the Food and Drug Administration (FDA) followed them much later in the United States. This information was available at the time of Harold's episodes, and if the family had taken action to find it, they might not have lost Harold in such a tragic manner.

When I (Lynn) was suffering from nerve trauma (which was ultimately found to be the cause of my mystery malady, as discussed in Chapter 8), my neurologist prescribed Neurontin, an antiseizure medication with the often-accepted off-label purpose of treating neuropathic pain (it allegedly "coats" the nerve endings). I subsequently had a major car accident due to the effects of the drug on my cognitive functioning. Needless to say, I went off the medication immediately!

The Changing Spectrum of Diseases

The Centers for Disease Control and Prevention reports that 62 million illnesses, 265,000 hospitalizations, and 3,200 deaths can be attributed annually to unknown infectious agents. A recent report from the Institute of Medicine claims that some thirty new diseases have cropped up since the mid-1970s, causing tens of millions of deaths. New microbes continually come into being and old ones can mutate or evolve rapidly, which challenges our immune systems' ability to resist them. Serious, sometimes lethal, infectious diseases such as various strains of influenza, acquired immunodeficiency syndrome (AIDS), and new drug-resistant strains of tuberculosis spread rapidly around the world, often from developing countries to industrialized nations. We're frequently beset by new strains of flu that set physicians on a hunt for ways to diagnose and treat them while researchers scramble to develop effective flu vaccines. For instance, we are seeing frequent cases of West Nile virus popping up.

Most recently, while severe acute respiratory syndrome (SARS) was dominating headlines, a virulent strain of avian flu in Belgium and the Netherlands quietly emerged, wiping out entire chicken farms, jumping from poultry to pigs and then to people. The victims began showing up in emergency rooms with eye inflammation and respiratory illness, which in eighty-three cases resulted in death.[3]

More people are traveling to more places than ever before, leaving behind their sanitized surroundings to explore remote areas where the local population has built up immunity to diseases that can knock travelers flat. In any airport in the world, you may be exposed to microbes the U.S. medical community has never heard of. Airplanes and cruise ships pump recirculated air, which may be harboring microscopic monsters, to their passengers.

Natalie Angier writes in the *New York Times Magazine*, "Today diseases as common as the cold and as rare as Ebola are circling the globe with near telephonic speed. You needn't even bother to reach out and touch someone. . . . Microbes travel by land, sea, air, nose, glove, love, sewage, steerage, rat backs, hat racks, uncooked burritos, overlooked mosquitoes. . . . Nowadays, a mosquito infested with the malaria parasite [or West Nile virus] can be buzzing in Ghana at dawn and dining on an airport employee in Boston at cocktail hour."[4]

Realizing they can't afford to ignore an epidemic in even the most remote areas, members of the medical establishment are seeking ways to solve this escalating problem. But there is no standard way to exchange up-to-the-minute information with researchers in other countries in spite of the existence of such organizations as the World Health Organization. As yet, no central symptom-based database exists in this country or in the world, though many experts are working to correct this deficiency.

Local governments are even being encouraged to harness computers for the task of identifying and tracking disease outbreaks (as reported in the

June 2003 issue of *Governing*, a magazine designed for states and localities). Clearly, though, we are still only in the infancy stages of gathering and exchanging data. It is easy to see how many diseases simply have not yet been identified and can be diagnostic mysteries.

The Immeasurable Effects of the Environment

The increase in mystery ailments may be related to factors we encounter in the environment, ranging from chemicals to microorganisms whose growth may be stimulated by changing climatic conditions. For instance, toxic mold can cause serious illnesses that not all doctors know how to recognize. They might expect to find such diseases in those who live in substandard housing but fail to ask pertinent questions of their well-heeled patients.

There are many unanswered questions about environment-related diseases and many aspects that must be researched, and without clear cause-and-effect statistics, physicians may be reluctant to link mysterious symptoms to such exposures. Even so, it is now estimated that forty million people have some form of environmental illness due to allergic or toxic reactions to hundreds of thousands of chemicals contained in our air, food, water, homes, workplaces, and schools. But until more studies are conducted, it is diagnostic guesswork at best.

Kathy, a hard-working executive secretary, had a complex of symptoms that started insidiously with flulike signs—chills, joint pain, and breathing difficulties—which ultimately landed her in the hospital emergency room gasping for breath. But no one could diagnose her condition until she found one smart doctor who was willing to look beyond the usual. He found that Kathy was suffering from a malady known as hypersensitivity pneumonitis—also known as farmer's lung or cheese lung—and more recently identified as a form of "sick building syndrome."

Hypersensitivity pneumonitis is a reaction to a specific type of mold—aspergillus—often found in air-conditioning systems that have leaked continuously over time. It is also found in hay stored in barns and in the fermentation process at cheese factories. For those who are sensitive to this type of mold, prolonged exposure to it can cause fibrosis of (a buildup of tissue in) the lungs. Initial symptoms may take time to accumulate.

Closely associated with sick building syndrome and other syndromes resulting from exposure to toxic mold is a controversial illness known as "multiple chemical sensitivity." This condition can cause a person to become allergic to almost anything that contains man-made chemicals. For an estimated 20–30 percent of the population (some thirty-seven million Americans), the symptoms of multiple chemical sensitivity can range from mild headaches, dizziness, short-term memory loss, nosebleeds, irritability, itchy eyes, and scratchy throats to possible damage to the nervous and respiratory systems. In its most extreme form, sufferers are confined to a plastic bubble world or one made up of only natural materials.

A different set of illnesses of an environmental nature appear to be a by-product of disturbance of ecosystems. This would include, for example, occurrences of Lyme disease in suburbia. Given that *Borrelia burgdorferi*, the bacteria that causes Lyme disease, has been around a long time, why are people suddenly being diagnosed with it? In open woodlands, foxes and bobcats keep a lid on the bacteria by hunting the mice that carry it, but when these predators vanish with our woodlands as developers clear lots for new subdivisions, the mice and their ticks proliferate unnaturally. Richard Osterfield, an animal ecologist at the Institute of Ecosystem Studies in Millbrook, New York, found in a recent survey that infected ticks were seven times as prevalent on one- and two-acre lots as they were on the fifteen-acre lots of yesteryear. The intriguing case study of a little boy who contracted Lyme disease while on a Boy Scout outing is described in Chapter 13.

In Malaysia, where pig farmers started pushing back the forest to expand operations, displaced fruit bats began spreading a pathogen now known as the Nipah virus. The pigs developed a cough so loud it became known as the "one-mile cough." Unfortunately, the virus spread from the pigs to their keepers, causing brain inflammation and death in 40 percent of those affected by it.

A full discussion of the medical consequences of disturbing the ecosystem is beyond the scope of this book. The point we are trying to make is how easy it is to have an undiagnosed disease that is quite real but remains a mystery until the root cause is found.

Potential Dangers from Genetically Modified Foods

Many scientists argue that we are creating a new kind of biological pollution by altering the genetics in food. Genetic manipulation of everything from corn to papayas may have unintended consequences, causing new drug-resistant diseases to emerge.

While biotechnology is likely to change the world for the better in ways we can only imagine, it's still in its infancy. Fears that genetically modified (GM) foods might promote drug-resistant "superbugs" have been fueled by some research findings. Dutch scientists recently discovered it might be possible for genes to jump from GM food into bacteria in the gut of farm animals. If the transferred genes are the antibiotic-resistant ones used in some of the GM crops fed to livestock, then there is a danger that antibiotic-resistant bacteria could spread from animals to humans.

The FDA assures us that GM foods are safe. But many people, including some scientists, are concerned that ingesting them may lead to changes in human cells and subsequent disease. Jane Rissler of the Union of Concerned Scientists says, "We know very little about the long-term impacts of genetically engineered food, so as a general matter, they should be subject to more scrutiny." The Royal Society in England, that country's leading scientific academy, issued a report in February 2002 that recommends implementing stricter safety checks before new GM foods are declared fit for human consumption.

Ravi Durvasula, an infectious disease scientist at Yale University, calls the possibility of laboratories unleashing potentially deadly disease the "Jurassic Park syndrome"—an assessment that he says "may be rooted in real concern."

Genetic Links to Disease Yet to Be Discovered

As research on the human genome intensifies, scientists are on the verge of innumerable breakthroughs that will link diseases to our genetic coding and offer the diagnostic and symptomatic help we need. But they are not quite there, even though genetic links have been found to some diseases such as dyslexia and certain types of high blood pressure. Likewise, physicians and their patients who suffer from little-understood conditions such as fibromyalgia, irritable bowel syndrome, and certain other inflammatory disorders have long suspected a genetic link to such conditions. Only recently has genetic research uncovered a common gene that doesn't allow certain patients to recover from inflammatory conditions as quickly or as well as those who don't have the gene. Scientists are now working on a drug to address the gene defect rather than the symptoms of the diseases.

The Human Genome Project, a consortium of scientists from the United States, Britain, Japan, France, Germany, and China, has established the complete human genome sequence, but much research still lies ahead. Gene testing already has dramatically improved lives. Some tests are used to clarify a diagnosis and direct a physician toward appropriate treatments, while others identify people at high risk for conditions that may be preventable.

Gene tests for Alzheimer's disease are available but are subject to debate. These tests are given to healthy people who have no symptoms but are considered to be at risk because of family medical history. The tests give only a probability for developing the disorder. One of their most serious limitations is the difficulty in interpreting a positive result because some people who carry a disease-associated mutation will never develop the actual disease.

A limitation of all medical testing is the possibility of laboratory errors. Many members of the medical establishment feel that uncertainties surrounding test interpretation, the current lack of available medical options for genetic diseases, the potential for provoking patient anxiety, and risks for discrimination and social stigmatization could outweigh any benefits of testing.

The promise of human genome research is great, but it will take time to develop inexpensive diagnostic tests for DNA markers. Doctors will need to take the time to understand predisposing factors that may render a patient vulnerable to a disabling condition. Awareness of these factors may eventually allow physicians to unravel complicated diagnostic problems.

Reasons for Hope in the Midst of the Diagnostic Dilemma

There can be little doubt that the diagnosis dilemma exists and persists despite the best doctors and medical technology in the world. Any one or a combination of factors contributing to this dilemma may be operating in your particular case. We trust you can see the essential need to take a more active role in the search for the diagnostic answers to your unexplained medical symptoms. In the next chapter, we'll define and describe just how easy it is for undiagnosed symptoms to become a mystery malady, and we'll share some examples and case studies. We will also call your attention to the need to develop a new mind-set as you learn the basics of medical detective work.

In Chapter 3, we'll reveal our revolutionary Eight Steps to Self-Diagnosis. You don't need to have a medical background to follow them. If you're willing to work through the steps and act as your own medical detective, you can find your way out of the diagnosis dilemma and be well on your way to solving your mystery malady.

My (Lynn's) mystery malady is described in Chapter 8. Dr. Rosenbaum's mystery maladies are shared in Chapters 6 and 16. We hope our personal experiences and the many case studies we present throughout the book will inspire you to work proactively with your doctors to find your diagnostic solutions.

2

All About Mystery Maladies:
A New Mind-Set

We grow up never questioning whatever is unquestioned by those around us.
—MARGARET MEAD

IN CHAPTER 1, we reviewed some research studies that support a fact many of us may already know or suspect: we are facing a diagnosis dilemma of critical proportions. We have dubbed the medical conditions that lead to a diagnosis dilemma "mystery maladies." So what exactly are these mystery maladies?

Definition of Mystery Maladies
- Conditions, syndromes, or symptoms that cannot be diagnosed easily or neatly despite advances in medical technology
- Misdiagnosed chronic conditions
- Symptoms that have no known cause or origin
- Conditions or syndromes that are now identifiable but until recently were considered "mysteries" and may still be unfamiliar to many physicians

How Do You Get a Mystery Malady?

Most mystery maladies develop in a deceptively simple way. Say, for example, that you have a persistent cough following what appears to have been a cold. You think you may have bronchitis. You make an appointment with your primary care physician and tell her your symptoms. She peers in your throat and ears, feels your glands, and listens to your chest. After asking some additional questions, she decides on a treatment plan based on an established protocol. She may prescribe a course of antibiotics, rest, and plenty of fluids, and she might advise you to avoid milk products that can cause mucus. Unfortunately, you don't get better—and so your mystery malady begins. The following scenario is not atypical for many mystery malady sufferers.

You call your physician again; she is somewhat perplexed but suggests a different antibiotic and perhaps an expectorant. Once again, you follow her directions, but your symptoms don't abate. Out of concern and in an abundance of caution, she refers you to a specialist, perhaps a pulmonologist, an allergist, or both, and you make the rounds. These physicians, in turn, may send you for x-rays, blood tests, and other medical tests. The end result is a laundry list of possible diagnoses, a fistful of medical bills, and a medicine cabinet full of prescriptions that offer you no relief. Perhaps you're now among the 65 percent of people who take prescribed allergy medications but don't actually have allergies.

At this point, you're confused, worried, and even slightly depressed because you're still coughing and you can't seem to get well. Now you may be thinking the real reason behind your medical problem must be "stress" or, depending on how fearful you've become, some undetected form of lung cancer. Soon your upbeat and generally good-natured physicians and their staff start to sound annoyed when you call yet again because they've been unable to help you. You're still coughing, still feeling sick and becoming frantic. Either you've given up entirely on doctors or you may still be searching for the right one who will have the answers.

Your friends and relatives encourage you to visit a renowned diagnostic clinic for yet another opinion. Although you are still coughing, at least you feel a temporary reprieve from your anxieties because surely these doctors will be able to make a definitive diagnosis. The day of your appointment arrives and so do you, along with all your records, a list of questions, and renewed confidence that your mysterious symptoms will finally be identified and treated. The clinic physicians review your records, perform their own physical exams, administer new tests, and repeat others.

After this visit, the doctors are absolutely certain of what you *don't* have, but they don't seem to know exactly what you *do* have. You diligently try to follow their treatment suggestions and obtain some relief, but your symptoms still don't go away completely. You now definitely have what we call a "mystery malady."

Rare is the person who at some time in his or her life has not had a mystery malady of one kind or another, but most of us are fortunate enough to see it come and go quickly. This book is for those who are not so lucky. The following table lists some examples of mystery maladies, and following that are some statistics of how many people suffer from them. We'll discuss many of these mystery maladies in case studies throughout the book.

Examples of Mystery Maladies

Adrenal fatigue	Fluid retention
Anxiety/somatization disorders*	Food allergies/sensitivities
	Headaches*
Autoimmune disorders	Heavy metal poisoning
Biomechanical pain*	Hemorrhoids
Blurred vision	Inflammatory bowel disease
Breathing difficulties	Interstitial cystitis
Burning hands	Lupus*
Chest pain	Mold allergies
Childhood diseases	Mood swings
Chronic fatigue syndrome*	Multiple chemical sensitivities*
Constipation	Multiple sclerosis*
Depression	Nausea
Diarrhea	Parasites
Digestive disturbances	Pelvic pain*
Dizziness or loss of balance	Reflex sympathetic dystrophy*
Fibromyalgia*	Sleep disturbances*

(continued)

*Statistics for these selected mystery maladies are presented in the following list.

Spondylitis   Vasculitis
Tension myositis syndrome   Viral syndromes
Thyroid disease*   Vulvodynia*
Travel-related diseases   Weakness
Urinary frequency   Weight loss/weight gain
Vaccination concerns/   Wilson's thyroid syndrome
    reactions   Work-related injuries*

Number of Patients Who Suffer from Mystery Maladies

• Twenty percent of patients attending general medical clinics suffer from chronic fatigue.[1] Conservatively, ten million Americans have been diagnosed with chronic fatigue syndrome (as defined by the CDC);[2] this is estimated to be less than 10 percent of the total number of cases.[3]

• Although an estimated eight million people suffer from fibromyalgia, the reported prevalence of fibromyalgia in some rheumatology clinics is as high as twenty percent.[4]

• In the U.S. urban population, between 15 and 50 people per 100,000 have lupus and the Lupus Foundation suggests a prevalence of two million.[5]

• Fifteen to thirty-four percent of the U.S. population suffers from multiple chemical sensitivities, a condition that has only recently gained recognition.[6]

• At least 1.1 million Americans have multiple sclerosis, with 3 to 5 per 100,000 Americans showing symptoms of amyotrophic lateral sclerosis (ALS), and this is often missed.[7, 8]

• Twenty percent of outpatient visits to neurologists are for chronic tension-type headaches with no known cause, yet there is a one-year prevalence of these headaches of 90 percent.[9]

---

*Statistics for these selected mystery maladies are presented in the following list.

- Five percent of patients who experience trauma to an extremity are estimated to have reflex sympathetic dystrophy,[10] but because of confusion over the diagnosis the true incidence is unknown.[11]

- Thirty-nine percent of all women of reproductive age have chronic pelvic pain that is poorly understood and often undiagnosed.[12]

- Thirty-five percent of patients with sleep disorders have their etiology in often undetected psychiatric disorders.[13]

- One million Americans have been diagnosed with inflammatory bowel disease, but it is estimated that the undiagnosed may put this figure at two million.[14]

- Fifteen to twenty percent of the female population has vulvodynia (pain of the vulva), a condition that most women can have for years before they tell their doctors—if they ever do.[15]

- Sixty percent of all work-related injuries turn out to be repetitive strain injuries, and those injuries account for the single largest cause of occupational health problems in the United States, but some refuse to acknowledge this genuine medical issue.[16]

- Autoimmune thyroid disease affects about 5–10 percent of middle-aged and elderly women with the annual incidence up to 4 per 1,000 women and 1 in 1,000 men. Thyroid disease is often subclinical and missed.[17]

These statistics are striking, and so is the cost of all this fruitless medical care in terms of lost time and money, and in suffering. Many of these mystery malady patients are told their medical problem is "psychosomatic." Conditions like blood sugar instability, chronic fatigue, candidiasis, hormone imbalances, nutrient imbalances, premenstrual syndrome (PMS), thyroid disorders, and pelvic pain are organic conditions that are commonly misdiagnosed as psychiatric disorders.

On average, patients with mystery maladies can take months and sometimes years to obtain a correct diagnosis. As these patients already know, there are some things doctors simply don't understand yet. But it seems like the medical community has only recently begun to admit this. According to R. A. Aronowitz, "We need to recognize and accommodate the essential continuity between persons who have symptoms that have been given a name and disease-like status and persons whose suffering remains unnamed and unrecognized."[18]

Worse still, today's mysterious illnesses are becoming notoriously more complex. Kurt Kroenke writes, "Clearly, the era of studying one symptom in isolation is over, and clinicians should know that patients who present with one [of these conditions] often have several other symptom syndromes as well."[19] The problem, as we discussed in Chapter 1, is that to look at a patient as a whole takes time, investigative effort, and ceaseless vigilance. More likely than not, no one but you (or perhaps your family or friends) is willing or able to make this effort.

Diagnosing Your Own Mystery Malady

So, you may ask, how can the lay public accomplish what the most highly skilled and expertly trained medical practitioners cannot? We know it's possible not only from our personal experience but also from observing the success of others who have used our revolutionary Eight Steps to Self-Diagnosis. This method was developed by a layperson (Lynn) with a physician's assistance (Dr. Rosenbaum). It has been used successfully by many people who have no particular medical expertise.

For example, eight-year-old David, whose case study appears in Chapter 13, developed numerous cavities in his teeth from an early age, and his mother's attempt to circumvent that problem ended up causing a mystery malady that no pediatrician could identify or resolve. Using the Eight Steps, his caring and persistent mother unearthed the solution, which none of their doctors may have known about at the time. Similarly, David's Uncle Gordon (in an unrelated case study told in Chapter 12) suffered from a lifelong and unending series of mystery maladies whose roots were eventually recognized as being psychiatric in nature.

Fortunately, both David and his uncle finally had their mystery maladies diagnosed correctly, and they are now enjoying good health because they and their physicians used many of the techniques and tools we describe in this book. But tools and techniques are only part of our self-diagnostic method; developing a new mind-set toward unraveling mystery maladies is the first threshold we must cross, so let's begin there.

Even though you're more than ready for some real answers and the information we've provided thus far may make sense, you may be still skeptical. How can you possibly be expected to solve your mystery malady when you are tired, suffering, and feeling sick? Your sense of hope or optimism may have eroded along with your physical condition. We understand that the mere thought of undertaking our program may feel so overwhelming that you may want to run for cover.

That's certainly how I (Lynn) felt several years ago, as I struggled with what seemed like a stunning aggregate of unexplainable physical symptoms. I was feeling exhausted and totally defeated because no one knew what was wrong with me. So allow me to share the story of how I stumbled onto a new way of thinking that I now understand is an absolute prerequisite to successfully undertaking our self-diagnosis method.

I had been dragging myself from one doctor to another without success, from work to home, trying desperately to perform my chores and take care of my kids, husband, house, and clients. I was beginning to wonder if perhaps I should just give up, lie down, and never get up again. I couldn't fathom whether I was a victim of bad genes, a malfunctioning medical system, or the sins of a past life.

I felt angry and betrayed. I had always tried hard to do the "right things" in life. I followed the rules; I stopped at stop signs, gave to charity, and never took a parking space that belonged to someone else. I didn't abuse drugs, cigarettes, or alcohol. I took care of my body: I exercised, ate properly, and even took vitamins. So why was my body not working? Why was this happening to me? The feeling that I was a victim of my illness was probably as intense for me as my actual physical problems.

Unable to create any meaning out of what was happening to me and why, I lost faith in my doctors and was swiftly losing my will to persist in finding answers. Desolate, I fell onto my bed and into the deep sleep of escape. When I opened my eyes two hours later, the radio was playing. An announcer was chattering; his gibberish just seemed to blend into the taste-less fate of my sickness. I lay motionless, drifting in and out of semicon-sciousness, until swiftly and distinctly as the clap of thunder that follows a snap of lightning, the announcer's last statement swooped down on my brain and shattered my listlessness. I had no idea in what context this declaration was made, but he said, "You have to keep an open mind." *You have to keep an open mind.* That simple phrase began tumbling around in my head like a single sock in the dryer.

Keep an open mind. Keep an open mind.

I flashed back to something I once read about the great sculptor Michelangelo. Prior to beginning to chisel, he would tap the stone lightly to determine if the marble was "true." If the tap revealed a dull or hollow sound, the stone was presumed to have faults and would crack when chis-eled in that place. If, however, it had a clear ring or one that "hung in the air" for a moment, it was true.

Like the sound of tapped marble, the phrase "Keep an open mind" was hanging in the air and ringing true in every cell of my body. Was I "tapping" into something that would prove profoundly useful in resolving my illness? Could hearing that phrase from an unlikely source at an unexpected moment actually bear witness to the very truth of the phrase? That would mean considering the possibility that the answers to anything, including medical solutions, could come from almost anywhere at any time. Maybe the solution to my mystery malady was to be found from listening to and looking in the least likely places. After all, I had already tried the usual ones. Maybe what I needed was to stop looking to my doctors alone for answers and start pursuing my own solutions from any source I could find.

Keeping an Open Mind

Certainly, we mystery malady patients can attest to the fact that even those physicians with the very best medical training come up short when put to the task of identifying and treating our complaints. We have to be willing to look elsewhere and rely on ourselves to do it.

This conclusion is not meant to imply that the principles of Western medicine and traditional diagnostic methods should be disregarded. On the contrary, it may actually be the case that for all the reasons we described in Chapter 1 the problem may arise from those principles and methods not being implemented as they were originally intended to be. In fact, most medical school textbooks, particularly those on the subject of diagnostics, will be the first place young medical students will hear that the practice of medicine is an art. But like any other art, diagnostic skill requires creativity on the part of its creator.

Creating any kind of art—whether it's music, painting, writing, dancing, or the practice of medicine—involves a process that combines the skills of the discipline with imagination, observation, thoughtful consideration and discernment, intuition, and an openness to all possibilities. In other words, keeping an open mind and allowing all possibilities to be considered.

From the physician's perspective, in certain cases, this may be as simple as taking the time to understand certain predisposing factors that may render a particular patient vulnerable to a disabling condition or considering potential precipitating and perpetuating factors that may maintain maladaptive illness behaviors. Such global thinking may create a consciousness of these factors that eventually allows the clinician to unravel the complicated problems that create the patient's distress.[20]

From the patient's perspective, we must start with a clean clipboard of our own, look at our medical problem with fresh eyes, and consider anything or anyone a possible resource that may assist us in identifying and solving our mystery maladies. We must be willing to take responsibility for gathering as much information as possible and to be persistent in this effort, regardless of the sources used. You can and should always check out this information with your physician. But the prerequisite is to have the open mind-set we are describing.

Every answer to every problem is a series of connections that are made in our minds after observation and the application of knowledge that may come from anywhere, whether it be formal education, life experience, happenstance, or creative thinking. If we are married to any preconceived notions, we may never find the answer to our mystery maladies.

A perfect example of where an open-minded approach could have saved thousands of dollars and many lives occurred in 1993 during an outbreak of an unexplained bleeding lung condition in an area known as the "Four Corners" (where the state borders of Arizona, Colorado, New Mexico, and

Utah all meet). Until the medical experts were willing to explore outside their own knowledge base, the case of Four Corners remained unsolved. This story, documented by the CDC's Special Pathogens Branch, involved a young, physically fit Navajo man who was admitted to the hospital suffering from shortness of breath and died almost immediately thereafter. It was discovered that this young man's fiancée had died with the same symptoms only a few days earlier. A series of laboratory tests failed to identify any known pathogen, including the one that caused bubonic plague in the Middle Ages.

The Special Pathogens Branch of the CDC was notified, and the state health departments of all four states—as well as the University of New Mexico School of Medicine—became involved in trying to solve what rapidly became an outbreak of the mysterious disease. During the ensuing weeks, as additional cases were reported and many people died, physicians and other scientific experts worked intensively to narrow down a list of suspected causes. These included exposure to herbicides or the possibility of a new type of influenza virus. Finally, the virologists at the CDC linked this pulmonary syndrome with a previously unidentified type of hantavirus. Researchers examined lung tissue samples from people who had died years earlier from an unidentified lung disease with similar symptoms. They estimated the first known outbreak of this particular disease to be as early as 1959.

Finally, someone had the bright idea of directly consulting with an outside, nonmedical source—the Navajos themselves. Interestingly enough, while the nationally renowned medical experts did not recognize this virus, the Navajos at once identified the disease which, while unnamed, was documented in their cultural records. Long ago, the Navajos had discovered a link between this virus and the animals involved in the dissemination of the hantavirus—mice. In fact, some of the Navajo elders had actually predicted the 1993 outbreak as well as earlier ones that took place in 1918 and 1933–34. The Navajo records reflected that each of these outbreaks had followed increases in rainfall, which subsequently resulted in larger piñon crops and accompanying increases in the numbers of mice feeding on them.[21]

If any of the medical experts had asked these Native Americans at the outset of the problem, they would have been told they were dealing with what came to be called hantavirus pulmonary syndrome, which is now identified and fully documented by the CDC. The moral of the story is talk to everyone, scrutinize everything, and keep an open mind!

As a mystery malady sufferer, you should seek as many alternative ideas from as many different sources as you have available. In other words, become proactive. Medical problem solving, particularly as it relates to mystery maladies, cannot be limited to only the "recognized" experts. Give yourself permission to think creatively, look at everything, and consult everyone, including sources that are not necessarily medical in nature.

We have been surprised by the consistency with which clinical solutions, especially in the case of mystery maladies, have come from places we least expected. If you keep an open mind, you make yourself available to help from all possible sources. And if you are open enough to allow your own creative thinking to emerge as you work through the Eight Steps for Self-Diagnosis, you are sure to help yourself.

Becoming Your Own Medical Detective

Diagnosing a mystery malady is much like solving a crime. The primary goal of any detective academy is to train officers to become capable and proficient investigators. While the crimes themselves may vary from burglary to homicide, the basic investigative techniques used to solve the crimes remain constant. Similarly, the exact nature of your mystery malady (whether it is gastrointestinal, dermatological, or neurological) is irrelevant for the purposes of self-diagnosis; the medical investigative techniques presented here will apply to all of them. Naturally, at different times during the investigation (whether it is criminal or medical), consultants with specific areas of expertise will be required, but the investigative method will not vary.

Here's what you generally need to know about basic criminal investigation: detectives, in responding to a crime scene, are trained to secure the entire immediate and surrounding area to preserve it. The investigative team then canvasses the scene, collecting and documenting the primary evidence of what's present or absent at the time of their arrival. That evidence includes the location of all actual and potential witnesses, as well as any physical evidence.

Detectives are also trained *not* to make a judgment about what is or is not relevant because they know from their training that even a seemingly insignificant clue might be the key to the whole case. Refraining from judgment will be equally important for you, as we will discuss in the next chapter.

The balance of the crime investigation is the following of every potential lead and clue down to the last detail. This may include in-depth interviews, research, fingerprints, photos, lineups, all-points bulletins, police sketches, subpoenas for more potential evidence, surveillance, computer crosschecks, and undercover work. It will also involve the processing and examination of all evidence by experts and crime labs with the latest crime scene investigative technology. The observational data will suggest a theory, or hypothesis, of the case. This theory is then tested against previously and newly collected data.

As information is gathered, the investigative team is committed to review the evidence again and again—in fact, as many times as is necessary—to solve the crime. As team members repeat this process, new leads often turn up and they are followed in the same manner. The process of probing, collecting and recording information, sorting and organizing it, researching and analyzing it is repeated. The theories are tested over and over until all the threads of evidence have been woven together into a coherent picture and the solution is found.

A similar process must be followed when solving a medical mystery through our Eight Step method. It too includes probing, collecting, recording, researching, and analyzing steps. It means formulating a hypothesis, testing it against additional data, and constantly reviewing the data and theories using deductive reasoning until the correct diagnosis finally emerges. Although not every crime is solved and not every mystery malady will be diagnosed, one thing is certain: unless the perpetrator of the crime comes forward or unless your malady simply resolves itself, the only opportunity to solve the mystery comes from the principles of good detection.

Our Eight Steps to Self-Diagnosis are your road map to good medical detection. Working through our program will uncover the clues necessary to correctly diagnose your condition. Each clue is like a piece of a puzzle. You gather the puzzle pieces and then assemble and reassemble them until an accurate picture appears. Each clue builds on the previous one, just as each puzzle piece locks into the next. However, it will be necessary for you to try several different combinations until you find the pieces that interlock. In working through the process, you may have to go back several times and repeat certain steps until you find the necessary clue.

Like police detectives, we start with the crime scene. In this case, the crime scene is your body in its past and present settings. Although the idea of a crime scene may seem like a negative way of looking at your body, it is absolutely not intended that way. In fact, if there is any negative connotation in your mind, we want to reframe this immediately. Why? We believe that part of striving for and maintaining good health is to nurture and appreciate our bodies for the complicated and miraculous instruments they are (even though they may be giving us a rough time at the moment). Viewing the body in its setting as a crime scene is to recognize that it is very fertile ground. Our bodies and the circumstances in which they are placed can provide a wealth of information if we know how to access it, listen to it, and try to understand it.

As a medical detective using our Eight Step method, you will begin by collecting and documenting the presence or absence of the primary evidence of your mystery malady. You cannot do this incorrectly, but you may do it incompletely. So perform each step and then do it again, as needed, partnering with your physician as you proceed.

In the next chapter, we'll reveal the Eight Steps to Self-Diagnosis. At the conclusion of that chapter, you'll have completed a diagnostic notebook that can help your doctor help you to solve your mystery malady. (If you have additional questions about how to apply any particular step, simply read on to the many cases contained in Part 2, where you will see exactly how each of the steps was used and how they were applied collectively to reach an accurate diagnosis.) In Chapter 4, we'll show you how to find the right physicians and create proactive partnerships with them. And in Chapter 5, we'll show you how to do medical detective work on the Internet as you continue the search for clues to solve your mystery malady.

If you're willing to spend the time and make the effort, the Eight Steps to Self-Diagnosis and the other tools and techniques we'll share in this book can help you not only find the solution to your mystery malady but live well while you're doing it.

3

The Eight Steps to Self-Diagnosis

It is certainly quite often the case that the physical aspect of disease, i.e., the pathology, can often be influenced in some way by the scientific approach, but in most cases the physical manifestation is only the final expression of a process which has been continuing a long time.

—Dr. John Ball,
Understanding Disease

In this chapter we reveal the revolutionary self-diagnosis model you've been waiting for. We've already discussed what mystery maladies are, how these conditions may develop, and the open mind-set that is necessary to begin to unravel them. Now you are ready to learn the specifics. In this chapter, we will outline the Eight Step method designed to help you become your own medical detective.

If you carefully work through the Eight Steps to Self-Diagnosis, you will uncover at least one or more important clues to solving your mystery malady. Each step builds on the one before it, and all the steps taken together will create a much clearer picture of your mystery malady.

Our self-diagnosis model is action oriented and goal specific. It requires a serious level of commitment on your part to work through the Eight Steps. Keep in mind that actually *doing* them is different from simply reading about them. The solutions you have been searching for can be discovered only if you work at the outlined tasks and do the required analysis (as many times as necessary) to piece together your diagnostic puzzle.

It won't necessarily be a quick or easy process, but we promise the benefits you'll receive will be directly proportional to the effort you are willing to make. We can guarantee that even if you don't actually solve your mystery malady, if you follow the Eight Steps and do the required work, you will have more information about your malady than you had before (which may even lead to some symptom relief).

If, at any point, you feel yourself becoming daunted by the work, remind yourself that until now you've probably left most of your medical care and decision making up to "the experts." Starting today, you have the golden opportunity to take a more active role in your own healing! As the wise physician Hippocrates said long ago, "If you are not your own doctor, you are a fool."

Before we get started, we want to share some general tips on how to work successfully through the steps.

Tips for Doing the Eight Steps

Some of the questions that you'll be asking yourself in different steps may seem to overlap or duplicate one another. This is deliberate, so answer them carefully and completely anyway. The overlap is designed to pick up things you might have overlooked earlier.

Take your time in working through each step. If you don't know the answers immediately, start paying more attention to your body and see if you can make the determination over time.

If you are not certain at first whether a "symptom" is really a symptom, record it anyway with a question mark. By the time you are done, you will be able to either remove the question mark or eliminate that symptom altogether. Pay close attention to the things you want to immediately dismiss as having no bearing on your symptoms, because these may be the very things that can give rise to an important clue.

Remember this model has worked for countless others who have little or no medical expertise, and it is likely to work for you if you'll do the necessary work.

So let's begin with the list of the Eight Steps to Self-Diagnosis. We will discuss each one individually in the remaining pages of this chapter:

- **Step One:** Record the exact nature of your symptoms.
- **Step Two:** Think about the history of your mystery malady.
- **Step Three:** What makes your symptoms better (or worse)?
- **Step Four:** Do a family medical history and determine if you have or had any blood relatives with a similar problem.
- **Step Five:** Search for other past or present mental or physical problems.
- **Step Six:** Categorize your current (and prior) significant medical problems by etiology.
- **Step Seven:** Investigate your lifestyle and belief system.
- **Step Eight:** Take your notebook to your physician and get a complete physical exam.

Step One: Record the Exact Nature of Your Symptoms

In this step, you'll be creating and keeping a notebook that will be used for all the remaining steps. In this notebook, you will begin to record and document your own medical case. You'll be compiling a detailed list of all the symptoms and signs of your mystery malady, using the detailed questions given. We recommend using a three-ring loose-leaf notebook rather than a spiral-bound one, because the better you become at detecting, the more likely you will be to return and add material (pages) to earlier parts of your notebook.

In order to record your symptoms, we first need to define signs and symptoms and understand the difference between them.

Symptoms Versus Signs

Medical textbooks describe *symptoms* as any perceptible change in the body or its functions that signals disease or phases of disease. A symptom is a sensation that only you can perceive and is normally not measurable (like pain or fatigue). A *sign* is an indication of illness that's actually observable and measurable (like a rash or a fever). For our purposes, it's irrelevant whether the bodily change is subjective (symptom) or objective (sign). We will refer to both generally as symptoms.

In observing and recording your symptoms, we urge you not to overlook any bodily change, no matter how insignificant it may seem to you.

It's extremely important to record *all* symptoms. Be as objective and factual as possible, but bear in mind that your objectivity may be compromised by your own unconscious feelings about being ill. Most people are afraid of disability, loss of independence, and, of course, ultimately death. Even if we are not consciously aware of these feelings, our fears may distort our perceptions, causing us to magnify or minimize our symptoms.

Case Study: Tim

Consider Tim, a mystery malady patient, whose hands and knees were swollen. He described his fingers as sausages—a big problem since he was required to use a computer keyboard at work. He was diagnosed with arthritis but was unable to gain any relief from the resulting treatment. After a year of suffering, he contacted us. We asked him to begin working through our self-diagnosis model by making a detailed list of all his symptoms.

As he answered the questions in each of the Eight Steps, he sharpened his thinking and found himself regularly returning to his notebook to add more symptoms. On his fourth return to Step One, he listed a symptom that had been present since the onset of his swollen fingers. He hadn't included it previously because it seemed to be an unrelated condition—scaly, white, dandruff-like patches of skin on both elbows. In his work with Step Five, he consulted his sister. She told him she also had this hereditary condition, diagnosed as psoriasis.

Tim returned with his symptom list to the physician who had originally diagnosed the swelling in his fingers and knees as arthritis. When he brought all his symptoms to the doctor's attention, she immediately made a connection: Tim probably had a rare form of arthritis known as psoriatic arthritis. When the psoriasis that actually causes the arthritis is treated aggressively, the arthritis improves. Tim's mysterious condition was solved! His case shows that even the smallest, seemingly irrelevant symptom can be a clue that leads to a diagnostic solution.

Why do we tend to do this? Anxiety over the possibility of disability can make us engage in catastrophic thinking, to perceive our symptoms as far worse than they really are. Conversely, some of us may be so afraid of becoming disabled that we defend against this fear by trying to minimize our symptoms, maybe even to the point of denying they exist or the degree to which they exist. Being aware of these possible subconscious feelings will help you evaluate whether or not you are accurately recording your symptoms.

Now try to locate your specific symptoms. For example, if your major symptom is stomach pain, narrow it down further. For example, is the pain in the lower left quadrant, just under the navel, or in the upper right side under the breastbone?

Continue to get more detailed, and record all your responses. Make a separate section in your notebook for each of the following categories:

• **Quality and Character.** Continuing with our example of stomach pain, is the pain best described as a dull ache or a sharp, shooting pain? If the symptom is a rash, is it raised, discolored, patchy?

• **Quantity and Severity.** How often do your symptoms occur, and how serious are they? How many times during the course of a day or night do they bother you? Does the severity differ? On a scale of one to ten, what number would you assign to your level of discomfort or pain? If pain is one of your symptoms, it is helpful to use a 1–10 scale to characterize it. Then you can rate it as a "3" in the morning and a "10" at night, for example.

• **Timing and Duration.** When did your symptoms first begin, and when do they occur now? How much time elapses between episodes? How often do episodes occur? For example, does stomach pain happen after you eat or at a certain time of day? Does it occur daily, weekly, seasonally? How long does it last each time?

• **Setting and Environment.** Where do your symptoms usually occur— in certain climates, in certain locations, at high or low altitude, at high or low barometric pressure, in sun or shade, or during periods of intense stress?

Case Study: Karen

After "living" on antibiotics because of recurrent urinary infections for two years and being exhausted from waking up several times a night to urinate, thirty-two-year-old Karen blurted out one morning, "I'm really pissed off!" At that moment, Karen had a gut feeling that she had hit the nail on the head. As soon as she allowed herself to acknowledge how angry she was about a particular life situation, she made the necessary change and miraculously her infections resolved.

Karen's infections were not psychosomatic; on the contrary, they had been objectively documented by urine cultures. However, it is entirely possible that resolving her anger released the tension she had been carrying in her body. Once her urethra became more relaxed, it allowed an uninterrupted flow of urine and a more complete emptying of her bladder. The less urine retained in her bladder, the less likelihood of the urine becoming infected. Going with her instinct was key to Karen's recovery.

• **Impact on Your Functioning.** How are the symptoms affecting your daily functioning? While you're experiencing the symptom, must you stop what you are doing, or can you continue your activities?

• **Other Factors.** Do you have any other thoughts, intuitions, or "gut feelings" about your symptoms? This is not about being right or technically correct but about keeping an open mind while you explore your mystery malady. Allow yourself to brainstorm.

Step Two: Think About the History of Your Mystery Malady

How long you have been having symptoms and when you first began having them are very important clues. The length of time a symptom persists can rule out certain conditions. For example, it is impossible to experience painful "gout" attacks that last for months because gout is a self-limiting disease, meaning that it evolves and resolves over the course of days (with or without treatment). If what you think is gout doesn't go away after a week or so, it's likely not that.

Associated Life Events

Ask yourself what was happening in your life when the symptoms began. Do you remember having the flu or starting a new diet, exercise program, medication, or vitamin supplement? Had you just returned from a vacation? Did you install new carpet in your home?

Case Studies: Gerald and Leah

Gerald's tongue had mysteriously turned black. When he got to Step Two, he suddenly recalled this condition had started when his heartburn began. Although one thing appeared to have nothing to do with the other, when he asked himself whether he had been doing anything unusual at the time his tongue turned black, the only thing he could think of was that he was taking Pepto-Bismol for his heartburn. Sure enough, "black tongue" is an unusual but listed side effect of Pepto-Bismol.

A similar thing happened with Leah, who was suffering from occasional dilation of one pupil, which affected her vision. While it never lasted very long and happened sporadically, she began to think something was seriously wrong. When she got to Step Two and thought about when this problem first occurred, she saw a relationship in the timing between starting treatment for her irritable bowel syndrome and the pupil dilation. On the surface, of course, these two conditions would appear to have no relationship. But with Leah's description of the history of the ailment, Dr. Rosenbaum solved the mystery: Leah's irritable bowel medication could cause pupil dilation if there was direct contact between it and the eye. Since Leah wore contact lenses, her pupil dilation was likely the result of her touching the pill and then, inadvertently, her eye. This mystery would not have been solved if Leah had not thought about the conditions surrounding the onset of her symptoms.

Step Three: What Makes Your Symptoms Better (or Worse)?

Observe what makes your symptoms improve and what exacerbates them. For example, are your symptoms affected by the presence or absence of medication, food, alcohol, sleep, sex, exercise, or hobbies? Do they seem to be affected by situational issues such as certain people, places, things, life events (or their anniversaries), dieting, or overeating? Go back over some of your earlier notes, like Setting and Environment from Step One, and think about them with regard to whether they are a factor in making things better or worse.

Time-of-Day Factors

Do there seem to be days or times when you are able to get some relief? These are important factors because sometimes the time of day when symptoms are worse can be a clue about what category your mystery malady falls into.

For example, if you see a pattern of your symptoms being worse in the morning or after prolonged sitting, your condition is probably inflammatory. If you observe that you experience more swelling with certain weather conditions, it is also likely to be inflammatory since changes in atmospheric pressure can cause contraction and expansion of the fluid responsible for swelling and discomfort.

As opposed to inflammatory conditions that are often worse in the morning, biomechanical problems (such as backaches, muscle contraction headaches, or eyestrain) often get worse as the day progresses. Nerve (neuropathic) problems are also usually more pronounced at night. We will talk more about these classifications in Step Six. But for now, be a good medical detective and just take notes!

Step Four: Do a Family Medical History and Determine If You Have or Had Any Blood Relatives with a Similar Problem

Your genes often predispose you to certain conditions. For example, it is less likely that the chest pain you are experiencing is a heart attack if you don't have a family member with this condition (although this generality is not true for all people). On the other hand, those bumps appearing on your knuckles are probably a form of familial osteoarthritis if your mother had them too. If you are wondering whether you or someone you love may be suffering from depression, check out whether another family member is or was depressed, since it tends to run in families.

The Importance of Degrees of Consanguinity

First-degree relatives (parents, siblings, and offspring) with similar symptoms are more relevant and revealing than second-degree relatives (grandparents, aunts/uncles, and grandchildren). However, the medical history of all your blood relatives should be examined, including their age at diagnosis of illness, significant lifestyle and environmental factors (if known), and their age at death.

Similar Backgrounds and Similar Conditions

We authors are not related, but we do come from very similar ethnic, religious, and cultural backgrounds. Our families emigrated from the same countries, and it is a documented fact that in past centuries there was much inbreeding within our religious and cultural groups. Consequently, we do not believe it is a coincidence that we have suffered from several of the same mystery maladies.

Step Five: Search for Other Past or Present Mental or Physical Problems

By now you've created your notebook, recorded your symptoms with some specificity and objectivity, and explored the history and circumstances of your ailment. If you've analyzed all this data and still haven't arrived at the solution to your mystery malady, then the time has come to pause and ask yourself, What am I missing here? What else could be going on?

Let's look at whether there is any relationship between your past and present physical and/or mental symptoms. It is fairly common for laypeople (and even some doctors) to see their conditions in a linear way, but the notion that you have only one condition at a time is a fallacy. You may have several active medical problems, any one of which may be contributing to your current malady even if it's not immediately obvious. The goal here is to uncover any other past or active problems that may be causing symptoms and to identify whether there is a relationship to what you perceive as your mystery malady. At the very least, consider the following questions:

- Has anything else been bothering you?
- Was anything bothering you just before the onset of your current mystery malady?
- Have you had any emotional or psychiatric problems in the past?
- What about current problems? (Sometimes it is difficult to separate your distress about your medical condition from other stresses, but try to be objective.)

Do a systematic review of your systems: digestive, respiratory, circulatory, skeletal, cardiovascular, lymphatic, endocrine, nervous, muscular, reproductive, and urinary. Are you having difficulties within any of your bodily systems?

For example, if apart from your mysterious chest pain, you are having respiratory problems that you believe are related to your allergy to grass and have nothing to do with your chest pain, list them anyway. If your neck hurts, but you feel certain that this resulted from lifting weights and you don't think there is a relationship between the neck pain and your inexplicably feeling hot and cold flashes, log both in your notebook.

Obtaining All of Your Past and Present Medical Records

You have a legal right to obtain copies of your medical records. A comprehensive review of all your medical records may help you see a pattern or similarity to your current ailment. As you sift through them, develop a chart for easy reference. Record in chronological order the dates of all office visits, hospitalizations or immunizations, and any laboratory and diagnostic tests performed (with their findings). List all medications or treatments you've had, including the dates they started and stopped.

When you review all your test results, bear in mind that testing and the instruments used in testing always have some degree of fallibility and limitations—just like the humans who perform them.* For our purposes, it is important not to assume that the diagnoses you recall being given were necessarily correct if they were based on testing or examination. It is better to rely on a statement of your symptoms at the time you sought medical attention and let your current doctor draw her own conclusions about whether your previous diagnosis was accurate.

Remember the importance of keeping an open mind. *Please make no assumptions yet!*

Step Six: Categorize Your Current (and Prior) Significant Medical Problems by Etiology

Etiology is the study of the causes of disease. This is a lengthy step, but it can be extraordinarily fruitful for your medical detective work. Illnesses may be classified in any number of ways. Most medical texts categorize disease and disorders by organ systems (which you reviewed as part of Step Five.) Sometimes, however, an analysis of organ systems is less useful in medical detection than a search for the possible origin or cause.

Take chronic headaches as an example. The organ systems usually involved are circulatory and nervous. However, with recurrent headaches, there can be any number of causes from bacterial (sinusitis to meningitis) to biomechanical (cervical arthritis or muscle tension) to traumatic (chronic subdural hematoma) to psychological (stress). Understanding the origin or cause of these headaches is most often key to treatment and resolution, and the same can be true with other mystery maladies.

---

*For example, rheumatologists commonly perform the antinuclear antibody (ANA) test, also known as the test for systemic lupus erythematosis (SLE). Countless patients have been referred to Dr. Rosenbaum over the years with a diagnosis of SLE based solely on a positive ANA result. That same ANA test performed by a second laboratory or possibly even the same laboratory on a different day could well have a different result. Certain medications can create a false-positive result (a positive test result in the absence of disease). Other conditions (such as thyroid disease and its antibodies) can also cause a false positive.

In this step, we are going to examine your symptoms from a different angle. In our self-diagnosis model, we have separated potential causes of disease and their symptoms into eight categories. The following list is not an exhaustive one, but it should get you started in the right direction:

- Genetic
- Infectious (viral, bacterial, fungal, or parasitic)
- Structural or biomechanical
- Environmental
- Metabolic
- Traumatic
- Iatrogenic
- Psychological

Just a reminder: as with most other things we've discussed, nothing should be viewed in an entirely linear manner. Even causation or origin of disease is not always a single event but rather a network of multiple factors that may intersect. Leukemia, for example, can relate to age, heredity, environmental issues, and behaviors such as smoking.* Nevertheless, examining your symptoms and determining what category they fall under may yield some important clues. Let's discuss each of the possible causes in detail.

Could Your Malady Be Genetic?

Genetic disorders are potentially the most important field of medical research. Such conditions account for approximately 10 percent of all pediatric and adult hospital admissions (not including diseases of a multifacto-

---

*In a recent case reported in Baltimore, determining the cause of a patient's complaint was confusing because it was multifactorial. A young woman was diagnosed as having the first case of autoimmune hepatitis when she was discovered to have all the symptoms of liver disease. A careful examination of possible origins revealed that this condition was likely induced by the use of black cohosh, an herbal remedy gaining popularity as an alternative to hormone replacement therapy.

Case Study: Justin

If Dr. Rosenbaum hadn't sought a comprehensive family history on an issue not normally considered "genetic," twenty-three-year-old Justin—who suffered from severe back pain—would still be undiagnosed and suffering. After months of treatment from a chiropractor, an orthopedic surgeon, and a physical therapist, Justin had experienced no improvement in his condition. In fact, bed rest and traction worsened his condition.

When he finally found his way to Dr. Rosenbaum, careful evaluation revealed that his pain was emanating from the sacroiliac joint. A thorough review of Justin's family history revealed several uncles with a long history of lower back pain that had no clear cause. Dr. Rosenbaum did a genetic analysis and found that Justin had the HLA-B27 gene, which predisposed him to an arthritic genetic condition called ankylosing spondylitis. Appropriate therapy for this diagnosis finally resulted in a reduction of Justin's pain.

rial nature). This number will surely rise with all the current research. Thus, you need to research your family history as first discussed in Step Four.

Is Your Malady Caused by Infection?

Biologic agents such as viruses, bacteria, fungi, and parasites cause the vast majority of disease, whether mysterious or not. Despite the virtual elimination of most infectious diseases in developed countries, parasitic disease is still quite common. A serious problem has developed with antibiotic-resistant bacteria, resulting in mutated and often deadly variants. Modern civilization has introduced other problems such as mass handling of foods, x-ray irradiation of food, immunosuppressive drugs, travel and encroachments into previously isolated locations, and biological agents used as weapons. Because of these many factors, infectious disease still thrives.

Think about where you've traveled recently. Did you experience any unusual smells or agents that stung your throat or eyes or skin, have you felt like you had a flu or virus, sore throat, difficulty breathing, drooling, muscle aches, swollen glands, increased heart rate, rash, or nausea? Has anyone

---

Case Study: Josh

When Dr. Rosenbaum's son was eleven years old, he suddenly developed diarrhea, abdominal pain, bloating, gas, nausea, and vomiting. He tried over-the-counter medicine to stop the diarrhea, but when it was discontinued, all his symptoms resumed. A trip to the gastroenterologist resulted in ten days of antibiotic therapy, but it was not effective. By going back and following the steps we've outlined, Josh's family realized that the symptoms started soon after a family white-water rafting trip. They remembered when Josh fell out of the raft and swallowed some river water. Dr. Rosenbaum also remembered that the Colorado River is known for containing a parasite named giardia. When a stool sample was tested, the infection was confirmed, and Josh's condition was cured with the correct treatment.

---

around you been experiencing similar symptoms (or even different ones) they consider unusual? Have you had an experience that is similar in time, place, or exposure to that of others?

Is Your Malady Biomechanical in Origin?

Biomechanics refers to the interrelationship between your body and its position or movement. For example, many sports injuries are biomechanical

---

Case Study: Dr. Katz

Consider the case of Dr. Katz, a hospital physician who developed a sensation of "burning acid" on his outer upper thigh when making rounds one day. Everyone focused on what was wrong with his thigh. But by not looking for a possible biomechanical origin, they missed the real diagnosis of meralgia paresthetica—a condition caused by wearing a tight belt under an obese abdomen. This, in turn, was pinching the nerve that goes to the thigh. Incidentally, this condition also accounts for the pain some younger women experience from constantly wearing hip-hugging, tight jeans!

(such as "tennis elbow," which is caused by an abnormal backswing, or foot pain from an abnormal gait).

Most, but not all, biomechanical maladies involve the primary symptom of pain. Yet biomechanics as the actual cause of pain is often overlooked—a sad fact since maladies of this origin are often the most simple to resolve.*

Could Your Mystery Malady Be Due to a Change in Your Environment?

One of the greatest current threats to our health is exposure to toxins in the environment—from the food and water we ingest to the air we breathe to the chemicals we're exposed to in cosmetics, toys, and household cleaners. Many people have concerns about the potential electromagnetic hazards of cell phones and computer screens. Environmental causes of disease are a new and expanding area of research.

Until more evidence emerges, we must be careful not to jump to conclusions. On the other hand, because the occurrences of chemical sensitivities, degenerative brain diseases, and many autoimmune disorders are clearly on the rise (some statistics say conservative estimates are now up to 15 percent of the population), it is difficult to ignore environmental factors as causes to be investigated. When considering such factors in your own case, find out if anyone else in your area is having the same or other significant symptoms.

Is Your Mystery Malady Metabolic in Nature?

Endocrinology is the study and treatment of glands (for example, the thyroid) and the hormones they produce. The endocrine system is often tested

---

*Mysterious pain often stems from the overuse of soft tissue, muscle, tendons, bursa, and ligaments. This may be due to poor posture or other improper body movements, such as sitting at a computer all day or talking with the telephone cradled between your head and shoulder. In women, it can be caused by constantly carrying heavy purses over the shoulders, and in men, it can result from sitting on a wallet.

by measuring hormone levels. Hormones communicate broadly with other organs through the nervous system, cytokines (proteins that regulate the immune system), and growth factors.

Endocrine disorders often cause imbalances in metabolism and as such are among the most difficult to diagnose; the metabolic system as a whole is a finely integrated network of an infinite number of chemical reactions occurring in all body cells, coordinated by signal systems such as hormones and enzymes. Common endocrine disorders include diabetes and other pancreatic disorders and pituitary, adrenal gland, and thyroid disorders. One metabolic condition in children that has only recently been identified was for many years believed to be the result of deliberate "bad" behavior and thus psychological in origin. Today we know that bedwetting is actually a metabolic disorder and can be treated successfully with a nose spray at bedtime that replaces the hormone necessary for regulating the reabsorption of water in the kidneys. Metabolic mystery maladies are discussed further in Chapter 9.

Was Your Mystery Malady Induced by Trauma?

A traumatic wound is an injury caused by an external force. Examples are fractures, sprains, dislocations, head trauma, eye injuries, and tooth loss.

Case Studies: Kara and Don

Kara suffered for years from vaginal discharge and dyspareunia (pain with sex). Her gynecologist was perplexed by the persistence of erosions (sores) on her cervix despite numerous attempts at therapy, including antibiotics, antifungals, cauterization, and even partial excision (removal of the cervical wall). Only years later, after doing research on the Internet, did Kara realize that she had been inserting her diaphragm upside down, resulting in chronic irritation (trauma) of her cervix.

Another case study is Don, who suffered from poor vision for a number of years. He was eventually diagnosed with keratoconus, an unusual cone formation of the cornea. By following the Eight Steps, he sharpened his powers of observation and discovered he was inflicting this condition on himself by consistently rubbing his eyes with a turning motion (trauma).

Because the word *trauma* implies a stressful injury requiring emergency treatment, it is easy to ignore the possibility that more subtle problems can also have their origins in a traumatic injury.

Was Your Mystery Malady Medically Induced?

A medically induced disorder is called *iatrogenic*. In the age of modern medicine we have some wondrous treatments and cures, but they can sometimes inflict a heavy penalty. Some iatrogenic effects are unavoidable and considered reasonable; they are known, expected, and endured because the benefits of the treatment outweigh the negative side effects.* Unfortunately, many side effects are not readily identified as possible causes of our mystery maladies.

As medical mysteries abound and solutions become even harder to come by, and as drug companies market aggressively and governmental regulations become more lax, growing numbers of doctors and their patients are experimenting with "off-label" medication use (prescribing medications for something other than their approved purposes). A recent study showed that more than 115 million such prescriptions were written in one year (2003) and thousands of patients have suffered serious, permanent, and mysterious iatrogenic consequences.

Also, there are documented cases of mistakes by overworked nurses and physicians, foreign sales of unauthorized drugs, self-treatment by patients, and an increase in elective surgeries and treatments to consider. All these factors can create medically induced conditions; unfortunately, most are not necessarily recognized as such.

Do a careful analysis of every medical intervention (physical therapy, medications, procedures, supplements, or treatments of any kind) you've had to determine if a possible relationship exists between the cause of your symptoms and that intervention. Recently, after years of use, Ephedra—a

---

*For example, the use of glucocorticoids (steroids, prednisone, cortisone) to control progressive immunological, hematological, or neurological conditions may produce side effects like truncal obesity, buffalo hump, stretch marks, fragile and thin skin, easy bruising, elevated blood sugar, and a rounded face.

common herbal supplement often used for weight loss—was removed from the market by the Food and Drug Administration (FDA) when it was finally linked to 155 deaths and dozens of heart-related conditions.

Is Your Mystery Malady Psychological in Origin?

Recent studies by the U.S. Surgeon General reflect the view that mental health and psychological illnesses are really just points along a continuum. For this reason, illnesses that are psychological in origin are difficult to identify. That, together with the fact that many such illnesses have very real physical or bodily symptoms, makes it easy to understand why they are often at the root of mystery maladies.*

In order for you to be objective about this analysis, it is important to remember that psychological illnesses do *not* arise from a lack of willpower or self-discipline. They are the same as other diseases like arthritis or diabetes. So do not rule out this potential source of your mystery malady until you've investigated it fully. This type of complicated mystery malady is explored in Chapter 12.

Step Seven: Investigate Your Lifestyle and Belief System

Sometimes a person's lifestyle and beliefs must be examined in order to arrive at a correct diagnosis. In some ways, this may be one of the most difficult steps to take and the most difficult clue to investigate. It can feel uncomfortable to consider the possibility that how we think or what we do (or

---

*In addition to the more well-known psychological illnesses (like depression and anxiety), other common conditions that often involve sustained, intense physical signs and symptoms include somatization disorder (the conversion of mental experiences or states into bodily symptoms); pain disorder (long-term chronic pain without physical findings); conversion disorder (signs and symptoms usually related to motor function, such as difficulty walking, swallowing, speaking, and even seeing); and hypochondriasis (a preoccupation with the fear of developing or belief that one has a terrible disease).

don't do, as the case may be) can actually be the cause of our medical problems—even if we are doing them in an effort to be more "healthy."

Lifestyles or beliefs are not "good" or "bad" in and of themselves, but they can become problematic if they affect our health. In order to examine this from a neutral position, it is important to *not* judge our behavior; we need to simply observe and document it. Remember our commitment early on to "have an open mind."

As you consider the following questions, keep in mind that this information is just for *you* right now, so be as honest with yourself as you can. Take your time to consider these questions, some of which are deliberately repetitious.

• What does an ordinary day entail for you, and has it been modified by your illness?

• In general, how do you cope with your illness? Have you coped with other illnesses in the same way?

• Are there financial problems related to your job or lack of a job?

• How do you unwind from the stress of daily living?

• How are you coping with difficult issues? Do you eat more or differently than normal? Do you drink, smoke a joint, pop a pill; meet up and go home with people at bars, clubs, and parties? Or do you prefer to be alone and avoid social contact, not eat, watch movies or TV all night, surf the Net for hours, or exercise excessively? Do you overspend or collect things and then refuse to return or discard them? What other things do you do to unwind from stress?

• Does it ever feel like your past sometimes affects your behavior in the present? For example, do you "stuff" your anger? Do you avoid social contact because you are afraid of getting hurt like you were in the past?

• Are you getting enough rest and relaxation? How do you feel about sleeping more than seven hours, napping in the afternoon, sleeping in late, relaxing in general, and leaving chores undone in order to have time for fun or relaxation?

- Do you feel you have to be perfect?

The next question is whether any of these beliefs or behaviors could possibly be causing your mystery malady or making it worse. For example, some people believe that it is "lazy" to sleep more than a certain number of hours, lie down for a while in the afternoon, or "have fun" before getting all their work done. Some of these people may actually be sleep-deprived, which can cause many different illnesses. Without recognizing the underlying cause, the constant illness may seem a mystery.

Another potentially problematic belief system and accompanying lifestyle is the opposite of having difficulty relaxing or getting rest. There

---

Case Study: Claire

Sometimes a belief system or lifestyle that leads to certain behaviors can obscure the identification of a mystery malady in a loved one. Consider Claire, the wife of a retired schoolteacher named George. At about the time of his retirement, George became a "collector" of things. He hated to throw anything away because he did not believe in wasting things. His favorite saying was "Waste not, want not." This included saving just about anything and everything that passed through their front door, including morning newspapers from the past decade.

The "collectables" were filling up every room of their home. Neither George nor Claire understood that this behavior was a coping mechanism for George—possibly deriving from the fear and belief that now that he was no longer earning an income they might not have enough money to survive past a certain age. His way of dealing with this stress was to hold on to as much as he could.

Unfortunately, this was disastrous for his wife. About a year after George's retirement, Claire began having difficulty breathing and developed "incurable" asthma. Although both George and Claire were terribly alarmed by this situation, neither associated his fearful belief system (and the collector lifestyle that accompanied it) with the dust and must. The piles of stuff were the root cause of Claire's life-threatening asthma. By examining their lifestyle and belief systems, the issue was finally brought to light.

---

are those who believe stress should be relieved but do it in ways that could cause a malady, such as drinking, drugging, or eating too much or too little. These activities (themselves an underlying disease) are often overlooked as a potential cause of a secondary mystery malady. This is because one of the symptoms of the underlying primary illness is denial.

In the privacy of your own room, without the need to disclose the information to anyone yet, allow yourself to consider the possibility that your particular beliefs and lifestyle might be a contributing cause or perhaps even the main cause of your mystery malady.

Step Eight: Take Your Notebook to Your Physician and Get a Complete Physical Exam

The notebook you began in Step One probably has many pages by now. If you have not done so already, now is the time to take the results of all your good detective work and consult the "experts." In addition to the consultation you will have with your physician, you will want to schedule a complete physical examination and ask your doctor to order whatever additional test(s) you may need to confirm or rule out conditions that may have been brought to mind by all your work and the clues you've uncovered.

In the next chapter, we will discuss how to create a proactive partnership with your physicians so you can more effectively enlist their help in your search for the correct diagnosis. And in Chapter 5, we'll show you how to continue your medical detective work on the Internet.

4

Creating a Proactive Partnership
with Your Physician

The patient, though conscious that his condition is perilous, may recover his health
simply through his contentment with the goodness of the physician.
—HIPPOCRATES, 1400 B.C.

THE LAST CHAPTER outlined in detail the Eight Steps to Self-Diagnosis.
The last of the steps is to take your notebook full of clues to your physician
and get a complete physical examination. Even if your doctor hasn't been
able to solve your mystery malady up to this point, a good relationship with
the right practitioner can be one of your greatest resources in your quest for
the correct diagnosis.

In this chapter, we will explore the special needs of the mystery malady patient and describe the traits you need to look for when selecting a
physician. This chapter will also identify ways to create a lasting, creative,
and productive partnership with that physician. Your role in creating such
a therapeutic partnership will be emphasized and discussed in depth. With
a willingness and commitment of both parties to make this vital collaboration work, the chances of reaching a diagnosis—and ultimately a cure—
increase dramatically.

Even if it takes some time, you'll find that choosing the right doctor
and creating a therapeutic partnership can have a dramatic impact on your
overall healing. Feeling a sense of support from, confidence in, and comfort

with your doctor will restore your hope during the search for a solution to your mystery malady.

Most educated consumers of medical care are generally familiar with the things to look for in selecting the right physician:

- Medical competence, including level of training, licensing, board certification, and experience in the diagnosis and treatment of the medical area related to your concern
- Good references, hospital privileges, and the respect of peers
- Ease in obtaining appointments, diagnostic testing, and prescriptions for medications
- Good listening skills
- Ability to give clear explanations
- Respect for patients (including not having patients wait more than twenty minutes without an explanation for the delay)
- Reasonable fees and/or acceptance of your insurance
- Belief in and practice of preventive medicine

Unique Needs of the Mystery Malady Patient

The qualities already listed are imperatives in any doctor-patient relationship. However, mystery malady patients have special needs and require some unique additional qualities in their physician.

Understanding and Extra Support

First and probably foremost, mystery malady patients become just that because no doctor has successfully diagnosed them. It is understandable, therefore, that you approach the task of finding the right physician already feeling disappointed and frustrated by the medical community. After all, you have been traveling from one specialist to another only to receive no diagnosis, misdiagnoses, or contradictory diagnoses.

Unless physicians have experienced a mystery malady firsthand or through a family member, few of them can even begin to know the often unspoken emotional burden of having an undiagnosed disease—the lack of control, the anxiety of not knowing if you will ever get well, the adverse impact on your relationships, the sense of isolation, and the abandonment and hopelessness you may feel. Nor do physicians necessarily appreciate the inordinate amount of patience, persistence, and inner strength required to deal with the chronicity of your symptoms, the decrease in your overall quality of life that comes with the uncertainty, and the physical as well as emotional impairment of function resulting from your mystery malady.

Yet it is not a psychiatrist you need; it is a medical doctor who is sensitive to the effects of living with an unidentified illness. To most physicians, illness is a disease process that can be measured and understood through testing and clinical observation. Period. To mystery malady patients, it is both that and the *dis-ease* of it all. You need a doctor who understands this and can give you the compassion as well as the support you need during the time it takes to pursue answers. You need to feel you're not being judged about your fears and anxieties. You need someone who is willing to give you extra time, extra patience, and extra effort as you seek symptom relief and explore alternatives while searching for a diagnosis. This is no small request in an era in which most doctors have doubled their patient loads in an effort to survive financially in a managed-care environment, despite their desire to give high-quality medical care.

Assurance of Continuity of Care

Many—if not most—mystery malady patients have a pressing, practical problem: these days, physicians live in a world of medical specialization where very few are willing to move beyond their niche. You, on the other hand, live in a world where your mystery malady may cross over several areas of specialization. The acupuncturist tells you your kidney meridian is the problem; the chiropractor states that your spine is out of alignment; the gastroenterologist says you have gastritis; the psychiatrist says it's in your head; the neurologist blames your problems on migraines. But none of these opinions is helping, and no one seems to be looking at the whole picture.

Generally speaking, this is supposed to be the role of your primary care physician. However, mystery maladies are often complicated and require more expertise than he or she can handle. You may need someone more specialized who is also willing to oversee your comprehensive medical care—

especially if other specialists are, or should be, involved in your treatment. In other words, you require a doctor who's willing to assume the "lead" in your care. If you don't already have a team in place, you may need this doctor to create one.*

The View of Medicine as an Art That Requires Creativity

Finally, to state the obvious, since your illness is not a textbook one and does not lend itself to easy diagnosis, you must have a doctor who is to willing to think "outside the box" and explore the possible answers that arise from the information you gather in working through the Eight Steps to Self-Diagnosis. You need someone who is willing to support you in following our revolutionary model. Your physician must be the curious sort—unafraid of a challenge and willing to go the extra distance to assist you in finding some answers. She must be willing to give you the extra time and energy that this will demand.

How Do You Find Such a Physician?

Once you have located a doctor who meets the basic criteria for a good doctor-patient relationship, you must make some basic determinations specific to your special needs.

• Does your doctor have an understanding of and empathy for the effects of living with a mystery malady? Is she willing to be patient and give you the support you need in dealing with this problem?

---

*For example, I (Lynn) had a condition that involved several areas of specialty—urology, gynecology, neurology, dermatology, and physical therapy and many other forms of treatment. My condition was far too complicated to have a general family practitioner take the lead. Fortunately, however, I was able to convince my urologist to assume the lead role in the diagnosis, treatment, and management of my condition. While I received treatment from my other specialists, my urologist maintained the "master file" and consulted with the other specialists involved. Before I entered into any treatment by another specialist, I always ran it by my lead doctor (see Chapter 8).

• Is your doctor willing to undertake a challenge beyond the area of his specialty? Will he help you create a team of specialists or work with your existing team as the lead physician in your care?

• Is this doctor willing to take the time and energy to explore solutions with you, listening to the information you have gathered on your own, analyzing and perhaps further researching any information you have derived from working through the Eight Steps to Self-Diagnosis?

How do you find these answers out? Very simply—ask! Be as direct as you can. This section provides some specific actions and questions that should help you decide whether this doctor is right for you. Start by scheduling an appointment or consultation so you can give your potential new doctor a "checkup." Remember you have taken back control of your own care and the responsibility to ascertain the necessary information and make the necessary judgments rests with you.

If you've never visited this doctor before, notice how the office staff responds to you. Are they abrupt or courteous, aloof or welcoming? A doctor's staff are generally—though not always—reflective of the doctors in the office. Even if you like the physician, problematic staff may affect your decision since you are looking for a long-term relationship and you will most certainly have to deal often with the staff.*

How soon can you get an appointment? If you have to wait longer than a month, it may imply that this doctor will not have the necessary time to devote to you. Try to determine whether the lengthy waiting period is

---

*I (Lynn) remember scheduling an appointment to see a medical specialist in another city. It and my plane tickets were canceled twice by his office staff. I waited several more months to see this doctor. When the day of my appointment finally arrived, I waited *three hours* in his waiting room. Once in the examining room, I was told by the staff, despite my long trip and my specific request for additional time for this initial consultation, that I had *ten minutes* with the doctor. On the way out, I checked with other patients in the waiting room and was told my plight was "standard operating procedure" in that office. Although the doctor was aware of the situation, he either wouldn't or couldn't change it. So, even though this well-recognized specialist was compassionate and extremely knowledgeable, I made a decision to not use him for my treatment.

because she tries to give her current patients all the time they need and hesitates to accept new patients until she can do the same for them. In addition, ask the front desk how busy this practice is and whether you will have to wait as long for a return appointment once you become one of her patients. If so, move on.

When scheduling your appointment, make certain you are allotted at least an hour so you will have the time you need to make a good assessment of whether this physician "has what it takes" to become your doctor and to see whether you actually receive that amount of allotted time. When you arrive at the office, how long do you have to wait? If it is longer than thirty minutes, find out if there is a legitimate reason (an emergency or delay in returning from surgery, for example, and not simply "scheduling problems"). If there is a problem, let the doctor know and see what his reaction is.

Generally, a physician's respect for your time or responsiveness to what you perceive as a problem is a good predictor of her respect for you as a patient and the overall quality of her care.* Take along all your relevant past medical records, your Eight Steps notebook, and a list of all your questions, including the ones we pose in this chapter. Then, in addition to assessing whether this doctor has the fundamental qualities everyone needs, you will want to make your special-needs assessment.

Here are some additional inquiries and observations you will want to make:

• During your interaction, do you get a sense of patience and support from this doctor? You will know this immediately by how he communicates with you and whether or not you feel comfortable communicating with him. Once you've talked to him about your specific case, plainly and directly raise the issue of your unique needs as a mystery malady patient as we've discussed them. Explain your need for a continuing relationship with him as you search for a diagnosis and/or cure.

---

* If time is a problem for you, make your appointments early in the morning or right after lunch, before scheduling backups grow exponentially. Also, for inexplicable reasons, studies show that Tuesday is the day of the week when doctors are most likely to be on time.

• Do you feel comfortable enough to share your fears, anxiety, or depression and what you might consider your "silliest" question or concern about your mystery malady with this doctor? If so, what is her reaction? Does she seem to acknowledge the difficulties of your illness and not make a judgment about it? Does she make any effort to help you through the emotions you may feel about having a mystery malady?

• Is the doctor doing more talking than listening? Are you able to state your concerns without interruption?

• How many cases of mystery maladies (as we define them) has he handled successfully? If he doesn't bring it up, ask.

• Do you feel that this doctor will support you in the special ways you may need? For example, would she be willing to write a letter to your place of employment or assist you in being exempted from jury duty if you are unable to serve, sign a form for handicap license plates, fill out disability insurance information, or even speak in support of you in a legal deposition, if necessary?

• When you talk about your feelings, does the doctor acknowledge them, or does he direct the conversation back to technical talk?

• When you ask questions, does the doctor take the time to respond in terms you can understand? Do you believe she will continue to make the effort to ensure that you fully understand your condition, medical directions, and treatment options?

• Does the doctor make you feel comfortable with his body language? For example, does he sit rather than stand during the visit, does he lean toward you rather than back while listening?

Share your work on the Eight Steps to Self-Diagnosis. If your prospective doctor hasn't already heard of this program, give her a copy of the book and ask whether she will lend her expertise to you as you move through the steps. Consider these questions:

- Is your doctor impressed with your willingness to do this detective work? Is she generally supportive of it?

- Is she willing and able to commit to taking the time to work with you? Alternatively, is there a member of her staff who is willing to do this and then will communicate with the doctor and get back to you with answers?

Trust your gut reaction. If, at the conclusion of your appointment, you don't feel a sense of caring, patience, support, and encouragement, this is probably not the right doctor for you. If you were made to feel rushed or that you took too much of the physician's time, even if he commits to giving you that time in the future, this is not the right doctor. If you didn't feel invited to talk, this may not be the right doctor. If his approach didn't make sense to you and didn't match up with information you've already received, this may not be the right doctor for you.

Let your feelings and instincts be your guide. If, for any reason, you have a negative feeling about a practitioner after you consult with him or if anything from his personality to the diagnosis and proposed treatment doesn't seem quite right to you, don't dismiss your reaction. If you're not sure and you want to give him another chance, investigate this physician further and have another consultation. If, however, after the second interaction, you're still not sure, move on.*

---

*Searching for the solution to the mystery malady involving his eyes, Dr. Rosenbaum found an ophthalmologist at a premier eye institute in another city who had been rated by a national news magazine as one of the best in the country. After waiting four hours to see this doctor, he felt rushed and was left with unanswered questions. Dr. Rosenbaum did not feel a sense of trust with this doctor, but desperate for solutions, he followed this expert's advice, had a risky surgical procedure, and found himself in excruciating postoperative pain. The doctor neither warned his patient that this would occur nor gave him medication in preparation for it. Dr. Rosenbaum wound up in an emergency room. Although technically competent, this ophthalmologist lost a patient because of his brusque, rushed attitude and his lack of empathy and bedside manner. Dr. Rosenbaum should have followed his own instincts, but extreme anxiety can cause even a physician to betray his medical and other instincts. Trust yourself!

Is Your Doctor Comfortable Moving Beyond One Specialty?

If you have a condition that involves more than one area of specialty, determine how active this doctor is willing to be outside her specific area. Although she may acknowledge that something is outside her expertise, will she continue to discuss it or does she go no further? If she suggests other areas of specialization you might look at and perhaps even makes a referral for another doctor, this is a very hopeful sign. She's obviously willing to give it some thought. If you really feel good about this doctor, pursue the idea of her willingness to assume a more active role in your medical care, despite the fact that other specialties are involved. Ask your physician these questions:

• If I bring in other specialists, would you be willing to consult with them? Would you be willing to assume the responsibility of managing my case?

• If I don't feel equipped to create my own team of specialists, are you willing to create or work with a team of different specialists and assume the role of lead doctor?

• Can you make this time commitment or arrange for your staff to assist me in communicating with you?

Is Your Doctor Willing to Think Creatively?

Clearly, yours is a complicated case with no easy solutions or you would have found them already. You need a doctor who is open to any number of ways to find solutions or potential treatment of your symptoms within the parameters of sound medical practice. This is where it is essential to have a physician of sound reputation as well as one who has run up against difficult-to-diagnose conditions and understands the need to use medical detective work. This includes his willingness to encourage and support his patient to take a proactive role in finding solutions. It's important to try to find someone who has had experience with conditions similar to yours for two reasons: (1) doctors who regularly treat certain types of conditions tend to get better results than doctors who treat those conditions only occasionally; and (2) doctors tend to want to continually learn new things about conditions of special interest to them even if they don't have a diagnosis yet.

Ask the physician these questions:

• Are you willing to treat my symptoms until a diagnosis is found? Since the known and prescribed therapies for my condition are not producing any improvement, are you willing, within the bounds of sound medical practice, to experiment and take a different approach in an attempt to gain some symptom relief for me if traditional treatments are not effective?

• Are you willing to do research and/or consult with other physicians for me?

• Will you share the latest information you come across relative to my symptoms and condition?

• Are you willing to evaluate the information I have gathered through the process of working through the Eight Steps to Self-Diagnosis and take it even further?

Then ask yourself these questions:

• Does this doctor display an intellectual curiosity and view my problem as one that needs to be solved?

• Is he known as a good diagnostician?

• Does he seem willing to have me seek more opinions and interested in hearing what they are? (If so, you have found a doctor who wants to get an answer just as you do.)

• Does he seem to have some enthusiasm with regard to his potential role in finding a solution? Or is there a sense of finality on his part that he doesn't know the answer, and rather than offering to find an answer, he either implies or says I should look elsewhere? (If so, then do!)

Finally, as part of your visit, make certain the doctor you are investigating gives you a thorough physical examination that includes nontroubled areas. The examination itself without further evaluation of clues and symptoms should take no less than fifteen minutes. If this is not done, do not return to this doctor. He will probably not make a good diagnostician.

Ultimately, no physician is perfect, but all you need is one who is "good enough." Choose the one who has as many of the traits we've discussed as you feel you need. Some of us will give up a compassionate personality for a person who seems extremely technically qualified or one who is simply willing to assume the role of lead doctor. Some of us may choose the compassion and support over an expressed willingness to take an active role. Some of us may simply want a doctor who is as curious as we are to find an answer and is willing to do the work with us even if she doesn't have a great bedside manner or lots of experience.

This is your judgment to make. But bear in mind that if after you've chosen, the physician turns out to be a mistake, choose again! You've gone this far, so just keep going and start the process again with someone else. The right doctor for you is out there; it's simply a matter of finding him or her. As with all the other work laid out in this book, persistence and patience pays off.

Your Role in Creating a Proactive and Productive Relationship

Now let's turn to your role in this new doctor-patient relationship. As in any relationship, including a therapeutic one, the needs of both people are important. Although traditionally a doctor-patient relationship is (or should be) patient-centered, the relationship between a mystery malady patient and a doctor involves some unique demands. Just as you need certain qualities and traits in your doctor above and beyond the norm, your doctor may need special considerations from you to be able to help you more effectively. (Incidentally, displaying sensitivity to those needs from the outset may be a key in locating the right doctor, and using the Eight Steps exactly as instructed will help your physician enormously.) So let's examine what you can do to create a proactive and productive partnership.

We've already discussed the enormous pressures on doctors who are trying to practice good medicine in a managed-care environment. No matter how deep their professional integrity and their commitment to keeping up with changes in medical information, physicians have as much difficulty as patients in creating a productive doctor-patient collaboration. It becomes even more frustrating in cases of mystery maladies—especially for doctors who want to be part of their patients' solutions.

Here's what you need to do to assist your physician and make yourself a more effective patient partner:

• **Give your doctor acknowledgment and respect.** Just as you want to be recognized as a whole person in conjunction with your disease, the experience, and the effects it has on your life, relationships, and functioning, your doctor is a person too, with frustrations, competing demands on her time and energy, and her own set of needs. She needs to know you have respect for these issues and will try to be a considerate patient.

Sometimes you might want to express your gratitude for her willingness to go the extra mile for you. Don't get angry at her when things don't work. Chances are she is equally frustrated, and you will want to acknowledge her frustration as well as your own. Indicate your willingness to stay the course and keep trying, which will encourage your doctor do the same. Remember you are in this together.

• **Clarify expectations.** Assure your doctor that you want to be a good patient and create an effective partnership. Ask what you can do to achieve this and what he may expect of you in this ongoing relationship. You'd be surprised how well received this question will be, and it gives both of you a sense that you are in this together.

Just as patients are affected by their doctor's attitudes toward them, studies show that doctors are profoundly influenced by the demeanor, comments, and attitudes of their patients. A patient who is routinely rude, irritable, or argumentative will not receive the same care as a patient who is more positive and treats her doctor as a human being. (Dr. Rosenbaum often felt closest to his patients who demonstrated care toward him by taking an interest in the camera collection he kept in his office or remembering his birthday, for example. It is only natural.)

• **Ask about the treatment plan.** Ask what happens if what the doctor proposes doesn't work. This will accomplish two things. It will give you hope that if one thing doesn't work, there are more things to try. It will also force your doctor to think ahead and be prepared for the next step, if he hasn't already done so.

• **Just the facts, ma'am.** When talking to your doctor about your symptoms or what is happening medically, try not to editorialize; just describe what is happening. Don't opine on your symptoms or self-diagnose ("I've begun having these headaches and I think they might be migraines."). Just describe the exact nature of your headaches, including other information you may have derived from doing Step One (for example, "I wake up with headaches once a week that hurt worst above my eyebrows and below my cheeks. They last for hours and aspirin or Tylenol does not seem to give me any relief."). Then let the doctor go to work, ask questions he deems pertinent, and suggest possible therapies or testing; then give him an opportunity to draw his own conclusions. Your doctor will be more willing to give you extra time and support if you stay on task, don't editorialize, and let him do his work.

Also, it has been shown that people who spend some time before their doctor's appointment thinking about their symptoms and concerns enjoy a more mutually satisfactory doctor-patient relationship. This is also where the Eight Steps are wonderful tools and enormously helpful in creating a good relationship with your physician.

• **Set parameters on the amount of time you will need and how best to handle your needs.** Since this will be an ongoing relationship that involves working through your Eight Steps, sifting through and analyzing information, doing some experimentation and reporting results, discuss with your doctor how best to handle this. Perhaps you will wish to schedule a regular twice-monthly appointment at which you can discuss all your accumulated questions and your progress. Perhaps you will arrange with your doctor to have a "point person" in his office—a nurse or physician assistant—through whom you can funnel questions. Ask about the best time to call if you need to speak directly to the doctor. Gather all your questions first and make one focused call rather than several.

If your doctor knows you have respect for his time in this way and you stick to agreed boundaries, it is more likely that he will also realize that if you call between appointed times, you are really having a problem and will respond quickly. Don't abuse this responsiveness.*

• **Be candid.** It is astounding how many honest people don't tell their doctors various things. One of the most common things people don't accurately represent is all the medications they are taking, lifestyle choices they make that might be hazardous to their health, other treatments or therapies they are receiving (such as acupuncture or massage therapy), or their fears about following directions the doctor has given. Your physician cannot help you if you are not completely candid about everything. Interestingly enough, the failure to be straightforward may be the very problem that keeps you from solving your mystery malady.

Lack of candor will clearly affect the efficacy of your doctor-patient relationship. Tell the doctor everything that might even remotely relate to your medical problem and let her be the judge. A good doctor knows what may adversely or positively affect your condition even if it's undiagnosed, and she also understands that anxiety, depression, and anger is normal in people with chronic illnesses and may cause them to do things they otherwise would not do. The right doctor will not be judgmental and will be able to advise you on what is beneficial or adverse to your health. She can talk you through these emotions during a productive visit.

• **Don't doctor-shop!** We know how frustrating it is to be ill and not get answers. But we are trying to create solutions, and doctor-shopping does not produce those. You cannot have an effective and trusting relationship

---

*I (Lynn) had a mystery malady that involved chronic pain, and my physician knew that. Yet whenever I called him, I always received a prompt return call because I had earned his trust over time. He came to know that if I called, it was urgent, and based on how often I refilled my prescriptions, he knew I never abused my pain medications. Thus, if I needed more medication, he was very responsive in prescribing it and trying new things to secure relief. Just knowing I had this support was enormously healing! But it was based on the relationship we, as doctor and patient, had worked to create.

with your physician if you don't keep him apprised of your actions. Even though you may be frustrated or experiencing anxiety in a search for answers, seeking opinions and treatments from other doctors while you are trying to create a proactive and productive partnership with your primary one can actually sabotage your recovery and make you both crazy. There are documented cases of patient deaths resulting from conflicting treatments by different doctors when one doctor did not know what the other doctor was doing.

Apart from being potentially hazardous to your health, it will certainly sabotage any chance you may have of creating that productive partnership you desire. In fact, it is likely to get you fired as a patient! You need to honor your commitments and stick with the treatment plan. This is not to say that you must stay with one doctor if you feel you are not making any progress or your doctor is not living up to his end of the relationship. But first you must give him an adequate chance. Try to resolve any difficulties you may be having with your current doctor; then and only then, move on if you cannot get what you need. Don't stay with that doctor and then not tell him you are working with someone else.

The surest way to lose the trust you have developed and commitment you have earned is to doctor-shop. Unless you are just lucky, you will not find your solutions by looking to other practitioners while you are in a relationship with one specific doctor.

• **Above all, communicate appropriately.** Apart from maintaining a continuing dialogue and line of communication, all interactions between doctor and patient must be handled with mutual respect—on both ends. While we are advocating a proactive relationship by taking action on your own and assuming responsibility for your own health care, being assertive in this way is very different from being confrontational or hostile. Oftentimes these approaches become confused when there is so much pain and frustration involved in the process of securing a diagnosis to a mystery malady.

It is tempting to scapegoat someone—either for the doctor to blame the patient out of frustration for not getting well or for you to blame the doctor for your continuing sickness. If you believe that she is becoming frustrated with you merely because she is not having success in treating you, address this with your doctor. Assure her that you are committed to staying the course until you find the solution. Likewise, if you think you have been inappropriately angry with your doctor for not "fixing" the problem, just admit it and apologize. It can be frustrating all the way around, but maintaining honest communication can salvage any damage.

While medical science may have its limits, hope does not, and that is sustained by maintaining a respectful, collaborative, and supportive relationship between mystery malady patient and doctor. It is worth remembering that you play a major role in fostering a productive and truly healing partnership. Developing this relationship is so important that it is the last of the Eight Steps for self-diagnosis. By following the suggestions in this chapter, you can do it!

5

Medical Detective Work
on the Internet

The best prescription is knowledge.

—Dr. C. Everett Koop,
former U.S. Surgeon
General

Throughout our discussion of the Eight Steps to Self-Diagnosis, including how to create a partnership with your physician, we have emphasized the need for you to assume a proactive role in sleuthing out the solutions to your mystery malady. In addition to observing and recording the exact nature of your symptoms, your sleuthing may involve outside investigation from whatever sources of information you have available. Many people, especially seniors, use the public library to learn about topics of interest. The library is an especially good resource when there is a reference librarian to help direct your research efforts, and the libraries at many medical schools are open to the public.

There is, however, a more convenient place to do your medical investigation—your own computer. The Internet can be a gold mine of medical information if you know how to use it effectively. Many hospitals now have computer terminals available for the community to use when researching health topics. Whether you grew up in front of a keyboard or you're a "surfin' senior," this chapter aims to help you do your own medical detective work on the Internet. If you're not computer savvy, we recommend that you enlist the help of family members or friends who are. Searching the Internet could turn up a unique and invaluable clue to your mystery malady.

Before You Start

For you library-card holders who are about to explore the Internet for the first time, understand first that there is no reason to be intimidated by the computer. Think of the Web as a library literally at your fingertips that is a little more challenging than the orderly world of library stacks. Although the Web may not be as rationally organized, it is without a doubt the biggest library you'll ever find!

It is also the quickest way to find information. It has been determined that it takes an average of five minutes and forty-two seconds on the Internet to find information relevant to specific health questions.[1] When was the last time you visited a library and found what you needed in such a short time?

We will suggest where to look and, more importantly, how to determine if the information you turn up is accurate and trustworthy. We will give you nine questions you should ask yourself to assess the websites you propose to use and point out some pitfalls to avoid.

A recent study found that physicians are increasingly encountering patients who have conducted online health searches. Some physicians even reported having changed their treatment protocols as a result of consumer requests. It is our opinion that physicians should be willing and able to help patients who want to research their own condition. The Agency for Healthcare Research and Quality (AHRQ) of the National Institutes of Health (NIH) echoes this view and recommends that every patient incorporate self-education into their treatment process.

According to a 2003 Pew Internet & American Life Project, 80 percent of U.S. adults eighteen and older (or about 93 million people) have used the Internet to research at least one of sixteen major health topics.

Two authors attempted to determine the prevalence of health-related searches on the Web.[2] They found that 4.5 percent of all Internet searches address health topics and estimated that 6.75 million such searches are conducted every day.

Another study published in the *Canadian Journal of Psychiatry* reports that a review of the most common search engines reveals that "the Internet has eliminated the distance barrier and has given the general public equal access to scientific articles, clinical trials, and guidelines."[3] Furthermore, it concludes that doctors should be in a position to mentor patients who want to research their condition further.

While you should be concerned or at least aware that potential harm can come from using poor-quality health information sometimes accessed on the Internet, studies have revealed very few cases of actual harm. The Montreal Children's Hospital group, for example, in studying 1,512 abstracts on this topic found few *reported* cases of such harm.[4] This may be because Web-surfing patients found the information to be either confusing or inconsistent and therefore more ineffective than harmful.

This is not to say there aren't some completely unreliable websites. We found some that, among other things, promote the health benefits of drinking one's own urine, oxygenation cures for AIDS, and use of colloidal silver as a cure for Gulf War syndrome. Knowing that such misinformation exists, researchers, organizations, and website developers are exploring alternative ways of helping people find and use the high-quality information that is available on the Internet.[5] Organizations such as the National Library of Medicine (NLM), which operates MEDLINEplus, and the Medical Library Association have developed guidelines and tips for consumers to use in evaluating health-related website content.[6] Many helpful articles are listed in the endnotes to this chapter, which highlights some of the guidelines and tips offered in these articles. We believe if you follow these recommendations and check the accuracy of any information you find with your physician, then any risk is substantially minimized if not eliminated.[7–9]

Since there is no formal watchdog organization that oversees or enforces the quality or accuracy of information on the Internet, it is up to you (and ultimately your physician) to be able to differentiate between accurate, scientifically based information and the advertising, hearsay, mere opinion, and other less reliable material you may find. But before we go into detail on the strategies that you can employ to make those distinctions, let's begin with a basic overview of research on the Web—especially for those who are used to researching at a bricks-and-mortar library. It's actually very easy and fast—it can even be fun!

Just Like the Public Library

When you use a major search engine such as Google, Yahoo, or AltaVista to locate websites and articles related to your health concerns, you will be given several links to "home pages" that contain the information you've requested. Think of each home page as a library catalog card. It has information to help you evaluate the relevance, authority, and accuracy of the information you are seeking.

Look at the site's name or home page sponsor or organization (what comes after the "www") the way you'd look at the publisher's name on the library's catalog card. Is it an established medical institution with a respected reputation? If the information is found in an article, look at the author's name and determine if he or she is an authority in the field. Would you buy a book from that author? Has the article or information been peer reviewed, meaning has it been subjected to the scrutiny of a group of medical authorities? If not, the information in that article may be less reliable.

Don't forget to check the dates on the information provided and whether that information has been updated recently. This is the equivalent of checking the copyright date on a published book. You probably wouldn't buy a health book (or check it out from the library) that's twenty years old; you'd want the latest edition that contains the newest discoveries in diagnosis and treatment. With these simple tips, the Internet can become your electronic reference librarian.

Now let's get into the actual medical investigation of your mystery malady. Finding health websites is easy; it's deciding which of those sites is worth your time that takes some savvy. When you send a query to a search engine, the number of links it churns out can be staggering. In the study mentioned earlier, physicians indicated that most of their patients have found fairly accurate information. However, some expressed displeasure about responding to information obtained online because it takes more time during the office visit and challenges their authority, especially when the information is inaccurate. The study concluded that the quality of Internet information is critical, as it influences both patient requests and physician responses.[10]

The concerns these doctors had about accurate information are certainly understandable. So how do you decide which sites are worthy of review?

Disclosures

One of the first ways to check out the validity of a site is to click on the "About Us" or "About This Site" section. For some reason, this section is not as widely appreciated as it should be. Participants in focus groups reported that when assessing the credibility of a website they primarily looked for the source. They rarely checked out the "About Us" sections where disclaimers or disclosure statements can often be found. We suggest that you do.

For example, if you were to click on medlineplus.gov and then click on "About Medline Plus," you would discover that the site has information "from the largest medical library, the National Library of Medicine. . . ." You would also learn that this site has extensive information from the NIH that is updated daily, and it has a policy of no advertising or endorsements of products or companies.

Also take a look at any disclaimers that might be found on the home page. Let's take, for example, a site that has produced results for some people—http://allexperts.com. From the home page and its name, it appears to be a place to locate experts of all kinds, including medical. However, one should use it with caution after reading the disclaimer. The owners of this site very specifically say that "[b]y using this service you understand that our volunteers have varying levels of expertise and haven't been certified as 'experts' (or anything else) by us in any professional way." Allexperts.com is telling you the credentials of its volunteers have not been independently verified. Knowing this, you can make a better decision about evaluating the information on the site and/or deciding to verify the information yourself.

Reading disclaimer statements can help you compare sites and make an intelligent choice about which you consider more reliable and want to discuss with your doctor. A number of excellent health care sites can be found in Appendix B.

Second Opinions

After finding information on one website, you might want to get a "second opinion" from another site. This is like getting a second opinion from

Case Study: Erica

After doing the first two steps of the Eight Steps to Self-Diagnosis, twenty-eight-year-old medical student Erica believed there was a link between her consumption of diet soft drinks containing aspartame and her frequent and severe headaches. After she found no such evidence in her medical textbooks or from her professors, she went to the Internet and first checked the Food and Drug Administration site (fda.gov), which had determined in 1981 that aspartame was safe for use in foods. According to the FDA, aspartame's approval status was investigated again in 1987 and that investigation supported the agency's previous conclusions. Although the site acknowledged that complaints are still forthcoming and investigation continues, as of the date of her search, no safety problems with aspartame had been identified with any consistency.

Still, Erica was convinced there was a link. So she went for a second opinion. Searching the Web randomly for information on aspartame was tricky. Her search on America Online (AOL) yielded 11,334 sites. Some sites touted the fact that the manufacturers attested to the safety of their product while other sites seemed to blame aspartame for every disease and condition on the planet.

Her first site was a "neutral" government site that had done its own studies, so Erica sought a comparable site. She didn't want to use the aspartame manufacturer's site since it obviously would be biased. Nor did she believe that a commercial site designed to sell a product, someone's personal Web page, or a chat room would be a good parallel source of information. She was looking for another neutral, objective site that would provide access to its own studies and would have no vested interest in the outcome of those studies. Thus, she decided to limit her search to sites ending in ".edu" (universities) and ".gov" (government sponsored).

Erica located the website for the National Institute of Neurological Disorders and Stroke (ninds.nih.gov). She checked the "About Us" page and found that NINDS was "the leading supporter of biomedical research on disorders of the brain and nervous system." Because this seemed to be an objective, pedigreed site that obviously did its own research, she decided to wander through it. There she found a statement that supported her hypothesis. It said "some people are sensitive to aspartame and may suffer headaches or fatigue." Erica decided she was, indeed, on to something. So she stopped drinking diet soft drinks containing aspartame and her headaches resolved.

another doctor. Surfing the Web actually gives you the ability to secure numerous opinions from any number of authoritative sites. If you can't find the answer you need in one place, you can go elsewhere—just make sure you are comparing apples to apples; you have to make certain the sites have an equivalent number of references or qualifications.

Erica's case demonstrates two things: more than one opinion is always beneficial, and comparing one research site with another site containing a neutral mission statement can give the scientific support needed to diagnose a condition.

Define Your Search

You may become overwhelmed by the sheer numbers of sites you bring up when searching a given topic. In order to avoid this feeling and maximize time efficiency, make your initial search as specific as possible. (You can always expand your search later.)

Nine Questions to Ask Yourself When Doing Internet Detective Work

In addition to the general information already discussed, here are nine important questions you should ask yourself before giving any website your full attention:

1. **Is the material on the website dated?** Old material is just that—old. Outdated articles may recommend a medicine, treatment, or supplement that over time has been shown to be ineffective or even hazardous to your health. Bruce Lewenstein, Ph.D., associate professor of science communication at Cornell University in Ithaca, New York, recommends that you always check the date on Web pages to ensure that information reflects current thinking in the field.

2. **Is the site loaded with ads?** "Sites heavy on advertising may have an agenda beyond pure education," says William Klein, M.D., codirector

Case Study: Ayeesha

Let's use Ayeesha's journey as an example of how to define an Internet search. When this twenty-two-year-old was told by her primary care physician that her hair loss and the new rash she developed weeks later were unrelated, she suspected differently. She had a great aunt who had been diagnosed with lupus—an autoimmune disorder—and even though her aunt's symptoms were different, she wanted to check it out.

Before scheduling an appointment with another doctor for a second opinion, Ayeesha went on the Internet and, using Google as her search engine, typed in the word *lupus*. It yielded nine hundred thousand results. The same search on Yahoo turned up eighty-five thousand results.

She needed to narrow the field to reduce the sheer volume of links. Having grown up using a computer, Ayeesha knew how to do this. Instead of using the single word *lupus*, she typed *lupus AND symptoms*. By connecting the condition and specifics she was looking for with the word *AND* (for example, *lupus AND rash*, *lupus AND etiology*, *lupus AND birth control pills*), more relevant sites came up.

If you use multiword phrases, place quotation marks around those phrases as well—certain databases have their own rules that must be followed.

Using this method, Ayeesha was able to link her hair loss and her rash. She was even able to determine that it was not a coincidence that her symptoms started when she began using birth control pills. Ayeesha wasted no time in going directly to a specialist in this area to verify the diagnosis and obtain the appropriate treatment.

---

of HealthBridge medical facilities in Long Island. "If you see a page where you can order products such as supplements and devices, the site should immediately be suspect."

A group from the University of Texas Health Science Center[11] used four common search engines to determine the availability, content, and readability of complementary and alternative medicine (CAM) pages on the Internet. They discovered that 78 percent of the sites were authored by commercial organizations and 52.3 percent had no scientific references. They concluded that consumers searching the Web for health information are likely to encounter consumer-oriented CAM advertising, which may not be supported by scientific fact.

3. **Who funds and promotes the site itself and/or the research studies?** Research costs money and someone has to pay. Is the sponsor an objective source such as a nonprofit organization (like the Lupus Foundation or the American Heart Association), university, or government agency? Was the study published in a peer-reviewed journal, or is it simply being touted in a company's press release? Pharmaceutical companies legitimately perform research as part of their development of new medicines. And some organizations fund research to further their own interests. However, just because a site is a commercial one does not mean it doesn't contain valuable and reliable information. Many for-profit hospitals and clinics have sites that advertise their facilities but also provide excellent information such as research results and treatment protocols.

4. **Does the site contain references?** Look for sources on the Internet that list references to research studies or published books. A legitimate study builds on prior information. Check the references periodically to make sure that they have not been made up by the author of the site. Again, this is a good time to click on the "About Us" section.

5. **What's at the end of the website address?** Dot-com (".com") or dot-net (".net") sites are more likely to be commercial. "Many good sites on the Web are dot-coms, but their primary reason for being is commerce. Seeing '.org,' '.edu,' or '.gov' as part of the address means the site is directly affiliated with what most likely is a credible, unbiased group; either a nonprofit organization, university, or government institution," says William Klein.

   In our experience, most mystery malady patients have great success with ".org," ".gov," and ".edu" sites. At one point, Dr. Rosenbaum found himself chronically exhausted. Fatigue was not exactly a specific symptom. Therefore, he directly went to a website for a certain university known for its excellent medical teaching facilities. When he clicked on the A-Z Health Encyclopedia and typed in *fatigue* he was led to the diagnosis of sleep apnea. The site gave him a precise description of his symptoms. He knew then he had to make an appointment at a sleep disorder clinic where this diagnosis was later confirmed and treated.

6. **Does this site have a seal of approval?** Some sites volunteer to be inspected and monitored so they can receive a seal attesting to the accuracy of the information they contain. Look at myphysicians.com to see what such a seal looks like.

    Health on the Net (HON) is an organization that monitors health websites to ensure they are secure, confidential, and backed by legitimate sources. If and when a site is approved, an HON button will appear on its pages. To validate the button's authenticity, try clicking on it to see if it takes you to the HON website.

    A seal from the Utilization Review Accreditation Council (URAC) indicates the site has met URAC's fourteen principles and fifty-three specific standards, including the use of credible sources, the ongoing updating of material, and security to ensure that no personal information can be revealed. To verify a site's seal of approval, search URAC's online directory at urac.org. The council does a full review of each accredited website once a year and conducts periodic reviews to verify that it remains compliant with the standards.

    We do not mean to imply that sites without seals of approval are necessarily inaccurate or dishonest. They may have simply chosen not to go through the validation process. Commercial sites—those dot-coms and dot-nets—may seek seals to validate their legitimacy, whereas sites from respected nonprofit organizations, institutions, and government agencies may not feel the need for such validation.

7. **What is the design of the research studies in question?** Abstracts of scientifically sound studies will include terms such as *double-blind, randomized, case-controlled,* or *placebo-controlled.* These terms indicate that the information is neither observational nor anecdotal. Anecdotal information and chat rooms can be helpful in pointing you in a specific direction; they should not be relied on for factual data.

8. **Is there more than one research study on the topic?** Most health topics you might be searching for will have multiple rather than single studies. Be sure to read several studies on the same topic before taking the first one you find at face value. If several studies duplicate the same results, these results can probably be trusted.

A single study could have turned out to be a dead end that no one continued to research, or it could be so new that the results haven't yet been duplicated. So if it's a single study, you can probably assume the results are not yet accepted by the scientific community.

9. **Can the study be found on PubMed?** PubMed is a premier Internet site maintained by the National Library of Medicine and the National Center for Biotechnology Information. It allows public access to the NLM's MEDLINE database, which houses articles from forty-five hundred journals from as far back as 1966. Go to pubmed.com to search this database. If you are unable to find a study mentioned there, the chances are better than not that the study was not published in a peer-reviewed journal.

It is often difficult to read and understand articles found on PubMed. However, it is not essential for you to read the complete article or abstract. In fact, many physicians do not always do so. They (and you) need to read only the title and the conclusion section, which usually contains short amounts of text.

Possible Pitfalls in Internet Detective Work

There are any number of problems in doing detective work on the Internet, which is why we always urge you to check the information you have found with your physician. Be careful of the following:

E-Mailing a Physician

Since it is difficult to understand the scientific language found in many medical articles, you can e-mail a physician on his or her website if this service is offered. But be aware that you may not receive an answer or you may get one that is not specific enough for you. Attorneys and malpractice insurance carriers have warned physicians about the amount of information they should give over the Internet. These physicians may be exposing themselves to liability, especially if the query is from someone who is not already one of their patients.

Most physicians have been advised to take a strictly educational approach and only answer general questions regarding a disease or condition. The reason for this is because when a doctor responds to specific questions, he or she creates a doctor-patient relationship. The physician now has a duty to this patient regardless of whether or not the patient has been seen personally in an office and regardless of whether or not monies have been exchanged. This can create the liability exposure that doctors want to avoid.

Keeping this in mind, you are highly unlikely to receive much help from e-mailing a physician or website for specific information about your particular condition. It is best for you to consult your personal physician. Remember, one of the qualities you examined in choosing your doctor (see Chapter 4) was your comfort level in bringing new information to him or her, so this a good time to exercise that prerogative.

However, rare as it may be, you might get lucky using Internet consultation. For example, Steve, a forty-five-year-old independent contractor who was self-employed, thought that he was having chest pain from heart disease. He was afraid to go to the doctor because he didn't have insurance to cover the office visit and expensive tests the doctor would probably want to order. By using the Internet, Steve was able to communicate his symptoms to a physician at allexperts.com. The physician was able to diagnose that his problem was from heartburn, and Steve's condition was successfully treated with over-the-counter medication.

Using Pharmaceutical Sites

The websites of drug manufacturers can sometimes be a good source of information in the same way as the *Physician's Desk Reference* (an annual compilation of information on and descriptions of prescription medications currently available). Although these sites appear professional and do contain a lot of information about the particular drugs the companies manufacture, you must bear in mind that they have an ultimate goal—selling their drugs. That goal does not necessarily include providing you with comparisons or a full study of the drugs. One group from the University of Iowa College of Medicine confirmed this by reviewing the material found on the websites of nine pharmaceutical companies that manufacture medication to treat depression. Most of the material on the websites consisted of advertising. None mentioned drug costs, and only one listed the percentage of adverse effects. The group from the University of Iowa concluded that the information pharmaceutical websites provided regarding the treatment of depression is limited and makes it difficult for consumers to compare drugs.[12]

After our review of such studies, we too have concluded there may be little value to using these sites for the comprehensive medical sleuthing we are encouraging you to do.

Commercial Versus Noncommercial Sites

Although you need to be aware of whether a site is a commercial one and whether the studies mentioned on that site are medically valid, the fact that a site is commercial does not mean it is not a good source of information. As we mentioned before, clinics, hospitals, and pharmaceutical companies often have websites that offer useful data. However, if you are looking for the most objective information or need to make comparisons, these sites are not necessarily the best. And obviously any site where the main objective is to sell you something should not be your first choice.

Testimonials

Beware of testimonials and "success stories." Most sites that offer the best investigative material for a mystery malady patient do not make such claims. Two researchers studied all the information available on the Internet for an herbal remedy called Opuntia.[13] They checked 184 websites and ultimately concluded that the majority of the health claims for success were based on folklore or indirect scientific evidence and could not be substantiated by medical research. The authors concluded that "the only way to assure high content quality was for the website to provide references to scientific publications."

Chat Rooms and Message Boards

Websites with chat rooms and message boards about illnesses abound, but many contain unreliable or misleading information. There is no doubt that chat rooms can be a great place to commiserate with fellow sufferers, gain support, and exchange ideas that can sometimes be valuable when dealing with a mystery malady. They are a great place to ask questions and hear what others have to say. After all, as we have said many times, answers may come from any source and you must keep an open mind.

Nevertheless, it is imperative to check out the information you find there with a trusted physician. Equally important is the warning that someone else's advice or experience may send you off in a direction that is not the most fruitful use of your time or may create a false expectation—be it positive or negative. Just use your discretion and don't take anyone else's advice without consulting your physician.

Conclusion

As you begin to explore the Internet on health topics, you will be amazed at how much information is available. You will be able to gain access to research studies and clinical trials. If you check the "About Us" sections, narrow your searches, ask yourself the nine questions we've outlined, avoid the possible pitfalls we warned about, use your common sense, and *always* consult with your physician, you are sure to find surfing the Web an invaluable part of your medical detective work. With the tools you've learned in this chapter in combination with the Eight Steps to Self-Diagnosis, you'll be well on your way to a correct diagnosis.

In the next section, we'll discuss different categories of symptoms and conditions and illustrate them with numerous case studies. We'll show you how our revolutionary model of medical detective work turned these diagnostic nightmares into treatment successes.

Part 2

DIAGNOSING YOUR MYSTERY MALADY

6

Are You Tired and Aching All Over?

MANY MYSTERY MALADIES are characterized by vague symptoms that could be associated with many different conditions. They are diagnosed by the absence of evidence of any other disease that could account for those symptoms. Some mystery maladies have not even been recognized until recently, and many more are yet to be named. For example, as we mentioned in Chapter 1, multiple sclerosis, once known as "faker's disease," was finally recognized because advances in medical technology (magnetic resonance imaging [MRI] of the brain and spine) finally allowed objective verification. Over time we will hopefully see more of these breakthroughs.

The disorder described in the following case study was still relatively unknown at the time it occurred. Although recognized today as a legitimate ailment, it is still not always easily identifiable by most physicians, and there remains disagreement among board-certified rheumatologists about its cause. Yet if left untreated, this condition can become chronic and debilitating. Ellen, the woman in the following case study, and I (Lynn) were friends. It so happened that I'd had the same condition years earlier. So when she told me about her symptoms, I shared the Eight Step method with her. Here is her story.

Case Study: Ellen

Within a year after the birth of her second baby, Ellen began experiencing fatigue, muscle soreness, and aches and pains all over her body. Until that time, apart from her inability to shed some unwanted pounds from her pregnancy, she had been in excellent health. Thinking perhaps her weight was causing her symptoms, she began working out at a neighborhood fitness center three mornings a week.

After a few days of vigorous exercise, her condition improved somewhat but babysitting problems made it difficult for her to keep a steady workout schedule. And since her thirteen-month-old daughter was still not sleeping through the night, Ellen was often too tired to go to the gym. It seemed that taking naps to get herself through the day was a better use of her time.

Ellen started feeling guilty about not getting more accomplished during the course of a day. She considered herself luckier than many; she had a helpful husband, a housekeeper who cleaned once a week, and a mother-in-law who always seemed available to babysit for the kids. She just couldn't get herself motivated to do things outside the house because of her pain, soreness, and fatigue.

When her daughter's ability to sleep through the night improved, Ellen hoped that at least her chronic fatigue would diminish. But it didn't, because now if she wasn't getting up at night for the baby, she was getting up to urinate frequently. Soon her aches and pains became so bad that it hurt when her husband tried to hold her. Her condition had deteriorated to the point that her mother-in-law became a fixture in her home. Ellen kept insisting it was probably "just a flu" and refused to see a physician. But after eight weeks, her husband called their family doctor himself.

Ellen shared her assumption with the family physician, and he agreed it sounded viral. Nevertheless, he ordered blood tests on the off chance that something else was going on. In the meantime, he told her to get extra rest and drink plenty of fluids. She followed his instructions, but staying in bed didn't seem to offer any relief. The blood tests confirmed that everything was normal. But Ellen didn't feel normal and began to wonder whether it was all in her head. When she shared her thoughts with her husband, he said he thought she was depressed. They both considered whether she had some sort of postpartum depression.

However, she soon realized that her depression had followed, not preceded, her mystery illness. Eventually, she returned to her family doctor who referred her to a specialist in immunological diseases. The immunologist believed she had Epstein-Barr virus, which was confirmed by a blood test that revealed the presence of a certain virus in her system.

The young mother was devastated because that diagnosis would probably mean fatigue for the rest of her life. Desperate, she began surfing the Web and found a peer-reviewed medical journal article on MEDLINE; it said everyone who had ever had the Epstein-Barr virus carried the same serologic evidence of an antecedent infection in their blood even if they didn't have symptoms. This gave her hope that her diagnosis of chronic infection wasn't a foregone conclusion.

Ellen and her husband decided they were unwilling to accept the diagnosis from the immunologist. Up until Ellen's illness, she had been healthy and their lives had been going well, so a chronic illness simply didn't fit into their game plan. But the doctors had nothing further to offer.

Weeks later, a friend suggested that she consult a well-known internist in Manhattan who had cured her own mystery illness and seemed to specialize in such maladies. This internist's waiting room was packed with patients who had been to doctor after doctor with no diagnosis or cure for their particular ailments.

Ellen felt sure she was going to get her answer there. After a thorough examination by the doctor, yet another blood test and a follow-up visit, he diagnosed her with Hashimoto's disease. He explained that Hashimoto's was an illness in which the thyroid gland begins to attack itself and prescribed thyroid medication. He also said she had the giardia parasite in her colon and told her to take grapefruit seed extract to cure it.

The thyroid medication afforded some relief from the fatigue and weight problems, and the grapefruit seed gave her indigestion, but otherwise, she continued feeling out of sorts for several more months. She was struggling just to get up in the morning, do her daily chores, mind the children, make dinner, and crawl back into bed. She felt like she was missing her children's lives, her husband's company, and any joy in living.

That summer, Ellen's husband rented a cottage in the mountains for two weeks. He thought perhaps a holiday from household duties and a change of scenery with the only thing on the agenda being play and relaxation would relieve Ellen's fatigue. Her mother-in-law went along and helped care for the children. It was a pleasant vacation. Nevertheless, Ellen still awoke each morning feeling unrefreshed and achy.

Worse still, new symptoms were beginning to appear—bright lights and noise were beginning to bother her and her clothes were beginning to feel uncomfortable. It seemed she was becoming sensitive to *everything*! She drew the blinds during the day and hushed the children constantly. She was becoming an invalid, wanting to be in a darkened room in loose-fitting clothes.

At this point, Ellen's depression worsened. She contemplated her worst fear that the Epstein-Barr diagnosis was correct. She decided she needed to take vitamins. She also ordered and consumed dozens of supplements and other "miracle cures"—all to no avail.

Her husband was becoming less sympathetic and supportive as Ellen withdrew into her private world of pain and illness. He insisted she go to another doctor. He called Ellen's mother, who lived in Florida, and apprised her of the situation. Ellen's mother sent her an airplane ticket to fly home to Miami. When Ellen arrived, her mother was very upset to see the deep circles under her daughter's eyes and her slumped posture. She gave Ellen one of her sleeping pills, put her to bed, and immediately made an appointment for the next day with her own primary care physician.

Remarkably, when Ellen awoke the next morning, she was feeling somewhat better, but her mother insisted they keep their appointment. Her mother's family physician referred Ellen to Dr. Rosenbaum, and he diagnosed fibromyalgia.

Using the Eight Steps

Had Ellen not found Dr. Rosenbaum almost one year after her symptoms first appeared, she might have been able to solve her problem on her own using the Eight Steps to Self-Diagnosis. Here's how Ellen could have found the same solution Dr. Rosenbaum did.

Step One: Record the Exact Nature of Your Symptoms. In her loose-leaf notebook, Ellen would have listed each symptom.

1. **Fatigue**
   - **Quality and Character:** Chronic and unrelenting
   - **Quantity and Severity:** All day, every day
   - **Timing and Duration:** The same even after a nap or a night's sleep
   - **Setting and Environment:** No different in any setting
   - **Impact on Your Functioning:** Can walk and do basic chores but cannot exercise or do anything too strenuous; have no motivation to do anything

2. **Joint Pains and Muscle Aches**
   - **Quality and Character:** Aching pain in fingers, elbows, and knees, as well as muscle soreness and tenderness in all major muscle groups; no redness or swelling
   - **Quantity and Severity:** All day with some days worse than others
   - **Timing and Duration:** Wake up feeling "creaky" and old, the aches and pains seeming to travel around my body; no change in timing or duration
   - **Setting and Environment:** Worse with weather changes, especially before it rains
   - **Impact on Your Functioning:** Same as above; can't think too clearly; can't lie on my side because my knees and shoulders hurt
   - **Other Factors:** Feels like a flu but no swelling of lymph glands, fever, headaches, or other flulike symptoms such as coughing

3. **Other Symptoms**
   - Sensitivity to light and noise
   - Clothes feeling inexplicably tight
   - Urinating frequently at night
   - Alternating diarrhea and constipation
   - Difficulty with memory and concentration

Had Ellen read Step One, she would know not to make any judgments on this information and continue on to Step Two with the understanding that she might have to return to her notebook to add more information later.

Step Two: Think About the History of Your Mystery Malady. If Ellen had thought about this and tracked her symptoms back in time, she would have realized the onset was earlier than she first thought. Her symptoms actually began before the baby was six months old. She just made an assumption that the first six months of fatigue were due to recovery from three days of labor, a C-section, and nighttime breast feedings. That would not have been an illogical assumption at the time. But by doing the remaining steps, she would also have realized it wasn't an accurate analysis.

Step Three: What Makes Your Symptoms Better (or Worse)? The first thing Ellen would have said is that after taking a sleeping pill, she awoke feeling better than she had in a very long time. Then given additional time and thought, Ellen would have recalled that when she went to the gym for a period of two weeks at what appeared to be her first "recognition" of her muscle aches, pain, and fatigue and before the onset of her other symptoms, she felt better. She would have realized that vigorous exercise helped her symptoms.

Step Four: Do a Family Medical History and Determine If You Have or Had Any Blood Relatives with a Similar Problem. Ellen would have determined that she had no blood relatives with this condition except for her father's sister, who described a similar problem that lasted for several years until she was sent to a psychiatrist, who said she was depressed. The psychiatrist prescribed medication and treated her with psychoanalysis until her money ran out. Her aunt would have suggested she was probably depressed and needed medication, which might have discouraged Ellen from inquiring further.

Step Five: Search for Other Past or Present Mental or Physical Problems. Ellen had been a very healthy person until the events of the past year. She would probably have agreed with her aunt that she was depressed, but she had already discussed this possibility with her husband. She knew the depression was brought on by chronic illness and feelings of helplessness and hopelessness as things got inexplicably worse. The only other condition of any significance she had ever experienced besides her thyroid disorder was alternating constipation and diarrhea. This condition appeared to come and go without explanation but never stayed for more than three weeks or so. This was an important clue.

Step Six: Categorize Your Current (and Prior) Significant Medical Problems by Etiology.

- **Genetic:** Depression seems to be the only illness that runs in the family, and my younger sister has some of the same symptoms but no one has diagnosed her either.
- **Infectious (viral, bacterial, fungal, or parasitic):** Prior blood tests revealed old virus infections but nothing conclusive.
- **Structural or biomechanical:** I'm somewhat double-jointed, but this doesn't seem to account for the fatigue and other symptoms.
- **Environmental:** A low-pressure weather system (before rain) seems to affect the symptoms, but it never brings them on.
- **Metabolic:** Thyroid was a problem but seems well controlled with my medication. (Possibility?)
- **Traumatic:** I've had no accidents or sprains or strains.
- **Iatrogenic:** I take nothing besides anti-inflammatory and thyroid medications that could account for this condition.
- **Psychological:** I'm depressed, but how does that account for the pain? Maybe it's related to problems with concentration. (Possibility?)

Step Seven: Investigate Your Lifestyle and Belief System. In honestly considering the various questions raised in this particular step, Ellen would have answered yes to the question about whether she felt she had to be perfect. One of the most difficult things in her belief system was that she wanted to be the perfect wife and mother. She felt worse about not being perfect than she did about her physical symptoms. She also felt guilty about asking anyone to help her before she became ill (because, of course, she had to be perfect).

Consequently, even when she would have liked to, she never asked her husband to feed the baby at night. After getting one night of total undisturbed sleep (because of the sleeping pill her mother had given her) she already felt a little better. For this reason, Ellen would have wondered if lack of sleep had any bearing on or relevance to her medical problems. This thought would turn out to be true.

Step Eight: Take Your Notebook to Your Physician and Get a Complete Exam. Ellen's notebook would have been filled with clues that would have been helpful to any physician she might have seen, even if her path had never crossed Dr. Rosenbaum's.

Making the Diagnosis

Ellen's story is typical of most patients diagnosed with fibromyalgia. Multiple tender points, muscle and joint soreness/tenderness, and achiness along with fatigue are the key symptoms.

You may recall Ellen not only noted widespread aches and pains in her muscles and joints, but she also experienced pain when her husband hugged her. She had trouble lying on her side with her knees together. These "tender points" are the key clues for this condition. In fact, when Dr. Rosenbaum examined Ellen, the first thing he did was press on what are known as the trigger points. There are between eleven and eighteen of these points that are extremely painful when pressed in a patient with fibromyalgia.

Other corollary clues that confirmed this diagnosis were sensitivity to light, noise, and tight clothing. (Some patients also complain of sensitivity to weather, odors, and foods.) In Step Five, Ellen described having had alternating bouts of constipation and diarrhea throughout her adult life, which are symptoms of irritable bowel syndrome; this syndrome is often associated with fibromyalgia and sometimes even referred to as "fibrogut."

While there is disagreement as to the cause of fibromyalgia,* Dr. Rosenbaum believes the origin to be a form of sleep disorder. There are two types of sleep: rapid eye movement (REM) sleep, also known as dream sleep, and non-REM sleep, known as nondream sleep. Non-REM sleep has four stages—one being the lightest and four being the deepest. Not achieving the right combination of sleep stages prevents the brain from producing endorphins. Endorphins are those "feel good" chemicals that get released when we are in love or after vigorous exercise. The phenomenon known as the jogger's high—a sense of extraordinary well-being—results from the flood of endorphins released postexercise.

---

*Researchers have suggested there may be a number of contributing factors, such as chemical changes in the brain that affect the regulation of substance P, a pain regulator.

Besides making us feel good, endorphins serve as the body's natural pain regulators, and with enough of them on board, pain signals to the brain can be overcome. (See Chapter 14 for more details.) For example, a prize-fighter can continue fighting and notice little pain after suffering a broken nose because his brain is functioning in "fight mode" and manufacturing endorphins and adrenaline, both of which can block pain signals. When the boxing match ends, the body ceases to function in overdrive and the boxer reaches for a painkiller.

Because they are natural pain regulators, endorphins allow ease of motion in the joints and prevent the pain and soreness associated with fibromyalgia. Without them, the muscle soreness, tender points, and generalized body pain occur.

In Ellen's case, she had not had a solid night's rest for more than thirteen months after her baby was born. Although the true onset appeared at six months after her baby's birth, the symptoms became too obvious to ignore at thirteen months. Dr. Rosenbaum firmly believed it was this sleep deprivation and the failure of her body to produce enough endorphins that caused Ellen's condition. The reason Ellen felt better during the short time she was going to the gym was because endorphins were probably being released after her vigorous exercise routine. Ellen's recollection of that time period helped prove this diagnosis accurate.

One type of medication used to treat fibromyalgia is the same class of drugs used to treat depression but administered in lower doses. These medications aid in achieving a better quality of sleep as well as boosting serotonin levels that also assist in pain management. (This may have been the reason Ellen's aunt would have been partially correct in thinking that her niece ought to be on depression medication. Ellen's depression, however, was not a primary cause but rather a secondary symptom that followed her debilitation and her inability to be perfect.)

Under Dr. Rosenbaum's care, Ellen was treated with an exercise program and received education about her condition. In addition, she was provided with a medication that restored her normal sleep pattern but was not the typical sedating and potentially addictive sleeping pill. Ellen recovered fully.

Dr. Rosenbaum was able to diagnose this condition for Ellen when fibromyalgia was known as a "wastepaper basket" diagnosis—one that was only made when everything else had been eliminated. The reason he could readily do so was because he himself had experienced it when he was deprived of sleep as a young intern.

Case Study: Dr. Rosenbaum

In the 1970s, Dr. Rosenbaum was a young intern. Like most interns and residents, he was often awakened by emergency code blues, beepers, alarms, telephone calls, talking, and all the other sounds of a busy hospital. Soon after he started his internship, he began to notice that all the noise caused him unusual distress and that the hospital's bright lights began to bother him.

Before long, his joints and muscles ached. It felt as if even his skin hurt. His knees ached as he stood up from a chair. When he slept on his side, like Ellen, his knees hurt when they touched. He had to turn down the sound on alarm monitors, and he was popping Tylenol and aspirin all day. At twenty-six, Dr. Rosenbaum felt creaky and old.

Like many other interns, he had his moments of hypochondria. When he couldn't figure out what was wrong, he became convinced his symptoms were the result of contracting some terrible illness from a patient. When he couldn't figure out which patient had such a disease, he decided that he must have metastatic cancer. He began weighing himself twice a day and had his blood drawn, his prostate examined, and his stools checked for blood. But nothing was proven. Before long, Tylenol failed to ease his pain. He tried stronger medications but then became afraid they might impair his judgment, so he stopped taking them.

As his illness became chronic, Dr. Rosenbaum stopped all athletic activities, which had previously been his best way of relieving stress. Without the physical release of exercise, he felt frustrated, agitated, and anxious. The pain persisted unabated. Soon he noticed that he was experiencing difficulties concentrating and making decisions.

He struggled to keep from losing his ability to be compassionate and understanding with his patients and questioned his ability as a caretaker of others. His suffering was so consuming, he doubted that he even wanted to be a physician. For almost a year, young Dr. Rosenbaum grappled with this and almost dropped out of his training program.

At last, the long, sleepless years as an intern ended and he went on to become a resident. No longer the low man on the totem pole, Dr. Rosenbaum resumed sleeping full nights. His symptoms diminished. As he felt better, he resumed tennis and other athletic activities. He remained without an exact diagnosis but strongly believed that his illness was somehow sleep-related.

Later during his fellowship in rheumatology, he read about a condition that sounded very much like his mystery malady. Medical texts defined the condition but did not identify its cause. Dr. Rosenbaum was almost certain sleep deprivation caused it. He had, after all, personally experienced both the illness and the cure within his own body. When he mentioned his theory to his professors, they laughed at him, but research later proved him right. He was acting as his own medical detective and was correct in the solution he found for himself and later for others such as Ellen.

Because of this experience with his own strange malady, Dr. Rosenbaum learned to listen carefully to the information his patients share with him. Over the years, he has seen young mothers with infants, men and women whose spouses snore, people with enlarged prostates, sufferers of carpal tunnel syndrome and nocturnal leg cramps, and frequent travelers who often sleep in a strange beds all presenting with the same symptoms. He has often found sleep deprivation to be the culprit.

The Importance of Sleep

Sleep deficits are an important issue. The American Sleep Disorders Association believes that sleep disorders affect more than seventy million Americans, with up to one-third of the population having symptoms of insomnia. The National Sleep Foundation suggests that up to 60 percent of Americans experience insomnia several nights a week. Whatever the cause, chronic sleep deprivation has been proven to significantly affect health and safety. Research indicates that even one hour's less sleep per night can reduce daytime alertness, productivity, and performance by 32 percent. Excessive sleepiness contributes to a poor quality of life, reduces memory and concentration, doubles the risk of occupational injury, and is a definitive contributing factor in obesity.

Recent research has linked lack of sufficient sleep with high blood pressure, heart failure, stroke, and psychiatric disorders. Studies show reduced sleep time is a greater mortality risk than smoking or heart disease. In fact, insomnia triples the mortality risk in elderly men.

Thirty years ago, many sleep-related complaints were treated with sleeping pills (hypnotic or sedating medications) without further evaluation. Today, however, a distinct class of sleep and arousal (awakening) disorders has been identified, and the field of sleep disorders medicine is now an established clinical discipline. Despite this, few physicians receive much education in sleep disorders during their training.

However, caution must be taken with sleeping pills because of the potential for addiction. These medications offer only a short-term solution and provide a window of opportunity to search for a more permanent and safer solution.

Disorders of sleep and wakefulness include insomnia or inadequate sleep, restless leg syndrome, periodic limb movement disorder, narcolepsy (excessive daytime sleepiness), sleep apnea syndromes, sleepwalking, sleep terrors, sleep bruxism (grinding of teeth), sleep enuresis (bedwetting), jet lag, and shift-work sleep disorders.

Failure to recognize and treat these conditions appropriately may lead to significant and often disabling exacerbation of existing medical and psychiatric conditions, including fibromyalgia, and difficult-to-diagnose diseases, including reflex sympathetic dystrophy, chemical sensitivities, and other conditions that involve pain. So when tracking clues as your own medical detective, be sure not to overlook the importance of sleep problems.

Conclusion

If your physician is among those who do not believe that diseases such as fibromyalgia or sleep disorders exist and you believe you have the symptoms, find another physician to consult. Do a thorough Eight Step analysis, making sure to address these specific questions:

- Is your skin painful and tender, or do you feel pain all over your body, even to the point of jumping when touched?
- Have you developed an intolerance for loud noise or light, perhaps even to the point of jumping?
- Do you find yourself urinating frequently?

- Do you have a sleep disturbance? Do you hardly ever feel refreshed on wakening after a night's sleep or even after a nap (although pain will rarely wake you)?
- Do you feel depressed?
- Do you have diarrhea, constipation, or alternating bouts of both?
- Do you sometimes experience headaches that feel like a tight headband?
- Are over-the-counter analgesics such as aspirin or Tylenol ineffective against the pain?
- Do you feel some relief after aerobic exercise?
- Does your clothing feel uncomfortably tight?
- Has your energy, memory, or ability to concentrate declined?

If you answered yes to at least five of these questions, ask your doctor to investigate whether you are suffering from fibromyalgia. Also, consider whether a sleep disorder may be the underlying cause of your symptoms even if it is not fibromyalgia. Remember, sleep disorders are one of the most commonly missed causes of mystery maladies.

7

Is Something You're Ingesting Making You Sick?

Treatments that are supposed to make us healthier or keep us well sometimes do just the opposite. More often than many of us realize, medications or natural remedies recommended for the treatment of certain ailments can become the cause of other maladies. Recent statistics show that reactions to medications and other remedies are the fourth leading cause of death in the United States, dwarfing the number of deaths caused by automobile accidents, AIDS, alcohol and illicit drug abuse, infectious diseases, diabetes, and murder. With 46 percent of Americans taking at least one prescription drug daily, 25 percent taking multiple prescriptions, and untold percentages ingesting over-the-counter products, there is a lot of potential for close encounters of an adverse kind.

There is no formal system for reporting the majority of such reactions because side effects or adverse reactions reportable to health regulatory agencies are narrowly defined as clear-cut responses that cause permanent disability, hospitalization, or death. Even the Food and Drug Administration (FDA) admits that serious side effects or medication reactions are grossly underreported and may be reaching epidemic proportions.

And what about "natural remedies"? Just because they are purchased from a health food store or their source is natural, it does not mean they may not be toxic for some people. Nutritional healing is becoming more and more popular because the traditional medical model of treating illness is not perceived as being as efficacious as it once was. There is much evidence to suggest that increasing numbers of yet unidentified maladies are resulting from nutritional supplements, vitamins and herbs, and many natural remedies. These remedies must be examined because very few controlled studies are performed on them.* Check Appendix B for websites on various alternative and complementary treatments and related studies.

As a result of all of these factors, it can take years (if ever) for a drug, vaccine, or natural supplement to be removed from the market as unsafe. Consider Propulsid, once the top-selling heartburn medication, which was on the market for seven years before the FDA finally withdrew it based on reports of hundreds of heart arrhythmias and scores of deaths. Or the very popular antihistamine Seldane, which sold for a decade before it was removed from the market, even though cardiac toxicities had been identified and exposed years before. Many patients who were using these medications and experiencing mysterious symptoms had no way of connecting one with the other—especially if their physicians had no knowledge of the possible side effects. This is likely to continue to be the case with other remedies.

Incorrect dosing has proved to be another major cause of mysterious symptoms. Carl Peck, M.D., former director of the FDA's Center for Drug Evaluation and Research, says, "There are numerous and noteworthy examples in drug development of failing to get the dose right when a drug is first marketed."

A perfect example of this problem is the newest class of antidepressants known as selective serotonin reuptake inhibitors (SSRIs) including Prozac, Zoloft, Paxil, Effexor, and Celexa. These medications are being prescribed for more than twenty million people at the manufacturers' recommended dosages. Prozac, for example, is recommended at a dosage of 20 milligrams a day, but recent research has shown that many patients need doses of only one-half or even one-quarter of that amount. How many people on these

---

*For example, Ephedra, the herbal supplement linked to heart attack, stroke, and sudden death was the first supplement banned since Congress severely restricted the FDA's authority to regulate herbal products.

medications are having side effects that are not being recognized as such? And how many people are having side effects from newly prescribed medications that are essentially being "overdosed"?

Undisclosed or unreported side effects and incorrect dosages of pharmaceutical medications (whether prescribed or over-the-counter), as well as of all natural remedies, must be examined as part of your medical detective work.

Without sufficient testing and/or reporting, it is easy to see how patients and even the most skilled medical practitioners can easily become victims of the profound lack of knowledge in this area. Doctors rely on the information disseminated by drug companies, whose tests are designed for specific outcomes and who spend billions in marketing their products. Their marketing strategies present information on the drug in the most favorable light possible. Patients rely on their doctors as well as the FDA, whose stated mission is to ensure the effectiveness and safety of medications. But the FDA is often rendered ineffective because of political pressures and funding shortfalls. Add to this the even greater lack of testing and reporting with respect to natural remedies, and we are all in potential trouble.

Nathan Pitman, M.D., a well-recognized radiologist in Boston, became a mystery malady patient under these precise circumstances. Even with his extensive medical knowledge, Dr. Pitman couldn't identify the cause of his problem until he employed the Eight Steps to Self-Diagnosis.

Case Study: Dr. Pitman

Between 2000 and 2002, fifty-two-year-old Dr. Pitman began having painful erections four or five times a night. It never happened during the day, and it didn't seem to affect his sexual functioning or libido. But his sleep was becoming terribly disrupted. The only thing that diminished the pain of these strange nocturnal erections was exercise, squatting, or urinating.

Within a couple of months after the onset and because the pain only affected him at night, Dr. Pitman developed a fear of falling asleep. He started taking sleeping pills and eventually developed an addiction to them. (We discussed the dangers of sleeping pills in Chapter 6.) Things went from bad to worse.

As there was nothing in the literature that named this mystery malady and because it was so disruptive to his life, Dr. Pitman allowed a urologist to convince him to have a partial prostatectomy. Unfortunately, it turned out to be a needless surgery. After suffering many more months, another urologist almost convinced him to have the remainder of his prostate removed. By this time, Dr. Pitman had become so desperate that he almost agreed. But something told him to stop looking at the problem from the surgical perspective and view it from a holistic medical perspective instead. (In good medical detective work it is always important to consider whether surgery, which so many doctors are prone to jump at, is necessarily the proper treatment.)

Dr. Pitman decided it was finally time to take matters into his own hands, even though urology was not his field of expertise. He became proactive. He engaged in some research at the hospital library as well as on the Internet. This led him to consider that he might have a hormonal problem, so he sought the help of an endocrinologist.

Like the urologists before him, the endocrinologist had never heard of this particular mystery malady. However, he had heard about our Eight Steps to Self-Diagnosis and advised Dr. Pitman to call Dr. Rosenbaum in Florida.

Using the Eight Steps

Dr. Rosenbaum then walked Dr. Pitman through the Eight Steps.

Step One: Record the Exact Nature of Your Symptoms. In his loose-leaf notebook, Dr. Pitman listed his single but clearly devastating symptom:

1. **Painful Erections**
   - **Quality and Character:** These erections are very hard and unrelenting.
   - **Quantity and Severity:** Every night, severe.
   - **Timing and Duration:** From one to three times per night lasting two to three minutes.
   - **Setting and Environment:** No different in any setting.
   - **Impact on Your Functioning:** Causes interruption in my sleep like a leg muscle cramp; I'm very fatigued.
   - **Other Factors:** I am afraid to fall asleep and have become addicted to sleeping pills.

Step Two: Think About the History of Your Mystery Malady. This began in May 2000. Nothing unusual happened that year except for two things:

1. I started riding a motorcycle. For my fiftieth birthday, I bought myself a Harley-Davidson and took a trip across several states, much to my wife's dismay. Later, she joined me, and I bought her a bike too. Now we ride together as a hobby.

2. I had an annual physical, including a stress test and blood tests. Except for my cholesterol and triglycerides, which were high, I was in very good health. The doctor told me to lose some weight and to watch my sweets and alcohol intake. He also prescribed cholesterol medication and Rogaine for male pattern baldness.

Step Three: What Makes Your Symptoms Better (or Worse)? Nothing makes it better except exercising, squatting, or urinating. On the other hand, nothing seems to make it worse, but it doesn't stop.

Step Four: Do a Family Medical History and Determine If You Have or Had Any Blood Relatives with a Similar Problem. [Dr. Pitman did what amounted to a medical genealogy chart, which was quite lengthy. We include here only the relevant portion.] I have determined that my cousin has priapism (a condition in which a patient has a sustained, often painful erection). This does not appear to be genetic, however, because my cousin's condition was the result of an inflammation of the urethra. My urologist had already eliminated this as the cause of my problem along with other possible causes, scuch as a reaction to medication used to counteract impotence such as Viagra.

Step Five: Search for Other Past or Present Mental or Physical Problems. Other than my painful erection problem, I had a cervical sprain after an automobile accident in my twenties, kidney stones several years ago, and now a high cholesterol problem which is currently being treated with medication. I have male pattern baldness which is being treated with Rogaine. There are no other past or present mental or physical problems.

Step Six: Categorize Your Current (and Prior) Significant Medical Problems by Etiology.

- **Genetic:** Some heart disease runs in my family. My father died of melanoma. My cousin had priapism, but it does not seem to be a genetic issue. Otherwise, my family has fairly good longevity.

- **Infectious (viral, bacterial, fungal, or parasitic):** I will have my blood drawn for infectious disease, but my symptoms don't indicate infection.

- **Structural or biomechanical:** There is no spinal cord disorder that would cause my condition.

- **Environmental:** Not relevant.

- **Metabolic:** I am not taking Viagra, so it could not be a reaction to that. Could it be another kind of medication reaction?

- **Traumatic:** Could I be experiencing trauma to this area as a result of my motorcycling?

- **Iatrogenic:** Could this be medically induced, that is, could my cholesterol medication or the Rogaine have anything to do with this?

- **Psychological:** I am anxious about sleeping now, but this is a result of the disorder. Before this problem started, I slept fine.

Step Seven: Investigate Your Lifestyle and Belief System. Could my new lifestyle/hobby—motorcycling—have anything to do with my medical mystery? Also, in trying to keep an open mind and thinking about my belief systems, there is a slight possibility that the symptoms do not indicate a disease or condition, which is why I can't find a diagnosis; maybe they are a side effect of some medication. I have listened to my patients who have from time to time complained about side effects of medications I prescribed, and I dismissed them if I couldn't find any literature or findings that would support their complaints. Now, since I cannot find a diagnosis for my condition—it's not in the medical books—I am wondering if I have been too quick to dismiss this issue.

I have long held the belief that if it wasn't in the literature, it wasn't so. Maybe I had more faith than I should have in the literature. Perhaps it isn't as complete as it needs to be. Maybe I'd better investigate this further even though I have not seen my condition listed as a side effect. It may not be an independent disease or condition, and my symptoms have to be caused by something!

Step Eight: Take Your Notebook to Your Physician and Get a Complete Physical Exam. Dr. Rosenbaum could not give Dr. Pitman a physical examination because they were located in different states, but the endocrinologist and urologists had already done so. However, Dr. Pitman raised two excellent questions that were brought forward as a result of doing the Eight Steps: whether motorcycling could be causing some trauma and possibly be a precipitating cause of his problem, and whether his problem was iatrogenic (medically induced by a medication). Although Dr. Pitman was not taking Viagra or any similar drug that had the potential for such side effects, the question remained as to whether the balance of his medications—his cholesterol medication or even Rogaine—could be causing this reaction.

On the surface, both questions seemed quickly answerable. First, no one could determine how, from a biomechanical standpoint, riding a motorcycle could impact penile function. It didn't seem the motorcycle was the likely culprit, but it was worth investigating. Dr. Rosenbaum asked Dr. Pitman to stay off his motorcycle for a while to see if there was any change in his condition.

As to an iatrogenic cause, while the literature did not indicate priapism as a side effect of either Rogaine or the cholesterol medication, Dr. Rosenbaum did not dismiss the possibility out of hand. He had already discovered firsthand that literature from drug manufacturers may be skewed for obvious reasons. The *Physician's Desk Reference* (*PDR*), which is a leading drug reference among not only physicians but millions of consumers, is mainly a collection of package inserts written by drug companies and as such may omit or underreport serious side effects of medications. In other words, information in the *PDR* is not complete. (Dr. Pitman was right to question his belief system on this subject.)

So Dr. Rosenbaum suggested he and Dr. Pitman should both get on the phone and call any and every doctor they could think of, in the hope of finding one who might have heard similar complaints from a patient who was using either Rogaine or the cholesterol medication.*

Making the Diagnosis

Dr. Pitman spoke with an endocrinologist who had a friend—not a patient—who had experienced erectile dysfunction from the same cholesterol medication that had been prescribed for Dr. Pitman. Although painful erections were not listed as a common side effect, Dr. Pitman agreed with Dr. Rosenbaum that he would stop the medication as an experiment and see if it made a difference. It did!

Dr. Pitman's symptoms did not disappear after he refrained from motorcycling, nor did they reappear after he discovered what he believed was the source of his condition. The difference came from not taking his cholesterol medication. His mystery malady was indeed an unlisted and perhaps unrecognized side effect of that particular medication. He consulted his internist to prescribe a different medication to lower his cholesterol.

In Dr. Pitman's case, four factors contributed to a successful outcome: working through the Eight Steps, keeping an open mind, talking to every physician he could about his problem, and a willingness to experiment and test his hypothesis by eliminating certain factors to observe whether this made a difference.

Case Study: Rosalind

Another medical practitioner, surgical nurse Rosalind, went through a less formal, deductive reasoning process to find the answer to her medical mystery. While not illustrative of the Eight Step method per se, it is a prime example of how things that might be healthy for some are unhealthy for

---

*At the time, Internet bulletin boards or websites were not as popular, but these are potential resources. We urge caution on their use, however. They should be considered one source to be verified along with all other information gathered. See Chapter 5 for more tips on using the Internet for medical detective work.

others and should not be ignored in the search for solutions to a medical mystery.

Approximately five years ago, Rosalind called in sick when she began having intolerable pain in her right side adjacent to her stomach. Being a surgical nurse, she thought the source of her pain might be her gallbladder because she had three of the "four Fs" likely to point to such problems— female, fair, fat, and over forty. While not fat, she fell into the other three categories. She consulted the doctor in the women's health center of the hospital in Reno where she worked. The doctor ordered a sonogram of her gallbladder. It revealed nothing abnormal. The doctor told her to change her diet anyway to eliminate fatty foods, which can play a role in gallbladder aggravation.

Rosalind followed the doctor's orders and lost a couple of pounds but had no relief from her pain. Her doctor then ordered an upper gastrointestinal series, which also had normal results. Rosalind's pain continued unabated. She was referred to a gastroenterologist. He was a wonderful and sympathetic physician, and after treating her with the usual antacid medications like Prilosec and Prevacid for several weeks with no results, he began to get concerned that he had missed something. So he scheduled Rosalind for a camera endoscopy. This is a procedure in which she would swallow a camera for the doctor to observe her gastrointestinal tract. When she did, he couldn't see anything of significance except a mild irritation of Rosalind's stomach lining. Satisfied that there was nothing seriously wrong, he gave her a diagnosis of gastritis.

The doctor may have felt better, but his patient did not. Rosalind was hesitant to call him again two weeks later with the same complaints, but when she finally did, he suggested that her problem might be stress-related since that is often a major factor in digestive disturbances.

So Rosalind scheduled a vacation with her grown son, his wife, and their small son who lived in Oregon. They all went to a wonderful bed and breakfast on the southern coast, and a few days into the vacation, Rosalind began to feel better. Her stomach pain eased and she thought perhaps the doctor was right. Ten days later, she returned home feeling wonderfully relaxed and healthy.

After the long flight home, she was tired. When she finished unpacking, she fixed herself a cup of tea. She had come to enjoy a certain herbal tea, which she began to drink in an effort to stop drinking coffee. (She had even taken a box of her special tea to work and drank it there too.)

Within fifteen minutes of drinking the tea, she sat up in bed and was suddenly doubled over with pain once again. She rushed into the kitchen and checked the ingredients on the tea box. It listed licorice root as a main ingredient.

Making the Diagnosis

As soon as she read this, Rosalind remembered an event that had occurred many years earlier when her son was little and they were visiting some friends in California. They had all passed an open field in which a licorice plant was growing. Their friend had broken off a piece of the plant, offering it to Rosalind's son to taste.

Within an hour, he was having a terrible stomachache. Later, he vomited. Rosalind was certain that his symptoms had resulted from ingesting the licorice plant, and chances were if he'd had a gastrointestinal reaction, her reaction was no coincidence. She surmised she was having a sensitivity reaction since they tend to run in families.

When she called the gastroenterologist the next morning to report what had happened, they concluded that Rosalind had probably started out with a simple case of gastritis months ago. She stopped drinking coffee because she knew coffee would further irritate an already distressed stomach. She went to the health food store to find a coffee substitute and purchased a tea that was supposed to be good for the stomach. She began drinking the tea instead of coffee, and before long her "solution" had turned into her real problem.

Conclusion

As you can see, anything we ingest, including things that are supposed to help us, can cause problems. How many times do doctors ask for the list of medications you are taking even though they are only aware of side effects listed in the *Physician's Desk Reference*? How often do doctors even think about asking about over-the-counter products or what vitamin supplements, herbal supplements, or nutritional products you may be ingesting? How much do we really know about the side effects of these products or even the medications listed in the *PDR*?

It is also important to remember that while Dr. Pitman and Rosalind got fast results when they discontinued the substances that were causing their problems, this may not be true in every case, and your symptoms may not cease the minute you stop taking a suspect medication or supplement. Keep in mind that it may take as long for the effect to wear off as it did for it to develop.

Likewise, it is not necessarily the effect of one drug or ingested product. It could be a combination of things—including foods and chemicals. You must eliminate the potential culprits one at a time.

Finally, as you can see, just because a product is "natural" does not mean it is harmless. For example, St. John's wort, which is used by people who are trying to treat their own depression, can cause rashes that are worsened by exposure to sunlight. St. John's wort can also interfere with the efficacy of certain prescription medications. Even something natural like grapefruit juice can interfere with certain medications and cause seizures in rare instances. Too much licorice, besides creating gastric distress for someone who's sensitive to it like Rosalind, can also cause a problem in your blood potassium level.

Keep an open mind as to whether the things you are ingesting might be a possible cause of your mystery ailment. Be proactive and your answer may be as simple as eliminating something.

Ask yourself these questions:

• Do your symptoms get worse immediately or even several hours after ingesting something, whether it is food, a drug, or an herbal remedy? Alternatively, do they improve after you eliminate that substance?

• Do your intestinal symptoms wake you up?

• Do others around you have similar problems? Could all of you be ingesting the same thing?

• Do you get headaches, jaw pain, or fluid retention after ingesting a product—especially one like monosodium glutamate (MSG)?

• Are you experiencing cramps, nausea, diarrhea, gas, or some change in your bowel habits?

• Are any other parts of your body affected, or are you experiencing any sort of rash or skin irritation? (Skin problems are often a symptom of an allergy or sensitivity.)

If you have answered yes to three or more of these questions, take an inventory of your diet, medications, vitamins, herbal remedies, or anything else you are ingesting and begin by eliminating one thing at a time for at least a week. Do not add the substance back in until you are certain you have eliminated it as the culprit. And by all means, seek the assistance of a gastroenterologist, allergist, or other physician or dietitian who may be able to help you. If you have determined that a substance isn't the cause of your problems, go back to the Eight Steps and continue working on them in your quest for diagnostic answers.

8

Do You Have Mysterious
Pelvic Pain?

THIS STORY IS personal and a perfect example of how the Eight Steps to Self-Diagnosis helped me (Lynn) to diagnose myself when no doctor could. It also demonstrates how creating proactive partnerships with my physicians helped me to finally find treatment for a very serious and painful condition.

Lynn's Story

In July 1998, I was invited to join friends for a class in what was then the newest exercise craze—spinning. Spinning is done on a specially modified, patented stationary bike that allows the rider to control pedaling resistance. Following an instructor's directions and the music, riders turn a dial to increase the pedaling speed with higher rpms to simulate road racing or hill climbing. The biker is either riding furiously, legs whirring like a frenetic eggbeater, or climbing hills and "jumping" (repeatedly rising out of the seat while pedaling).

As I was in fairly good athletic shape, I dove right in. I placed my feet in the foot straps, adjusted the tensions, and began biking according to the orders being barked out by the instructor.

At some point, the Velcro strap that held one foot on the bike pedal began coming loose, repeatedly causing my foot to fall off the pedal. This, in turn, caused me to slam involuntarily onto the bicycle seat. This happened at least a dozen times during the course of the workout. At the conclusion of the class, I walked out of the gym bow-legged and feeling oddly injured. Inside of a week, I found myself experiencing a painful, burning sensation "down there" that felt like a roaring fire. Little did I know that this was the beginning of a six-year process of trying to solve a mystery malady. (It was this ordeal that actually prompted me to develop this self-diagnosis model and enlist the assistance of Dr. Rosenbaum.)

At first, I thought I had a yeast infection, so I purchased an over-the-counter cream. The application of that cream just made the intolerable pain even worse. Tears streamed down my face as I made an appointment to see my gynecologist. He found not a yeast infection but a bacterial one and prescribed a gel to be inserted vaginally. The medication may have treated the infection, but it didn't relieve my pain.

That pain prompted me to seek the advice of my primary care physician. She suspected a urinary tract infection (UTI) and cultured my urine; it was positive for infection. She treated me with antibiotics and assured me I would feel better in a few days. I didn't.

After weeks of continuous and distracting pain, I was cultured again for a urinary tract infection, and once again, the culture was positive. After treatment, the infection was gone, but my symptoms persisted. By this time, in addition to the almost stinging sensation of a thousand small cuts, I sometimes felt painful "squeezing" in the area as if my bladder were spasming. It seemed that no matter what I did, I couldn't get any relief from the pain.

Finding it difficult to talk about my extreme pain in this very private area, I sometimes felt it was difficult to even acknowledge it was happening; it seemed almost surreal. When the spasms worsened to the point of almost crippling me, my primary care physician sent me to a urologist who, as I lay on the treatment table, dilated my urethra without warning—a shocking and painful experience! (For those who are unfamiliar with the process, dilation involves placing a surgical sterile rod into the urethra, ostensibly to stretch it.) In the weeks of pain and several office visits that followed, the physician did this several times as well as putting me on medications to help what he diagnosed as bladder spasms. When I didn't get any better, the doctor just kept increasing the dosage to the point that I found myself dazed and drooling in the supermarket. I needed better medical help and switched urologists.

This time I made an appointment at a well-regarded teaching hospital. I waited for several weeks to get an appointment to see the head of the urology department. I sat in the waiting room for one and a half hours and was eventually seen by this highly respected specialist. He dismissed me (after a five-minute consultation and two-minute examination) with the diagnosis of urethritis. He said that he dealt mainly with male prostate cancer patients, and there was nothing further he could do for me except to encourage me to see his partner, who specialized in female urological problems. So I made the appointment.

Three weeks later, I saw this specialist. He took my history again. I ventured an opinion that maybe I was not actually having bladder spasms since the medication prescribed to treat them didn't work. He surmised that I was actually experiencing muscle spasms in the pelvic area. While he didn't give it a diagnosis, he explained that he was doing research on this condition and was beginning to perform an experimental surgery that involved implanting an electrical device in what he called the pelvic floor. So far, he boasted, it was having positive results.* In fear, I switched urologists again.

I called Dr. Rosenbaum. Even though I knew this wasn't his field, I trusted his judgment and he referred me to another urologist. This one was a lot kinder, but he was also perplexed about my condition. Sometimes when I was in pain, I tested positive for infections; at other times, I didn't. At this point, I was no longer able to wear jeans, pants, or panty hose because my vulvar area had become too sensitive. Although actually having sex did not hurt, within an hour afterward, I was again having full-blown symptoms. On any day, I couldn't sit for any length of time nor could I bicycle or do anything that put pressure in this area. I was running to the bathroom at least twelve to fourteen times a day. This actually created a small groove in the carpet running from my office to the ladies room! I was also waking up several times per night to void. This latest urologist, in a moment of candor and probable frustration, told me that he believed me to be a "credible

---

*Remember we advised you in Chapter 4 to trust your instincts about doctors. This "experimental surgery," while providing relief to some, would produce horror stories later on. This is not to say one shouldn't try new things, but you must use your judgment and common sense. This procedure seemed extremely invasive and was too untested for my taste. My instincts saved me from potential disaster.

person" and "not a fabricator," but my level of intractable pain was simply not consistent with urinary tract infections. And even stranger, the pain, frequency, and urgency seemed to persist even when I didn't have an infection.

He then asked me how my sex life was before all this began. I didn't like what I perceived to be his implication. I told him it had been just fine, thank you, and that my sex life was not the issue here. The issue was finding out what was causing my pain because *it* was affecting my sex life.

He suggested I undergo a cystoscopy, in which a fiber optic tube is inserted into the urethra and bladder for diagnostic purposes. Although it was less than pleasant, it was the first pain relief I had since it was the *only* time I was given pain medication. The cystoscopy revealed the presence of pseudopolyps in my urethra, which the doctor surmised could be the cause of my many bouts with cystitis (infections). He suggested surgery to remove them. I was agreeable to anything at that point. Just prior to my undergoing that surgery, the surgical nurse assured me that many cystitis patients got well after the polyps were removed. Unfortunately, I didn't.

My symptoms persisted, and soon, I was inexplicably having some numbness in my right leg and arm. This caused the urologist some alarm because bladder spasms together with the numbness suggested the possibility of multiple sclerosis (MS). At this point—almost a year into the problem—my husband at that time, who until then had been my only comfort, was losing faith. He sarcastically remarked that I had MS all right, but it wasn't multiple sclerosis—it was "many symptoms." The strain my condition was placing on our marriage was becoming evident, and I was beginning to lose any hope I had of finding the cause or cure.

The urologist referred me to a neurologist who ordered a magnetic resonance imaging (MRI) of the brain and also performed a nerve conduction test. The nerve conduction (electrical current) test greatly exacerbated the pain in my vulva. The neurologist concluded I did not have MS but indicated he did believe I had nerve trauma, probably as a result of the spinning injury or possibly from all the bladder infections. He didn't have a diagnosis but recommended I take a strong medication that is often given to epileptics, designed to "coat" a patient's nerve endings. He said in large enough dosages, it might give me pain relief.

At this point, *desperate* was an understatement of my feelings. I tried the medication. Even though the starting dose was minimal and did not minimize my pain, it was enough to affect my cognitive functioning to the point that I would be driving my car one moment and forgetting where I was going the next! Eventually, I had a car accident from the effects. I called my primary care physician in a panic. She told me unless I wanted to have another accident or was ready to give up practicing law, I should immediately stop the medication, as loss of cognition, memory, and drowsiness were its most common side effects. I felt I had no choice but to stop the medication, and I did not return to the neurologist.

My chronic pain and repeated infections continued for several more months. At this point more than two years had elapsed with no relief in sight. I was frightened, anxious, and feeling hopeless. When I finally complained for what would be the last time about my pain to this particular urologist and he refused to prescribe anything stronger than over-the-counter pain medications (explaining that his diagnosis was cystitis and he knew cystitis would not normally cause such pain), I lost my cool.

I knew my symptoms were real and his diagnosis was wrong. I needed to find out what was really happening to me. I refused to continue living in agony. Here's how I got my true diagnosis and ultimate treatment, which was as long a process as finding the diagnosis itself.

Using the Eight Steps

Step One: Record the Exact Nature of Your Symptoms. As the pain was so intense and diffuse, it was difficult to separate the exact nature of my symptoms. Doing this exercise made me focus on it objectively.

1. **Pain in Vulva**
   - **Quality and Character:** Pain is of a burning nature; sometimes feels like the sting of a thousand microscopic cuts. Occasionally, it's a "squeezing" pain.
   - **Quantity and Severity:** Pain is minimal in the morning but becomes severe by nighttime. On a scale of one to ten, I'd say eight at its worst, three at its best.
   - **Timing and Duration:** Pain is always present, but it gets worse with infection and recedes some when the infection is treated; worse for two weeks after sexual intercourse or vigorous exercise.
   - **Setting and Environment:** Better when standing or lying down. Worse when sitting, wearing pants or pantyhose, exercising, or after sex.

- **Impact on Your Functioning:** I am becoming nonfunctional from the pain. My job and marriage are being affected.

2. **Urinary Tract Infections**
   - **Quality and Character:** Ranges from mild to severe.
   - **Quantity and Severity:** Every other month; see above.
   - **Timing and Duration:** Always after sex but sometimes for no reason.
   - **Setting and Environment:** No change in different settings.
   - **Impact on Your Functioning:** After a course of antibiotics, I am somewhat better for a few days and try to get most of my activities done then.

3. **Bladder Spasms**
   - **Quality and Character:** Feels like the muscles in my perineal area are squeezing tightly and then sometimes release.
   - **Quantity and Severity:** Sometimes the spasming is severe enough to make me cry, but it is not constant.
   - **Timing and Duration:** Always before and during an infection.
   - **Setting and Environment:** Same as above.
   - **Impact on Your Functioning:** Can hardly sit anymore.
   - **Other Factors:** I have a gut feeling that this symptom is in reaction to the others. It doesn't stand alone. Also, I am not certain if the doctor who wanted to perform the experimental surgery might not have said something right—it isn't bladder spasms but muscle spasms.

4. **Urgency and Frequency of Urination**
   - **Quality and Character:** Feels like muscles in my perineal area are squeezing around the bladder, worse when infected.
   - **Quantity and Severity:** Sometimes it is severe enough to make me cry, but it is not constant.
   - **Timing and Duration.** Always before and during an infection.
   - **Setting and Environment:** Same as above.
   - **Impact on Your Functioning:** Can't be away from a bathroom for long.

Step Two: Think About the History of Your Mystery Malady. It was clear to me that this condition began after the spinning class, so the neurologist's conclusion that there was probably trauma to my perineal area sounded like a plausible hypothesis. Before that time, I had had perhaps one urinary tract infection in my entire life; now I was having them at least once every two months. I explored "associated life events." I remember going on vacation the day following the spinning class and participating in a lot of physical activities, including increased sexual activity. This may have further exacerbated the trauma. I made a note of it, recognizing that as I went through the steps, I might need to return to this one.

Step Three: What Makes Your Symptoms Better (or Worse)? This was easy to answer. All my symptoms were fairly constant, but they would become worse if I had an infection, sat for prolonged periods of time, wore tight pants, had sex, exercised, or even applied a cream or ointment designed to improve the situation. If I had an actual UTI and it was treated, my symptoms improved. *Any* pressure applied to the area made all my symptoms worse. Even the slightest touch provoked an unreasonable amount of pain. Worse still, if I woke up without pain and did any of the problematic activities, the pain was triggered and I couldn't turn it off. On the other hand, if I woke up without pain and just lay in bed (applying no pressure to the area), I could go for a few hours without pain. My anxiety level skyrocketed with the thought that I would be laid up just to get pain relief; with those thoughts, the pain seemed to get worse. Hence I discovered that pain would worsen with anxiety.

Step Four: Do a Family Medical History and Determine If You Have or Had Any Blood Relatives with a Similar Problem. After a survey of my family's medical history, I found a half-aunt who had a similar condition. Hers was diagnosed as dermatological in nature and was treated with cortisone creams. She had none of the myriad other symptoms I did, but her treatment gave me something to think about. I ventured an examination of the skin in that area and found it to be raw and red. So now in addition to urological, gynecological, and neurological implications, perhaps there were dermatological aspects to examine—something no doctor had yet suggested.

Step Five: Search for Other Past or Present Mental or Physical Problems. I
wasn't sure if any prior condition was related, but a good medical detective
does not prematurely rule something out. I was very aware that I had a history of allergies and wondered if I was having some sort of allergic reaction.
I made a note to myself to explore this further. (Perhaps I needed to examine whether coming into contact with detergents, panty liners, or fabrics
other than cotton could be causing the problem.)

Also, I'd had fibromyalgia earlier in my life (see Chapter 6) and Dr.
Rosenbaum had treated me for this condition. He had defined myalgia as
diffuse muscle pain and possibly an inflammation of fibrous tissues of the
muscles, fascia, and sometimes nerves. This made me wonder about my
"bladder spasms." Maybe they were, in fact, muscle spasms since the bladder spasm medication did not help much. I put an asterisk by this step. I
would have to consult Dr. Rosenbaum about this.

Some years previously, I also had been diagnosed with Hashimoto's disease (a chronic inflammatory condition resulting in thyroid malfunction).
It struck me as I proceeded with Step Five that all my prior conditions had
something in common—inflammation and/or autoimmune disease.*

Securing my old medical records reminded me of the several gynecological surgeries I'd had, including the removal of ovarian cysts, the removal
of a fibroid tumor before I had my first child, and a C-section. I didn't know
if these surgeries had anything to do with my current mystery malady, but
since it was not time to start ruling anything out, I simply made a note of
them. (These past gynecological surgeries also became relevant to my diagnosis. Remember, list everything!)

*Step Six: Categorize Your Current and Prior Significant Medical Problems
by Etiology.* I looked back at everything I had recorded in my notebook and
made some additional notes. Then I formulated some questions and theories to go over with my physician.

- **Genetic:** Were my prior conditions genetically based, and were they
  related?

---

*This observation would later prove my diagnosis conclusively. One or more of these condi-
tions were often associated with the correct diagnosis I finally received.

- **Infectious (viral, bacterial, fungal, or parasitic):** Although UTIs were bacterial, should we check for these other categories, as obvious as it might seem?
- **Structural or biomechanical:** I believed there was more to discover about the spasming (whether bladder or muscle), as one urologist had indicated, even though I rejected his experimental surgery for it.
- **Environmental:** I needed to explore this in terms of substances and things in the environment such as a detergent allergy.
- **Metabolic:** I would have to determine if there was anything I was eating or medications I was taking that could cause this problem, although it seemed highly unlikely.
- **Traumatic:** I think this was the origin (the spinning exercise).
- **Iatrogenic:** Did my prior surgeries have anything to do with this condition?
- **Psychological:** I had discovered anxiety made my symptoms worse, but was anxiety the real cause?

Making the Diagnosis

My medical detective instincts were telling me to stop here. Working through Steps One through Six had yielded a lot of potential clues. I needed to do some research and inquiry. I decided to use the Internet as a resource. (Refer to the information in Chapter 5 for tips on using the Internet to research your mystery malady.) Using the key words the doctors had used—*cystitis* and *bladder spasms*—in an attempt to match some of my clues with any information available, I found that one website described a condition no doctor had yet mentioned—interstitial cystitis (IC). I was stunned to learn that IC patients had many of the symptoms I'd listed in Step One. The only problem was that IC normally involved bladder pain *without* an infectious process. Since I was invariably in and out of an infectious process, IC didn't seem to apply to me and perhaps that's why no doctor had thought of it. (I later learned it was either that or because few doctors know about it.)

We mystery malady patients must be willing to keep an open mind and think outside the box. I reasoned that since my symptoms were so similar to IC, I should continue to explore this condition. I secured a number of articles and suddenly ran across a condition often associated with IC that sometimes stands on its own—pelvic floor dysfunction.

According to the articles posted on the websites, this condition involved muscle spasms in the pelvic floor, nerve inflammation, and bladder urgency and frequency. Symptoms also included high levels of pelvic pain and decreased urinary flow (which is known to sometimes cause infection).

I became very excited; I knew I was on to something. I called my primary care physician and asked if she had ever heard of this condition. To my amazement, she told me that in the past year she had attended a lecture given by a physical therapist whose entire practice was devoted to treating this problem and that it was one which, up to this point, had been virtually unrecognized and unidentified in the medical community.*

She immediately referred me to this physical therapist.** Although this health practitioner was not a physician, she knew more about my condition than any doctor I have met before or since. When I asked her to tell me more about it (and without my saying very much about my own symptoms), she began to describe for me in exact detail what I had been experiencing since my accident occurred. She even ventured to guess that, at this point, I had probably stopped wearing pants or pantyhose, had difficulty sitting for any length of time, and was probably very hesitant about having sexual intercourse. As I listened to the details of my own experience from a complete stranger and after so much untold suffering, I started crying. Someone finally knew what was wrong with me, how it felt, and the consequences of this terrible condition.

The physical therapist said the greatest problem with this condition, in her experience, was how often it went undiagnosed. She indicated that she had many patients who came to her after *a decade or more* of pain. The other difficulty was that there was often no easy or definitive way to cure it. The treatment was as varied as each individual. In my case, she thought it might be difficult to rehabilitate me in part because my prior gynecological

---

*I asked my doctor why she had not referred me to this physical therapist before. She responded, "Well, I thought we were dealing with nerve damage, not muscle or biomechanical issues." Had I done my Step One earlier, I might have gotten some help sooner!

**For anyone who believes this condition applies to them, the name of the physical therapist is Mary Lou Cokl, and she is located in South Miami, Florida.

surgeries were sure to have compromised my pelvic floor long before that spinning class caused the trauma.

The factors controlling what treatments worked and for whom depended on many elements, ranging from a person's particular chemistry, the cause of onset, the duration and severity of symptoms, and how much of the condition was caused by nerve or muscle involvement. It was her opinion that the spasming, or musculoskeletal response to the trauma and pain, was a natural bodily defense to protect and guard the injured area. This defense mechanism then became its own source of aggravation and pain.

The entire process evolves, as it had in my case, into a vicious cycle—trauma causing nerve injury, nerve injury causing pain, pain causing muscle spasms, and spasms causing the failure to void properly, which led to urinary tract infections. These in turn further irritated, eroded, and compromised the skin, making it both painful and more susceptible to infection, thereby perpetuating the cycle.

Clearly, she explained, this cycle had to be addressed on multiple levels—neurologically (and psychologically) for the chronic pain, biomechanically for the pelvic floor muscle spasms, immunologically for the chronic urinary tract infections, and dermatologically to treat my damaged vaginal skin. (Yes, there are gynecological dermatologists.) She ventured that *pelvic floor dysfunction* was the umbrella term for my condition, but the largest component of my pain was another condition labeled *vulvodynia*.* The pain of vulvodynia can be quite severe and is typically felt by the patient as a burning, irritation, or rawness that may be constant or intermittent, local or diffuse, and can last for months or even years. In any case, it is certainly worsened by infection.

Armed with all this new information, I went back to the Internet and researched vulvodynia and its many forms. Each is a type of neuralgia in

---

*While little is known about these chronic, focal pain conditions, there are actually many kinds of "dynias," including glossodynia (painful tongue), carotidynia (headache pain), coccygodynia (pain in the coccyx), prostatodynia (also sometimes referred to as prostatitis), and proctodynia (pain in the rectal-anal area).

which the etiology may be unclear but is usually neuropathic (that is, they are pain syndromes that are often treated with medications for neuropathic pain). Because patients' etiologies vary, different treatments work for different patients. Recent research is even speculating that vulvodynia may be a form of fibromyalgia, a prior condition of mine (as discussed in Chapter 6).

In consulting with Dr. Rosenbaum, who as I have mentioned before, practices medicine as an "art" and not just a science, he suggested based on my newly acquired information that this condition sounded very much like complex regional pain syndrome or reflex sympathetic dystrophy, a condition that occurs in most cases after a traumatic injury. This opened up a new area for inquiry.

All the pieces of my medical puzzle were coming together to form a clearer picture. In time, I discovered that my medical history had actually "set me up" for the final blow—no pun intended. While my full diagnosis was not pretty, it made sense, and it would allow me to start on the road to finding a cure.

My physical therapist referred me to both a urologist who was experienced in treating my condition and a gynecological dermatologist who treated the vaginal skin with varying strengths of cortisone creams to calm the inflammation and then a compounded estrogen cream to regain elasticity and strength. This aided in the rehabilitation of my skin. (At one point, this doctor insisted I take the same medication the first neurologist had prescribed, which I'd been taking at the time of my car accident. When I refused to do it, she "fired" me as a patient because I wouldn't listen. Months later when I returned, hoping she would forget her directive, she off-handedly remarked what a terrible drug that medication was and that she was no longer prescribing it! I declined to comment, since my goal was not to say "I told you so" but to continue to get the good dermatological expertise she did offer.)

Treating this complicated mystery malady that crossed so many areas of specialization was like waging a major war. It had to be fought on several fronts. I assembled a medical team consisting of my gynecologist of thirty years, Dr. Kenneth Baer; Dr. Rosenbaum; my urologist, Dr. John Mekras; a neurologist; and a dermatologist. I asked Dr. Mekras to become the team leader and he agreed. I didn't make a move without consulting him, and I followed the advice that was detailed in Chapter 4 to create a proactive partnership.*

Still, finding the right treatment was no easy task. First and foremost, I learned that untreated pain can lead to ongoing, intractable pain (as we will explain in Chapter 14). I began to address my pain with medication, but I explored every other avenue as well. I turned myself into a human guinea pig because I was determined not to live in pain or on pain medications forever. As in any war, one must use whatever strategy has the best chance of prevailing and be open-minded. In my case, this included a great deal of brainstorming and eclectic experimentation, including injecting Botox into my pelvic floor muscles to stop the spasming and pain.

Eventually, however, the most effective treatments were the result of deductive reasoning, good detective work, and creative thinking. As I'm writing this book, the residual effects of this condition are still with me; however, I began writing standing up and I am happy to report that I have finished sitting down! My infections have stopped, and I have actually had not only days, but sometimes weeks, without pain. Sex is fun again. I am even wearing jeans, albeit not too tight. It's not over yet, but backing out of a vicious neuropathic pain cycle takes time. Whereas once I almost lost hope, as a result of working through the Eight Steps, I now have complete faith that my pain will one day simply disappear.

More on Pelvic Floor Dysfunction and Vulvodynia

Sources indicate as many as 15 to 20 percent of women suffer with this little-known condition. There is even an International Society for the Study of

---

*Although I consulted with two of the foremost recognized experts in the country on this condition, I felt my urologist was very competent to handle my case; willing to consult with other experts, when necessary; and most of all, willing to try whatever made medical sense to find a cure for me. This is why I selected him to be my lead physician and will be forever grateful to him for this.

Vulvar Disease as well as the National Vulvodynia Association, both organizations dedicated to the sharing and learning of collective scientific study. Nearly any woman can develop this condition and although there is a substantial amount of scientific information documenting the clinical causes and demonstrating the absence of any psychopathology, many doctors still think of vulvovaginal pain disorders as a form of hysteria. Another sad truth is that most doctors have never even heard of this ailment.

The lack of medical knowledge is coupled with the fact that most women are embarrassed to report their symptoms, and if and when they finally do, they discover the condition crosses so many medical subspecialties that getting proper treatment is difficult. Treatment options include anticonvulsants (antiepileptic medications), antidepressants (for alteration of pain impulse transmission, not depression), a low-oxalate diet,* antibiotics, anti-inflammatories, anxiolytics, biofeedback and physical therapy, estrogen/testosterone creams, immune system modulators, vestibulectomy,** acupuncture, and pain management.

Conclusion

If you think you may have such a disorder, ask yourself these questions:

- Have you had chronic, burning pain in the vulvar area for more than three months?
- Have you been treated for various infections (yeast, bacterial, urinary) but the pain still persists?
- Have you had recurring and repeating cycles of infections with pain?
- Does even the slightest touch to the vulvar area create extreme pain?

---

*Oxalates are natural by-products found in urine. There is some belief that these oxalate crystals are produced by the consumption of certain foods and act as irritants that can cause vulvodynia.

**Vestibulectomy is a surgical procedure to remove the vaginal tissue known as the vestibule and replace it with less sensitive tissue. It is only prescribed for those whose pain is localized in this area of tenderness.

- Have you ever been diagnosed with allergies, irritable bowel syndrome, fibromyalgia or other neuralgias, or other inflammatory or autoimmune disorders?
- Have you been to the doctor with symptoms of what you believe are a yeast infection, but no definitive cause can be found?
- Have you experienced any incontinence?

If you've answered yes to at least three of these questions, you may have pelvic floor dysfunction and/or a form of vulvodynia. (Pelvic pain with other symptoms might well be pelvic inflammatory disease, fibroids, ovarian cysts, endometriosis, pelvic congestion, periformis syndrome, irritable bowel syndrome, and interstitial cystitis.) Work through the Eight Steps. Remember that the origins of these conditions can be different and everyone's body systems are different, so keep searching until you find the right treatment for you.

9

Is Your Weight Problem Really Diet-Related?

WE ARE A nation obsessed with weight and diets. It may be understandable since more than 60 percent of Americans are overweight, about 33 percent of all adults and 15 percent of all children are classified as obese,* and government researchers are now blaming obesity for at least three hundred thousand deaths a year.[1]

Obesity and two illnesses linked to it, heart disease and high blood pressure, are on the World Health Organization's list of the top ten global risks.[2] Despite these facts, obesity is a subject that many physicians are hesitant to raise. Unless patients bring up their weight problem or there is a disease process such as diabetes or heart disease associated with it, it will likely not be addressed in an office visit. If weight does become the subject of discussion and the doctor advises the patient to lose some pounds, they both often assume that weight loss will occur with a reduction in caloric intake. Yet obesity is not always a result of overeating or eating improperly. Consider the case of Ruth. Her extra pounds were always a source of unnecessary torment but were never successfully addressed by any doctor. Here is her story and the solution she finally found.

---

*Obesity is defined as being more than 20 percent (25 percent in women) or more over the maximum desirable weight for a person's height.

Case Study: Ruth

Ruth had hated her body ever since she was a teenager, which was when she first became overweight. Since her mother had died when she was very young, she had no one to help her understand how to make herself more attractive. Her father, especially when drunk, was abusive and would refer to her as "the fat pig." Occasionally, when her two older brothers were angry, they'd do the same.

As soon as she had saved up enough money, she moved away from her family to Los Angeles, lost some weight, and fell in love and married a man she believed was totally unlike her dad. Life was good for the first two years of marriage. Because her husband said he wanted a big family and Ruth wanted to please him, she began having babies—three to be exact—one after another. She never had much chance to lose weight between births, and with each pregnancy she gained another twenty pounds that she couldn't drop later. Being occupied with her children's needs, she had little time to care for herself or her husband, Rick, who she knew was cheating on her with other women. Ruth was miserable but felt she couldn't leave him since she had three children and no marketable skills.

She tried desperately to lose some weight and dreamed of the day the kids would be old enough for her to leave her husband, but that day came and went. When the last of her kids was eighteen and on his own, Ruth was still with her husband and fifty pounds overweight.

Even though Rick rarely came home anymore, Ruth felt too defeated to go anywhere. Besides, she figured, who would want her? One evening, however, her husband did something he'd never done before. He struck her and called her a "fat pig" just as her father and brothers had before him. The sting of both the slap and the words finally motivated her to leave him.

She decided to move to Philadelphia, where her mother's sister lived, and begin a new life. She practically starved herself to lose some weight and got a job with benefits, which allowed her to seek psychological counseling. In therapy, she was treated for low self-esteem, depression, and poor body image. Ruth and her psychiatrist talked a lot about her body, which she clearly regarded as her enemy.

In the course of one of those sessions, Ruth discussed her other physical ailments, one of which was a mysterious condition that left her weak, tired, numb, and in pain. While weakness and fatigue are common symptoms of depression, the psychiatrist knew numbness of the limbs was not. These symptoms raised the possibility of some other condition like a pinched nerve, multiple sclerosis, and even certain cancers. He referred her to a well-regarded internist.

At the internist's office, Ruth related that her hands and feet would sometimes feel like clubs and her lower legs would get very painful, especially at the end of the day. Sleeping was also difficult because she would have to get up frequently to urinate, which often deprived her of a good night's sleep. She awoke feeling unrefreshed and achy.

Although she had always hated to look at herself in the mirror, it became worse because she would wake up every morning with dark shadows and swelling around her eyes. Additionally, she noted that she had to take her shoes off at the end of the day because her feet had become so swollen. Sometimes her rings would slide easily off her fingers, while at other times she had to use soap to remove them.

Ruth's internist considered and ruled out a dizzying array of possibilities from multiple sclerosis, thyroid disorder, lupus, and other autoimmune disorders to heart disease. She underwent a battery of expensive diagnostic tests and consultations with specialists that left her insurance company aghast. While Ruth's psychological condition appeared to be improving with psychotherapy and support, her physical condition was not. She was still overweight and not feeling well.

After months of listening to Ruth's physical problems, her psychiatrist secured the Eight Steps to Self-Diagnosis from a friend who had used them successfully. He passed them on to Ruth. Since it appeared that her medical doctors had ruled out the most serious possible conditions and she was yo-yoing from one unsuccessful diet to another, he hoped that working through these steps together might help them solve her mystery ailment. Ruth was very fortunate to have such a good relationship with her psychiatrist. She immediately sat down to begin work on her Eight Steps to Self-Diagnosis notebook.

Using the Eight Steps

Step One: Record the Exact Nature of Your Symptoms. Ruth recorded the following facts about her mystery malady:

1. **Numb Hands and Feet**
   - **Quality and Character:** Feels like they are "thick" and swollen, sometimes feels like prickly pins and needles.
   - **Quantity and Severity:** By the end of the work day I have trouble pushing buttons and even using utensils. I sometimes drink soup for dinner as a result.
   - **Timing and Duration:** Always worse at the end of the day and after eating certain foods.
   - **Setting and Environment:** Setting doesn't seem to matter, although I get worse after traveling.
   - **Impact on Your Functioning:** I've given up anything that requires what you'd call fine motor skills like sewing, knitting, even cooking.

2. **Numbness and Pain in Lower Legs and Forearms**
   - **Quality and Character:** They feel heavy and sometimes even burn.
   - **Quantity and Severity:** Keeps me awake.
   - **Timing and Duration:** Worst in the evening and lasts until morning.
   - **Setting and Environment:** Worst after I eat out for some reason.
   - **Impact on Your Functioning:** Don't feel like socializing—I look bad and feel bad.

3. **Swollen Eyes**
   - **Quality and Character:** Bags under my eyes with bluish discoloration that looks worse in the morning.
   - **Quantity and Severity:** See above.
   - **Timing and Duration:** Worse in the morning, usually better by evening.
   - **Setting and Environment:** Worse when traveling or eating out.
   - **Impact on Your Functioning:** Have to wear sunglasses and lots of makeup.
   - **Other Factors:** Like I said, I look bad and feel bad so I don't do much.

4. **Frequent Urination**
   - **Quality and Character:** Just a lot of running to the bathroom but no burning or irritation.
   - **Quantity and Severity:** At least three or four times per night.
   - **Timing and Duration:** Mostly at night.
   - **Setting and Environment:** Worse after eating in restaurants.
   - **Impact on Your Functioning:** I have trouble getting a good's night sleep.

Step Two: Think About the History of Your Mystery Malady. I have been overweight my entire life, but I have not always had the other symptoms. The first time I experienced them was with two of my three pregnancies. But the doctor always told me it was normal. I'm not pregnant anymore, so they can't be normal!

Step Three: What Makes Your Symptoms Better (or Worse)? I always feel worse after I eat out or if I travel. I feel worse in warmer weather. My leg numbness and pain and my ankle swelling decrease when I lie down. I also feel better when I swim in my apartment complex pool on Sundays. I definitely feel worse as the day wears on.

Step Four: Do a Family Medical History and Determine If You Have or Had Any Blood Relatives with a Similar Problem. I don't really know much about my mother because she passed away from kidney disease when I was very young. My father is an alcoholic, and my two brothers suffer from migraine headaches. My three children are in good health.

Step Five: Search for Other Past or Present Mental or Physical Problems. I am somewhat depressed. I have hypothyroidism, but I am on Synthroid for that and feel better. I had high blood pressure, severe headaches, and swelling (like I have now) during two of my three pregnancies. I stayed in bed, got better, and fortunately had normal deliveries. I have food allergies—especially with milk, egg, and wheat products—as well as hay fever. Occasionally, I suffer from gastroesophageal reflux disease [also referred to as acid reflux, a condition in which partially digested food in the stomach backs up into the esophagus and causes a burning sensation and pain].

Step Six: Categorize Your Current and Prior Significant Medical Problems by Etiology.

- **Genetic:** I think my weight problem might be genetic because my mother was also heavy. My whole family seems to have allergies, and I think this might be a factor in my brothers' migraines.
- **Infectious (viral, bacterial, fungal, or parasitic):** Could a parasite cause this? But I haven't done any foreign travel.
- **Structural or biomechanical:** I don't do a lot of exercise because I can't move my body too well, but I think this is because of my other problems.
- **Environmental:** Although I had these problems while I was pregnant, they didn't start to be persistent until I moved to Philadelphia, so maybe it is environmentally related.
- **Metabolic:** I am told my thyroid has been normal since I've been on medication. An endocrinologist checked my hormone and insulin levels. She said my weight could become a problem because I could develop adult-onset diabetes.
- **Iatrogenic:** I am taking an antidepressant, thyroid medication, anti-inflammatories for my aches and pains, and antihistamines occasionally for my allergies. Could any of these be causing my problems?
- **Psychological:** My psychiatrist says my physical problems are not psychological.

Step Seven: Investigate Your Lifestyle and Belief System. I read this step and I've tried to answer all the questions related to my stresses and the way I cope with them honestly. Yes, I have financial problems and family problems, and sometimes I am lonely—especially because of my weight. Also, I know that my weight problems—or my problem with dieting and losing weight—is related to the way I cope. My psychiatrist refers to them as "intimacy problems." But even though my mystery symptoms have something to do with my weight, I don't think my intimacy problems have anything to do with the cause of my symptoms.

Step Eight: Take Your Notebook to Your Physician and Get a Complete Exam. Ruth had received a complete physical several times while her doctors ruled out serious or life-threatening conditions, including heart, liver, kidney, central nervous system and hormonal disorders (and before she completed her Eight Steps). So she decided to use her notebook to research her condition on the Internet.

Ruth went to a search engine and entered her first symptom, numbness of hands and feet. This brought up a huge volume of material. However, most of it referred to parethesias, peripheral neuropathy, diabetes, polyneuritis, and other neurological disorders. She also found a number of health products for sale. She looked up the symptom of swollen eyes and found mostly allergy-related diagnoses.

Ruth went back to her psychiatrist in frustration. He referred Ruth to another internist and told her to take her notebook. He promised to follow up with this doctor.

Making the Diagnosis

[What follows is an account of the new internist's thought process and how Ruth's notebook was helpful in discovering the correct diagnosis.] After seeing all the conditions that had been ruled out, I wasn't altogether sure Ruth's problems were not psychological, but I was willing to look at whatever other avenues remained unexplored. I used Ruth's symptom chart but not for her main symptoms. All her other doctors had already heard these. I tried to look beyond that to her specific descriptions under the symptoms. I derived some important information from them. For example, I noted that in the first symptom, besides her hands and feet being numb, she said they were "thick" and "swollen." That was difficult to see because of her weight. I also noted that she described burning or prickly sensations in her arms and legs.

These facts, together with her observation that her pain was worse at the end of the day, seemed to indicate a neurological condition, even though most of those disorders (confirmed from her prior medical records and testing) had already been ruled out. And while a neurological diagnosis would not explain her other symptoms—"thickness" of her digits, swollen eyes, and frequent urination—it could not be summarily dismissed.

I noticed under her description of "frequent urination" that she was not getting a good night's rest and she had aches and pains. I checked for secondary fibromyalgia but she didn't have the usual tender points indicative of this condition *except* in the areas that were swollen. The tenderness in those areas raised the possibility of periostitis or shin splints but I ruled those out based on other factors.

I examined her hands and feet and listened for symptoms of carpal tunnel or tarsal tunnel syndrome, but she didn't complain about any of the classic symptoms for those. There had to be other clues to this mystery, so I referred back to her notebook.

Four things popped out as I marked up her notebook with a yellow highlighter. Ruth had had these symptoms with two of her pregnancies. Her rings were tight and she couldn't button her clothes—the swelling again. Also, her pain and swelling improved after she lay down and when she swam. Finally, she indicated that two of her existing physical problems were hypothyroidism and food allergies.

I was beginning to see a picture now—one that was really quite obvious. But in searching for a complicated answer everyone, including myself, had missed it. I asked Ruth if she had ever mentioned these things to her other doctors. She responded that she'd reported her thyroid issues, but no one had ever asked her about the other four things and she hadn't thought about them before she worked on the Eight Steps.

The picture that was forming as the puzzle pieces of Ruth's story were put together finally compelled me to ask about her weight. I had not wanted to pursue what I already knew from Ruth's psychiatrist was a painful subject, but it was impossible to avoid it now if she really wanted an answer to her mystery malady. I asked her specifically if her weight at night was different from her weight in the morning. Ruth seemed angry at me for having raised this issue that haunted her every waking hour. She said, "I never look at my weight anymore. . . . It's too depressing! Besides, I'm on thyroid medication for it."

I reminded Ruth that she'd mentioned she felt worse at night, and there were several indicators of a condition that I could confirm and actually demonstrate to her if she would make this determination. She was reticent until I told her I was uninterested in the actual number of pounds she weighed; I simply wanted to know if she weighed more at night than in the morning and how much. She reluctantly agreed to observe this before her next visit, which we scheduled for a week later.

I called her psychiatrist and enlisted his help because I wasn't sure she would come back after this discussion, and I had a strong inkling I might be on to something. At her next appointment, Ruth indicated there was somewhere between a four- and six-pound difference between her night-time and morning weight! That was a lot of fluctuation. I asked her to raise her lower leg for me and said I was going to tell her what was wrong and how she could definitely lose some weight. Now she seemed alert and interested. When she extended her leg, I pressed on her lower leg and showed her the indentation mark it left for several seconds after I released it.

This physical finding, together with all her other symptoms, indicated a medical condition known as edema, or the abnormal buildup and retention of fluid. It is often associated with pregnancy (when it's known as preeclampsia). It is commonly seen in the feet and ankles, usually because of the effect of gravity. As the fluid accumulates, it often pinches off the nerves temporarily to the hands and feet, causing neurological symptoms such as numbness. Fluid also builds up in the front of the shins where it makes the skin tight and causes pain. It also accumulates in the hands—which is why Ruth's rings were sometimes tight and she couldn't perform fine motor functions.

Clearly, this condition was also the reason for her constant urination during the night. As fluids build up during the day, the body naturally tries to rid itself of all this extra fluid at night. Difficulty in sleeping is common, since the bladder needs to be emptied frequently. The bloating and swelling can turn into muscle aches and pains. Ruth's unexplained weight gain and especially her enlarged abdominal girth were a result of this problem.

Finally, loose skin may result, especially under the eyes, hence her "bags," bluish coloration, and swollen eyes in the morning. This is aggravated by high salt intake, which causes further water retention, and is the reason Ruth was worse when she traveled or ate out at restaurants (fast foods are notorious for their high salt content).

Edema can be a symptom of another disorder and is often associated with kidney, bladder, heart, liver, and other conditions already mentioned. Since all these conditions had been ruled out with diagnostic testing, when Ruth's doctors knew there was nothing seriously wrong, they dismissed her. Also, because her weight probably made it difficult to detect the swelling, they made certain assumptions.

Edema, however, can also be caused by food allergies, thyroid disease, or medications. It can be idiopathic (of no known origin) and while not life-threatening, if left untreated, it can cause the kind of discomfort Ruth was experiencing and become progressively worse.

I treated Ruth with a low-salt diet and diuretics, also sometimes referred to as "water pills." Gradually her physical symptoms disappeared, as I hope her psychological ones did, for she was a nice woman who had been through more than her fair share of troubles.

As a point of information, there are also many natural remedies that can help with water retention, including simply eating lots of parsley, alfalfa, strawberries, rose hip tea, and mostly raw foods. However, the use of diuretics—whether prescription or "natural"—can lead to electrolyte imbalances (as we will discuss in Chapter 10). Be sure to have your potassium levels checked and take a potassium supplement if it is indicated.

Case Study: Pedro

Pedro, a very successful car salesman, always made people laugh. So at the age of forty, when he first started gaining a lot of weight, he would joke about it and say he was getting so fat he had time zones around his belly. Sometimes he would tell his customers they could find better bodies at his used car lot. Everyone would laugh, but inside, Pedro was not happy about it. He loved his flan and *dulce de leche* ice cream desserts from time to time but he knew he didn't eat enough of them to justify this weight gain.

He decided to take action. He eliminated all desserts and undertook a strict exercise routine—running a mile every day for six months. This increased his endurance but didn't decrease his weight. He noticed he was still getting rounder by the week. He'd go on the offensive rather than have anyone say anything to him about his significant weight gain. He would ask his coworkers if they could take a picture of his toes so he could remember what they looked like. Or when someone would ask if Pedro was "around," he'd say, "Yep, I'm getting rounder and rounder." And so he was. Everyone would laugh and think Pedro was a great guy. But Pedro wasn't happy about his face, which was looking more and more moon-shaped.

He tried every diet under the sun, including Atkins, South Beach, and even Weight Watchers. He went to all the Weight Watchers meetings. There he made everyone laugh with his self-deprecating weight comments. The problem soon became that the other folks at Weight Watchers were all losing weight even though Pedro wasn't.

He was so frustrated; he was certain everyone was thinking he was a "closet eater," but he wasn't. Soon after, he developed another bothersome symptom: he became weak and sluggish. His wife finally put her foot down and told him that it was time to go to the doctor.

The family doctor was shocked when he saw Pedro. His patient had become morbidly obese. Pedro tried to explain that he was gaining weight inexplicably and that it wasn't a function of his overeating. The doctor ordered blood tests and gave Pedro a complete physical. He found Pedro's blood pressure to be elevated.

When the results came back, the doctor called Pedro. He advised him that his thyroid function was normal but that he had better lose some weight to bring his blood pressure down or there might be serious consequences. Pedro reminded the doctor that he was doing everything he could and now he was feeling weak and tired. The doctor responded by saying, "If you weren't so overweight, then you wouldn't be so weak and tired."

Pedro was now more than frustrated—he was becoming depressed—but once again he tried to lose the weight. Nothing worked. It wasn't until his son Pete made a joke about his weight that Pedro moved into real action. When he asked his son about what Pete wanted to do when he became as big as his dad, the little boy replied, "Diet!" At that point, Pedro had lost his sense of humor about his condition. He got hold of the Eight Steps to Self-Diagnosis and made a decision to do them.

Using the Eight Steps

In working through Step One and doing a disciplined analysis, Pedro realized a few things he hadn't considered before.

Step One: Record the Exact Nature of Your Symptoms.
  1. **Weight Gain**
      • **Quality and Character:** Mostly face and belly, not arms and legs.
      • **Quantity and Severity:** Thirty to forty pounds overweight.
      • **Timing and Duration:** Started at age forty.

- **Setting and Environment:** Not from overeating.
- **Impact on Your Functioning:** I have trouble getting around because I'm so big.

2. **Weakness**
   - **Quality and Character:** Both arms and legs.
   - **Quantity and Severity:** Moderate.
   - **Timing and Duration:** Started with weight gain.
   - **Setting and Environment:** Stairs are a problem; I have to use my arms to help me get out of a chair.
   - **Impact on Your Functioning:** It takes longer to navigate stairs.

3. **Stretch Marks**
   - **Quality and Character:** Bright red ones on belly and buttocks.
   - **Quantity and Severity:** Numerous.
   - **Timing and Duration:** Same time as weight gain.
   - **Setting and Environment:** Not applicable.
   - **Impact on Your Functioning:** I have to cover them up; they're embarrassing.

4. **Other Symptoms**
   - **High blood pressure:** Doctor blames it on my being overweight, which is not my fault.
   - **Thick beard:** My beard requires two shaves a day now, and I had to get a new shaver.
   - **Fullness of face and neck:** Like a moon face.
   - **Hungry all the time:** Even after I've just eaten.

Pedro was concerned about his stretch marks because of how red they were, but he thought maybe most fat people had them and that's why his doctor didn't say anything during the physical. He also never thought about the fact that his beard was now so thick that he'd needed a new shaver and always had to shave twice during the day. Nevertheless, he knew the Eight Steps required him to list everything and not make a judgment about how important it was or what it all meant.

Pedro went further with his Eight-Step notebook. In response to Step Seven (Investigate Your Lifestyle and Belief System), he created a calorie consumption journal. From that, he realized he wasn't consuming more than one thousand calories per day, yet he still wasn't losing any weight. He knew there was something seriously wrong. He decided it was time to do some research, and following the suggestions in Chapter 5, he signed on to the Internet and located every educational site and article he could find on obesity.

He learned that if his calorie consumption chart was even close to accurate, his diet and eating habits were definitely not the cause of his obesity. He also learned there were other possible causes. He immediately made an appointment with a well-known internist in town because he felt his family doctor was not responsive.

Making the Diagnosis

On the day of his appointment, Pedro took his Eight Step notebook, his blood test results from the family doctor, his calorie journal, and his sense of humor to the internist's office. He told the doctor he wanted to be so thin he'd have to jump around in the shower to get wet. The internist laughed and after reviewing Pedro's notebook, he responded that he didn't know if he could get Pedro *that* thin, but he was reasonably sure he could make him a lot better. He said he was very impressed with Pedro's hard work and then gave Pedro a blood and urine test and a computerized tomography (CT) scan. The doctor felt reasonably sure he could give his patient not only a diagnosis but also a cure.

Fortunately, Pedro got both. When all the test results came back, the doctor told Pedro he had developed Cushing's syndrome, also known as hypercortisolism. This is a metabolic disorder that occurs when excess cortisol circulates in the bloodstream.

All the key indicators were found in Pedro's notebook: the round face and extra fatty tissue in the neck; the thinning skin (which accounted for the bright red stretch marks); the excess beard growth; his obesity, weakness, and fatigability. In fact, Pedro's metabolic condition causes a certain peculiar pattern of obesity that results in a round (moon) face and obesity around the trunk (centripetal obesity). The tests the internist ordered simply confirmed the diagnosis.

He explained that Pedro's adrenal glands were producing too much cortisol, which in turn caused all his symptoms. The CT scan revealed a small adrenal adenoma, or benign tumor. This tumor was subsequently removed and eventually all Pedro's symptoms, including his obesity, disappeared.

Case Study: Lincoln

Fifty-two-year-old Lincoln was a middle school math teacher. Toward the end of the school year, he began to feel sluggish and generally run down. He noticed he was having problems focusing on his lesson plans and was randomly forgetting things. He attributed it to simply needing his summer vacation after a long, tough year.

What he couldn't explain, though, was his gradual weight gain over the past three months. He knew that he had stopped exercising since his heart attack in March, and even though the doctors told him it was perfectly fine for him to start exercising again, he was a little anxious about resuming any activity that required a lot of exertion. He thought this might be the reason for his weight gain, but it just wouldn't level off and the pounds kept slowly creeping on. He recalled that when he had stopped smoking years earlier, he had gained weight but even that had leveled off after a couple of months.

At the last school health fair, he was checked out and was told he was fine. Several times, he visited the hospital clinic where he'd been treated for his heart attack; they drew his blood and even checked for thyroid disease. The results were normal. Lincoln was told it was anxiety after his heart attack, but he *knew* there was really something wrong with his body.

When summer vacation finally arrived, Lincoln made a concerted effort to get back into his weight lifting and daily two-mile walks around the river in the city where he lived. But after two months of this regimen with no abatement of his symptoms and no weight loss, he decided to take matters into his own hands. He was given a copy of the Eight Steps by a teacher friend and decided to try to solve his mystery malady.

He filled up a notebook, precisely answering all the questions posed by all Eight Steps. He called some of his fellow teachers to get recommendations for the best family doctor on the school's health plan. Several of his colleagues suggested a very bright woman only a few years out of medical school. He made an appointment with her and took his notebook to the appointment.

This doctor's waiting room was packed with patients. But as it turned out, Lincoln didn't need much of her time. After taking a brief history, the doctor knew her new patient had had a heart attack and mentioned with concern that he really needed to lose weight. Lincoln told her that was one of the reasons he was there. He said he couldn't seem to take off the weight, and he enumerated his other symptoms. She said it sounded like he had developed thyroid disease but dismissed it when Lincoln told her he had been tested for this several times at the clinic and the results were negative. She was perplexed. She said that maybe he just needed to find a different way to lose weight and the other symptoms would disappear. (That's what the doctors had said at the clinic but Lincoln knew very well he had already made every effort to no avail.)

With some hesitation, Lincoln showed her the Eight Step notebook, and she appeared impressed with his effort. She decided if her patient had put in this much time and effort to try to solve his problem, he deserved the same from her. She told him she didn't have time to review the notebook while he was there, but if he left it, she would look at it after office hours.

The next day, Lincoln received a call from the physician's office to come in for yet another blood test. After reviewing his notebook, the doctor understood immediately what the problem was. When the blood test result was "positive," she called her patient with his diagnosis.

Making the Diagnosis

The doctor told Lincoln his notebook was the key to her finding his diagnosis because she was able to make certain connections that she otherwise could not have. When she had read Steps One (the exact nature of symptoms), Two (history of the malady), and Five (other past or present mental or physical problems), she knew that Lincoln's diagnosis was probably hypothyroidism despite the negative results on initial tests.

The notebook revealed that while Lincoln was being examined for his heart problems in the clinic the prior April, he'd developed a cardiac arrhythmia (a dangerously irregular heartbeat), passed out, and "coded." The doctors had administered an emergency dose of a commonly used antiarrhythmic drug called amiodarone. She researched this drug to confirm her suspicions: although it is very effective, it can cause hypothyroidism in 13 percent of patients because it contains 39 percent by weight iodine. This would explain all of Lincoln's symptoms, including the puzzling weight gain over time. The problem was complicated by the fact that the medication also classically yields negative test results for thyroid disease at first. This is known as "silent thyroiditis." With these negative findings, everyone—including Lincoln—simply attributed his weight gain to his lack of exercise and his other symptoms to the anxiety from his heart attack. She prescribed thyroid medication, and within weeks, Lincoln was returning to his normal weight and feeling much improved.

Without having the written clues from his notebook, the physician might not have been able to put together the pieces of the puzzle, and it would have been easy to miss the real connection between the events in April and Lincoln's weight gain several months later. Taking the time to get a detailed medical history during an appointment with a busy doctor with a waiting room full of patients like this one would have been difficult. Clearly, the Eight Step notebook allowed Lincoln to receive the correct diagnosis much more quickly than might have happened otherwise.

Conclusion

Not all obesity is caused by overeating and inactivity. Regardless of cause, however, weight is a serious health issue and one that should not be ignored, whether or not your doctor raises it with you. It is often associated with high blood pressure, diabetes, coronary artery disease, stroke, sleep apnea, osteoarthritis, and several types of cancers. Being overweight can be an integral factor in determining the cause of a mystery illness. Use the Eight Steps to help you and your doctor find the underlying cause of your medical problem. But if either of you has been avoiding the issue because of the stigma about being obese, you need to muster the courage to raise it.

Remember, weight is not a judgment on a person's character, worthiness, or anything else. It is simply a physical—and more often than not, a genetic—characteristic like brown hair or fair skin. However, when dealing with a mystery malady, it could very well be the missing piece of the puzzle. Work through the Eight Steps, carefully unearth your own clues, and keep an open mind—even if the medical and other experts insist on keeping theirs shut!

Ask yourself these questions:

- Have you reduced your caloric intake, done a written tracking of your calories, and still been unable to lose weight?
- Have you started a regular exercise regimen (at least thirty minutes a day) with no weight loss?
- Are you experiencing other symptoms along with weight gain?
- Was the onset at a particular time in your life that did not correlate to changes in caloric intake?

If you've answered yes to these questions, it is time to raise this issue with your doctor and work through the Eight Steps if the answer isn't easily identified.

10

Are Your Ways of Staying Healthy Making You Sick?

THE PUSH TO achieve greater health, wellness, youth, energy, and a toned physique is all around us. Articles abound, books are hyped, and TV commercials prompt us. The trend toward patients taking greater responsibility for their health and health care is an important and positive one, and this book is obviously premised on it. But sometimes in our zeal to maximize our health, we may take our efforts to an extreme and unintentionally harm ourselves. Failing to stay alert to things that can go wrong in our efforts to stay healthy and trim can result in mystery maladies. This is sadly demonstrated by the following two case studies.

Case Study: Maria

Maria was a forty-eight-year-old Miami homemaker whose last child had just entered college. With time on her hands, too many birthdays behind her, and an ob-gyn husband who was on call and often not at home, Maria decided it was time to take care of herself and get in shape. She joined a local fitness center, hired a personal trainer, and worked out at least five times a week. Some would say Maria became almost obsessive about her exercise program and the shape of her body. Over the next ten months, however, all her hard work seemed to be paying off as she transformed herself into a svelte, muscular woman.

Since she spent so much time at the gym, she developed many friend-ships there with women who were also fanatical about their exercise, diets, and personal trainers. They all loved to party and frequent the hottest South Beach night spots. When they invited Maria to join them, she began to drag her husband, Burt, along as they went clubbing on the weekends.

While Burt was happy his wife looked so good and was filling her new-found time without the kids in a seemingly healthy manner, he was not so thrilled to be spending his weekends off with her new friends. The clubs didn't start hopping until midnight, and unlike most of Maria's new friends—many of whom were considerably younger and certainly not obste-tricians who were expected to deliver babies at all hours of the night—he needed his rest when he wasn't working. Maria was not happy when he refused to join her in her new social life, so she began to party without him.

As time went on, Burt became concerned that his wife might be cling-ing to her youth in an inappropriate way. He suggested counseling. She laughed it off, retorting, "With the amount of sex you get—with a body like mine—I shouldn't hear you complaining." That would usually end the conversation.

Two years into her exercise routine, when she was about fifty and her friends thought she looked fabulous, Maria started to gain weight. Being married to a gynecologist, she knew the symptoms of menopause and also knew her husband would probably suggest hormone replacement therapy, which she thought would only make her gain more weight. She decided not to mention it to Burt but instead worked harder at the gym and added nat-ural supplements (including soy, evening primrose oil, and other vitamins and herbals) to her diet to help with the symptoms of menopause. She also started eating less.

She was successful in curbing her weight gain, but she was becoming chronically tired and weak. In time she also developed muscle cramps and became depressed. Burt noticed that Maria had stopped going out in the evenings. There were no more personal checks being written to her personal trainer. While he was secretly delighted in this change, he was also concerned about her fatigue and depression.

He questioned Maria carefully, and she responded somewhat evasively that she had simply become bored with it all. Burt was skeptical. Not only had his wife put on a few pounds (which he reasoned could have been a nor-mal result of having given up the exercise), but she had become less interested in sex as well. Burt assumed menopause might be setting in and suggested that Maria might want to check her estrogen levels. She replied she was still getting her periods and everything was fine. Because Burt was not altogether unhappy with this turn of events—Maria was at home more, seemed less hyper, and actually looked better with a couple of extra pounds—he tried to deny the muscle weakness he was also observing in his wife.

Finally, when he could ignore it no longer, Burt told Maria to make an appointment to be examined by their friend and family physician and at the very least to have her thyroid checked. Maria refused. Just to prove there was nothing wrong with her, she had her personal trainer start coming to their home to help her return to a physical fitness routine.

Her trainer was shocked to find Maria in such a weakened state. She tired easily and had definite low energy. He also attributed the change to menopause and tried to work her harder. Maria would keep her act together until he left and then break down in tears. Eventually Maria had to tell him that she could no longer train, but she made him promise not to tell her husband something was wrong. (She even went so far as to write him checks and have him pay her back in cash so Burt wouldn't get suspicious.)

Soon she found she could hardly climb up into her SUV. Rather than tell Burt, however, she tried alternative healing methods, including Reiki, acupuncture, and massage. When all of them failed to work, she tried Rolfing, which was extremely painful. At that point, Maria's situation turned from bad to worse as her muscles began cramping without any precipitating cause. When she finally became concerned that she had multiple sclerosis or some really terrible disease, she confided in her husband.

Burt swung into action; he immediately took Maria to his office and drew her blood to check her thyroid, estrogen, and other blood levels. When he received the results, he noticed a dip in Maria's estrogen levels, indicating the onset of menopause. Her thyroid levels were being successfully handled by the thyroid medication she had been taking for years. However, he also observed oddly elevated muscle enzymes and low potassium levels. That needed a further workup, but the next round of testing revealed no answers. Burt sent his wife to his colleague, Dr. Rosenbaum, who started Maria working through the Eight Steps. Dr. Rosenbaum suspected he was dealing with a case very similar to that of eighteen-year-old Jennifer, whom he had seen the year before.

At fifteen, Jennifer was a gifted scholar and a star gymnast. She competed in shows nationally and won several competitions per year for the next three years. After high school, she left home for college since her parents wanted her to become a doctor. They thought a professional athlete could not earn a good and lasting living. They also believed getting married shouldn't be the "be all, end all" for a smart young woman like their daughter.

Jennifer would have preferred to simply continue with her gymnastics, but she did her parents' bidding. At college, she had less and less time for physical training—something she had not anticipated when she agreed to attend. Gradually, she got into the college lifestyle and began to ease off her rigid diet and exercise regimen. Even though her classes were difficult, she was actually more relaxed and happier than she had been for three years, possibly because she didn't feel quite as compelled to win. Her grades were decent, but she didn't mind settling for Bs and even an occasional C.

She began having a social life, hanging out in bars with her friends. Then her physical problems began—the first was a change in her energy level. She assumed that sedentary activities like studying as well as the weekend partying were the cause of her problems. Her lack of energy, though, soon turned into weakness.

It was then that Jennifer decided it was time to go back to the gym. She also put herself back on a diet—as much as the school cafeteria food would allow—and supplemented her salads with a variety of nutritional supplements. Nevertheless, she continued to grow weaker, was chronically tired, and developed muscle cramps. At first, the cramps occurred just when she worked out. Later, though, they happened even after she stopped exercising. Her parents became worried and took her to see Dr. Rosenbaum, who gave Jennifer the Eight Steps as "homework."

Using the Eight Steps

When Dr. Rosenbaum received the information in Maria's notebook, it looked very similar to Jennifer's, but Maria was too weak to fill out much of it. Scant as the information was, it was enough to help Dr. Rosenbaum solve her mystery malady.

Step One: Record the Exact Nature of Your Symptoms.

1. **General Weakness**
   - **Quality and Character:** Overall muscle weakness as if I had the flu all the time.
   - **Quantity and Severity:** All day.
   - **Timing and Duration:** Even when I wake up; there is no variation.
   - **Setting and Environment:** I feel it worse when I exert myself in any way.
   - **Impact on Your Functioning:** Cannot climb into my SUV and have trouble just walking around. Definitely can't exercise. No interest in sex anymore.

2. **Muscle Weakness**
   - **Quality and Character:** I feel like a straw doll but have no aches or pains that go with it.
   - **Quantity and Severity:** All day.
   - **Timing and Duration:** All day and no variation except for one day when I fasted and just drank water all day; for some reason I felt a little better.
   - **Setting and Environment:** Same as above.
   - **Impact on Your Functioning:** Couldn't even get on the scale this morning.
   - **Other Factors:** There is no pain or any other symptom with weakness.

3. **Chronic Fatigue and Depression:** Same as above on everything.

Step Two: Think About the History of Your Mystery Malady. This began after I turned fifty and went into menopause. That's when I started gaining weight, so I began eating less; exercising more; and taking soy products, evening primrose oil, and other food supplements. I lost the weight but felt worse.

Step Three: What Makes Your Symptoms Better (or Worse)? Exercise used to give me more energy; now my weakness is persistent and nothing makes it better although exercising now can make it worse. I have no energy or strength.

Step Four: Do a Family Medical History and Determine If You Have or Had Any Blood Relatives with a Similar Problem. My father died of colon cancer at the age of seventy-one, but he was heavy and never took care of himself. My mother's brother also had cancer, and my mother had skin cancer from which she ultimately died. My sisters are living and generally healthy, although my elder sister is obese like my father and has high blood pressure.

Step Five: Search for Other Past or Present Mental or Physical Problems. In the past, I considered myself a healthy person but never felt better than when I started working out. After my last child left for school, I was treated for depression with Prozac. I believed I had empty nest syndrome. When I started working out, I stopped Prozac and felt better. Unfortunately now, with my poor health, I'm depressed once more.

Step Six: Categorize Your Current and Prior Significant Medical Problems by Etiology.
- **Genetic:** None that I'm aware of.
- **Infectious (viral, bacterial, fungal, or parasitic):** Occasional cold or flu.
- **Structural or biomechanical:** I have a weak lower back, but exercise has made it stronger.
- **Environmental:** None.
- **Metabolic:** I have hypothyroidism.
- **Iatrogenic:** I am not taking any prescription medicines other than for my thyroid.
- **Psychological:** Depression when last child left for college but I felt better after getting into my exercise. Now I am depressed that I am so weak.

Step Seven: Investigate Your Lifestyle and Belief System. I used to think my worth was about being a mom so when my last child left home, I felt lost.

Building myself up at the gym, losing weight, gaining muscle tone, and looking young and beautiful again took my thoughts away from this. Going to the clubs on South Beach and having younger men act interested in me also helped me feel good about myself. Don't get me wrong; I have always been happy with Burt and love him dearly. I knew he wasn't happy about what I was doing, but it felt like something I needed to do for myself.

Now I am very frightened. I went from fit and trim to feeling haggard and even having muscle weakness and spasms like an old person. I didn't want to acknowledge this because I was afraid I might have cancer like my mother and father or just be dying—and maybe I might or should be if I am just going to be fat, weak, and old.

Step Eight: Take Your Notebook to Your Physician and Get a Complete Exam. Dr. Rosenbaum gave Maria a thorough physical exam after his nurse reported to him that his patient was so weak she had difficulty getting up on the scale to be weighed. Although Maria brought her prior lab results, Dr. Rosenbaum did his own laboratory testing because different laboratories sometimes yield different results. He too found elevated muscle enzymes indicative of muscle inflammation as well as a dangerously low potassium level. In fact, it was low enough to cause electrocardiogram (EKG) abnormalities.

Making the Diagnosis

The first thing Dr. Rosenbaum did was to encourage Maria to begin eating foods rich in potassium and take potassium supplements. However, this didn't help her to the extent he expected. There was no identifiable medical condition that could explain what was going on with her.

Maria's journal revealed her fear of becoming overweight and menopausal and how strong her feelings were regarding this subject. Given this and the fact that her potassium levels had dropped made Dr. Rosenbaum suspect that diuretics, or "water pills," were playing a role in Maria's mystery malady. These medications increase the volume of urine formation, helping the body to decrease excess fluid. Unfortunately, they can also "wash out" essential minerals and electrolytes like potassium and cause muscle spasming and weakness along with an elevation in muscle enzymes. Dr. Rosenbaum asked Maria directly if she were taking any diuretics to help her shed water weight. She denied it.

Most doctors, as matter of routine, will inquire about what medications a patient is taking, but there was nothing else in Maria's medical records or even in Dr. Rosenbaum's subsequent questioning of her list of medications, that would be related to her condition, particularly since her thyroid levels were normal. Then Dr. Rosenbaum remembered his college-aged patient Jennifer. He reviewed Maria's notebook again. While it was pretty sparse—only a half-hearted effort at best—on a second look, it turned out to be good enough.

Under Step Two relating to the history of her ailment, he noted that Maria had scribbled she was taking soy, evening primrose oil, and other supplements. He questioned her about these other supplements. When she didn't remember what they were, she was instructed to return home and call Dr. Rosenbaum immediately to read all the ingredients to him.

Among her supplements was one "specifically formulated to prevent and treat cellulite." This particular supplement, she enthusiastically informed Dr. Rosenbaum, even came with instructions on how to massage certain cellulite-prone areas. Unfortunately, it also had an ingredient that was essentially the same as a diuretic and, taken on a daily basis as she was doing, would deplete her body of essential minerals and electrolytes like potassium.

After months of deteriorated health and worry, Maria's mystery malady improved dramatically *within one week* of stopping her anticellulite supplement and starting on magnesium, calcium, and potassium.

An essential question with any natural supplement is to determine the plant from which the supplement is derived. It may have side effects that are known and easily identified to a trained medical practitioner. In your Eight Step notebook, take special care to note every time you began ingesting any new supplement so you can correlate the possible onset of your symptoms with it.

In Jennifer's case, Dr. Rosenbaum was able to determine that supplements were also causing her symptoms because she did list all her supplements in her notebook. Dr. Rosenbaum was immediately able to link the ingredients that were acting like diuretics to the symptoms that were so debilitating. Jennifer also got immediate relief with treatment. Neither Maria nor Jennifer might have had such an immediate treatment success without working through the Eight Steps.

Case Study: Leonard

Leonard's story is similar in that his mystery malady resulted from his efforts to stay trim, but the cause in his case was quite different. He was a sixty-four-year-old investment banker who lived in the suburb of Westchester, New York. After long workdays in the city, he would commute home on the Grand Central Railroad and unwind by running through the quiet suburban streets after dark. When his two kids entered high school, he and his wife, Erica, decided to embark on a new adventure. They enrolled the kids in a private high school in Manhattan and bought a loft in Soho. Erica was thrilled to have Leonard home each evening at an earlier hour than when they lived in the suburbs. In place of the hilly roads of Westchester he'd once jogged, he bought a treadmill and several weights. His wife joined him in his exercise routine.

Life was interesting for the family as they spent their weekends in Central Park and museums and exploring the ethnic neighborhoods of New York City. Living near Chinatown and Little Italy was especially fun, and the family ate out regularly. Within a year of their move, however, Leonard developed severe pain in his shoulders, especially while doing his two-mile run. The pain began interfering with mundane activities, even causing him difficulties while dressing and undressing. Rolling over in bed at night was a chore. His shoulders became "bound" and lost their normal mobility.

After several visits to his internist, a physical therapist, and a chiropractor and a great deal of diagnostic testing ordered by an orthopedic surgeon, Leonard finally underwent surgery, but his pain was unabated and the cause remained undetermined. Leonard tried to continue his exercise routine, but instead of maintaining his strength, he became progressively weaker. Desperate for answers, Leonard's physician contacted Dr. Rosenbaum, who put Leonard to work on the Eight Steps to Self-Diagnosis.

Using the Eight Steps

Here is a sampling from Leonard's notebook.

Step One: Record the Exact Nature of Your Symptoms.
  1. **Shoulder Pain**
     • **Quality and Character:** Usually sharp; other times it feels like a
       dull ache or burning.
     • **Quantity and Severity:** All the time, but when I use the treadmill
       or move my shoulders it is worse.
     • **Timing and Duration:** The pain is sharp when I move my shoul-
       ders and a dull ache the rest of the time. I've had this for eight
       months now.
     • **Setting and Environment:** Anywhere.
     • **Impact on Your Functioning:** I feel crippled and have limited my
       physical movements. I still work, but I am becoming more seden-
       tary so I try to at least walk on the treadmill. It's impossible to
       even comb my hair. I have a hard time dressing and even brush-
       ing my teeth.

  2. **Neck Pain**
     • **Quality and Character:** Dull ache.
     • **Quantity and Severity:** All the time.
     • **Timing and Duration:** It gets worse at night.
     • **Setting and Environment:** Same as above.
     • **Impact on Your Functioning:** Same as above.
     • **Other factors:** Feels like chills from a flu but there is no accom-
       panying fever; maybe it's the constant pain; otherwise same as
       above.

Step Two: Think About the History of Your Mystery Malady. This started
when I moved to Manhattan, but I don't think this is related. There is no
difference in weather from Westchester. Am I allergic to the city? This
doesn't seem relevant, but I am recording everything without judgment.

Step Three: What Makes Your Symptoms Better (or Worse)? I am better
when I am immobile, but I am losing my endurance and gaining weight so

I still try to exercise. Exercising makes me worse, especially doing my weights after the treadmill. Physical therapy and my anti-inflammatory medications help, but the problem never really goes away.

Step Four: Do a Family Medical History and Determine If You Have or Had Any Blood Relatives with a Similar Problem. My father died of a heart attack. My mother, however, died of old age and Alzheimer's disease. My brother is healthy.

Step Five: Search for Other Past or Present Mental or Physical Problems. I have been in relatively good health all my life. I was treated for depression and anxiety after my father died of a heart attack when I was nineteen, but I was okay after about six months. I had a knee operation from a college football injury, but I recovered fully. Other than that I have had the normal amount of colds and flu.

Step Six: Categorize Your Current and Prior Significant Medical Problems by Etiology.
- **Genetic:** None.
- **Infectious (viral, bacterial, fungal, or parasitic):** Occasional cold or flu.
- **Structural or biomechanical:** I had knee surgery but no problems since. My shoulders are "frozen" now.
- **Environmental:** Am I allergic to living in the city?
- **Metabolic:** No problems.
- **Iatrogenic:** Maybe the unnecessary surgery for my shoulders has created a bigger problem for me.
- **Psychological:** Depression and anxiety after my father died. Otherwise I've been lucky until now.

Step Seven: Investigate Your Lifestyle and Belief System. My lifestyle is very straightforward. I don't feel my beliefs have anything to do with this problem.

Step Eight: Take Your Notebook to Your Physician and Get a Complete Physical Exam. Leonard returned to his physician with his Eight Step notebook in hand. In Leonard's case, it was helpful in eliminating many things. And a single factor he kept repeating became the main clue and basis, not for his diagnosis, which was fairly clear, but for the cause of his condition.

Making the Diagnosis

Leonard's notebook accurately described a fairly typical case of "frozen shoulder," sometimes known as adhesive capsulitis, which is characterized by stiffness, limited range of motion and pain. The ligaments and tissue around the shoulder capsule or joint become inflamed and stiff. Usually this occurs after surgery or a fracture of the arm when the limb is immobilized. It also usually occurs in one shoulder. In Leonard's case, it was both shoulders, which was atypical.

Leonard's history didn't seem to have any of the things that normally cause frozen shoulder. But his notebook repeatedly made mention of this problem occurring after he moved from the suburbs to Manhattan. He even joked about possibly being "allergic" to the city as a cause of his problem. Dr. Rosenbaum asked him to return to his journal, act like a medical detective, and specifically list what in his life had changed since he moved to the city, using what he now knew about the causes of frozen shoulder—surgery, immobilization, or a physical trauma or injury.

Leonard realized that the change from suburb to city was mainly in the form of exercise. Leonard used to run for two miles on country roads. Then when he moved to Manhattan, he ran his two miles on the treadmill.

Suddenly it occurred to Dr. Rosenbaum that both shoulders were being affected so Leonard had to be doing something with both arms. He asked Leonard to do an experiment using the treadmill: to run and describe exactly what he did with both arms while he ran. He reminded Leonard not to make any assumptions and to keep an open mind.

Leonard did what he was told and immediately realized he was leaning *both* his arms on the support bars of the treadmill while running. This clue was the missing puzzle piece! By using his shoulders to support his weight, Leonard was probably causing progressive microtrauma to both shoulder joints. As the pain from the trauma intensified, Leonard began guarding against the pain by not using them. Progressively, his shoulders became more bound down, or frozen. First he was immobilizing them as he leaned on them while running. Then he was immobilizing them further by refusing to use them because of the pain, giving himself a double whammy. His mystery malady was clearly biomechanical in origin.

Conclusion

Attempting to stay healthy through diet and exercise is certainly recommended. However, as with Maria, Jennifer, and Leonard, exercise and dieting can be hazardous to your health if not done properly and with supervision. Always check with a medical professional before attempting either. And don't forget to analyze your own so-called healthy habits when searching for clues to your mystery malady.

Ask yourself these questions:

- Have you begun any new routine or regimen in an attempt to get or stay healthy?
- Did your symptoms begin after that?
- Have the symptoms gotten worse?
- What exercises, programs, foods, supplements, diets, medications or practices are you doing or taking now? Could they have any relationship to the onset of your problems?

If you're not sure, work through the Eight Steps to find your clues.

11

Do You Have Unexplained Back, Neck, or Joint Pain?

NECK, BACK, AND joint pain affects a whopping 60 to 85 percent of the population at any given time. John Sarno, M.D., professor of clinical rehabilitation medicine at New York University School of Medicine, wrote, "The pervasive concept of vulnerability of the back, of ease of injury, is nothing less than a medical catastrophe for the American public, which now has an army of semi-disabled men and women whose lives have been significantly restricted by fear of further damage or bringing on the dreaded pain again."[1]

This observation about the fear of pain pertains not only to backs; it also applies to necks, shoulders, and other joints and major muscle groups. Musculoskeletal and joint pain often starts without warning and for no obvious or easily explainable reason. Sometimes it can stop without treatment. In other cases, it becomes recurrent and we don't know why we are hurting or how to fix it. Most of the time, with this kind of pain, people just assume they have injured themselves, and the injury was the precipitating cause of their pain. But this is not always true.

In this chapter, we share several interesting cases of seemingly unexplainable muscle or joint pain. Once these frustrated patients used the Eight Steps, they finally found the correct diagnosis and obtained relief from their pain.

Case Study: Brad

Brad, a twenty-seven-year-old mortgage broker and avid tennis player, developed a terrible lower backache one Sunday morning after his weekly game of tennis. He assumed that he had somehow sprained his back during the game. Being an active young man and having injured various parts of his body at one time or another, he knew the drill. When he got home, he iced the most painful area of his back, laid down, and later applied moist heat. He felt reasonably certain the pain would diminish before he went back to work on Monday.

But it didn't. In fact, the pain remained fairly intense and persisted the entire week. One week turned into several, and he finally went to his doctor. He was x-rayed and when it was determined his pain was probably a soft tissue injury, he was treated with nonsteroidal anti-inflammatory drugs and given a prescription for physical therapy, which he pursued twice a week for several weeks. He was told to rest as much as he could. He gave up playing tennis and working out altogether.

The drugs and physical therapy helped somewhat, but they didn't completely resolve his problem. In fact, he found that resting actually made him feel much worse. He figured out that if he kept moving around—walking, riding a bike, or doing any other activity (including sex), he had less back pain. Lying down or sitting in a chair or car for some reason caused his back to become stiff and hurt even more.

This reality was rapidly becoming a real problem in his job. Even though he would get up and stretch periodically, by the end of each workday, he was close to tears from the pain. He was ready to give up his job to become a construction worker or anything that was less sedentary and more physical.

Worse still, sleeping was a problem. Every morning, he awoke with increased back stiffness, and the pain in the lower left quadrant of his back was excruciating. His friends suggested some alternative therapies, which Brad tried. Massage therapy felt great but did not afford him any long-lasting relief. Acupuncture lessened the sensation of pain, but the relief only lasted for a few hours. His doctor examined Brad again and discovered that his patient was, indeed, "tight." He referred him to an orthopedic surgeon who suggested a routine of back stretching exercises. They helped until Brad stopped moving for a while, and the pain that felt like a hot poker in the lower left side of his back started up again.

Brad tried a number of other things in an effort to help himself, including wearing magnets. He dropped a few pounds because he was afraid he was getting sciatica like his uncle whose condition had improved with weight loss. But when he discussed the problem with his Uncle Ben, they both agreed Brad's pain didn't seem the same since it didn't radiate down his leg. Brad now understood why his own doctor hadn't suggested sciatica as a diagnosis. The only relief for Brad, besides the anti-inflammatory medication, came from physical exercise.

Eventually, Brad visited another orthopedic surgeon who prescribed strong pain medication. Brad took this medication for a while but soon stopped for fear he would become like his father. Brad remembered his dad, who'd also had back pain, living on pain pills for most of his life. Brad was afraid of becoming addicted like he thought his father might have been.

Finally, Brad considered quitting work and going on disability, but he knew he would have a big problem getting disability coverage. How was he going to explain to the insurance company that he couldn't work but he could still play tennis, exercise, and be extremely active? The whole thing was a huge mystery.

Fortunately Brad's uncle described his nephew's problem to a friend with whom he played cards and who happened to be a retired physical therapist. This therapist had heard about the Eight Steps from his daughter. He had a copy of them sent to Brad.

Using the Eight Steps

This is a sampling of Brad's notebook, which finally led to a correct and admittedly unusual diagnosis.

Step One: Record the Exact Nature of Your Symptoms.
1. **Back Pain**
    - **Quality and Character:** One-sided lower back pain that feels like a hot poker. Pain does not radiate like a pinched nerve or sciatica.
    - **Quantity and Severity:** Often and severe on one side of my back unless I am physically active.

- **Timing and Duration:** Worse in the morning or after prolonged inactivity.
- **Setting and Environment:** Anywhere and everywhere when I'm inactive.
- **Impact on Your Functioning:** It sometimes wakes me up at night. Now I can barely sit at my job.

Step Two: Think About the History of Your Mystery Malady. The back pain started one Sunday after a game of tennis. The only other possible cause of this sprain that happened about the same time was that I was dating this girl, Lydia, and we were into some heavy-duty "sexual gymnastics." Maybe this had something to do with my injury.

Step Three: What Makes Your Symptoms Better (or Worse)? Activity and exercise makes the pain better. Rest makes it worse. Pain killers and anti-inflammatories help, but if I stop taking them, the pain returns.

Step Four: Do a Family Medical History and Determine If You Have or Had Any Blood Relatives with a Similar Problem. My father was always complaining about low back pain but I think he just liked to complain and this was a great excuse for him to take prescription drugs. Eventually he died from a heart attack. My uncle has sciatica. My mother is fine but has arthritis in her fingers. My two sisters are in good health. My grandparents were in fairly good health until they died.

Step Five: Search for Other Past or Present Mental or Physical Problems. Other than the tennis elbow I developed two years ago which got better, and other muscle strains and sprains from playing football and other physical activities, I have been fairly healthy other than an occasional cold. About eight months ago, after I started dating Lydia, I may have caught something from her. She had some gynecological problems which she said she took care of, but I developed a horrible burning sensation when I urinated. I went to a urologist who gave me some pills and eventually the burning resolved.

Around the same time, I also had an episode of red-eye, which my eye doctor said was conjunctivitis. He prescribed some eye drops, and it went away.

Step 6: Categorize Your Current and Prior Significant Medical Problems by Etiology.

- **Genetic:** My father had back pain but I don't know if this was true and possibly genetic or an excuse to take drugs. My mother has arthritis and her brother (Uncle Ben) has sciatica. Is this related or genetic?
- **Infectious (viral, bacterial, fungal, or parasitic):** I had the two infections I mentioned—urinary and conjunctivitis. Sometimes I have ulcers in my mouth, but I forgot to mention this to my doctor or in Step Five.
- **Structural or biomechanical:** My back pain does not get worse with activity or exercise; it gets better. Pain does not radiate like a pinched nerve or sciatica. The massage therapist said I have few, if any, muscle spasms anymore. Is this back pain biomechanical?
- **Environmental:** No change with traveling to different locations. No change with different chairs or driving different cars.
- **Metabolic:** Not that I can tell.
- **Iatrogenic:** I don't think so.
- **Psychological:** This is driving me nuts!

Step Seven: Investigate Your Lifestyle and Belief System. I see I may not have told my doctor everything that I've described in these steps. I will take this notebook with me and go through it with him.

Making the Diagnosis

Brad's regular physician was able to diagnose Brad's condition after a careful review of his notebook. Most cases of low back pain last only a few days because it is usually caused by the tightening or spasm (severe tightening) of the muscles that are used to support the spine in an upright position. Rest, certain therapies, and medication will usually alleviate the problem.

What was strikingly different about Brad's condition was that it persisted beyond a reasonable time, and instead of rest alleviating the problem, it made it worse. Conversely, exercise improved his condition. This is typical for conditions that are caused by inflammation rather than by tight muscles. So this was the first clue to be derived from Brad's notebook. While it appeared to be muscular, Brad's condition was probably inflammatory in nature and consequently more related to his joints than his muscles.

There were several other important clues in Brad's notebook. The fact that Brad's father also had low back pain, despite the son's strong opinion about his father's condition, was not only relevant but a significant factor in making Brad's diagnosis. His condition was likely genetic.

Further, two seemingly unrelated conditions listed in Brad's notebook but not revealed to any of his physicians—his urinary tract infection and his conjunctivitis—were also significant. Related to these incidents was Brad's mention of Lydia, his girlfriend at the time. He noted this relationship because he was assuming a possible link between what he perceived to be his back sprain injury and their "sexual gymnastics." Interestingly enough, what was more important about his reference to Lydia was that his infection likely came from her, and this was most probably the precipitating cause of both his condition and his off-the-cuff observation abut his mouth ulcers.

Everything described in Brad's Eight Step notebook pointed clearly to Reiter's syndrome. This condition is most common among young men and has been linked to the HLA-B27 gene (probably inherited from his father) as a potential genetic predisposing factor. While some patients report painful arthritis affecting the knees, ankles, and feet as part of this condition, low back pain is also common, particularly if there is evidence of sacroiliitis. This was confirmed in Brad's case.

Although it seemed muscular in origin, Brad's back pain was due to inflammation of one of his sacroiliac joints. These joints are relatively immobile. They connect the pelvis to the bottom of the spine (the sacrum). But this inflammation did not come from an injury. The sudden onset after his tennis game on that Sunday many months before was simply coincidental.

Reiter's syndrome is sometimes referred to as "reactive arthritis." The arthritis is a response to infection elsewhere in the body. In Brad's case, the arthritic inflammation of his sacroiliac joint occurred as a reaction to his urinary tract infection, which had also triggered his eye infection. In many men, the infection begins in the genitourinary tract (bladder or urethra) just as it did with Brad. In women, it can be an inflammation of the cervix, fallopian tubes, or vulva. Joint symptoms, eye involvement, and mouth ulcers or other rashes can be observed with this ailment.

Based on his notebook, it was fairly clear that Brad exhibited the stereo-typical pattern of Reiter's syndrome. He was genetically predisposed to develop this syndrome from his father. Although it's just speculation, evidence points to the fact that Lydia's gynecological issues caused Brad's genitourinary infection, which in turn triggered the inflammation of his eyes (conjunctivitis) many weeks later. Weeks after that, his lower back inflammation began.

Brad, like most patients, thought his back pain was the result of an injury from his tennis game. In fact, it was not. Although there is no cure for Reiter's syndrome, when Brad's condition was treated with prolonged use of anti-inflammatory medications, antibiotics, and a supervised strengthening exercise routine, he improved greatly. But without working through his Eight Step notebook, diagnosing this syndrome would have continued to be extremely difficult.

The following case study describes another mystery malady that took an enormous toll on the patient and her family and confused even the best doctors. Since it involved chest pain, it did not seem to be musculoskeletal in origin. Yet it just took some basic detective work, using the Eight Steps, to determine that it was not cardiac in nature.

Case Study: Anna

Anna, a married mother of three, suffered from severe chest pain and feared she might have a heart problem. Several months earlier when the pain first started, she thought it was gas because she was always eating out at the fast-food places her kids enjoyed. But she hadn't received any relief from antacids or other over-the-counter preparations. She ended up in the emergency department where an electrocardiogram (EKG), arterial blood gases, and a chest x-ray were taken. When the doctors there were unable to find the cause of her pain, she was admitted to the main hospital for observation and evaluation. She subsequently received a stress test, an echocardiogram, and ultimately a cardiac catheterization. When those tests turned out to be normal, her physicians brought in an attending gastroenterologist to evaluate her for a possible abnormality in her stomach, gallbladder, or esophagus. After the gastroenterologist tried certain strong antacids and ulcer medications, he administered nitroglycerin. When these medications failed to relieve her pain, she was placed on narcotics. Without question, Anna was suffering from a mystery malady. Her doctors sent her home and suggested to her husband, Tim, that she should see a psychiatrist.

Although relieved to know that his wife didn't have a heart problem, Tim felt more than a little angry about the situation. He had missed two weeks of work, for which his pay was docked. He was in debt as a result of Anna's hospitalization. He had been living with his mother-in-law for the past two weeks, and the kids were acting up without their mother.

Anna felt ashamed and embarrassed that she had caused all these problems over what was apparently nothing. Her chest pain continued, but she was simply too humiliated to see a psychiatrist or complain again. Within a matter of days, she was in a car accident. Then she found herself doing things she had never done before. She left the stove on, burning a pot and subsequently her hand. She almost left her two-year-old child behind, alone in the house, when she departed for the supermarket. Now, in addition to being in physical pain, she was suffering from a crisis of confidence. Anna was terrified that she was now unable to handle the children or her life.

Fortunately, Dr. Rosenbaum was the preceptor for the medical resident who was assigned to evaluate Anna after her discharge from the hospital. As he listened to her medical history, Dr. Rosenbaum applied the medical detective method and made some very basic observations that a number of well-trained and well-meaning physicians had failed to do. The key was the exact nature of Anna's symptoms (specifically location, timing, and duration—from Step One) and what made those symptoms better or worse (Step Three). She was fine in the mornings and worse in the evenings. Strenuous activities did not seem to make the pain any worse.

When Dr. Rosenbaum gave Anna a physical exam, he noticed that she had very large breasts. He found out that she didn't wear her bra at night and connected that to the fact that she began each day without pain. So Dr. Rosenbaum asked her to go braless for a day as an experiment. Much to Anna's amazement, the pain did not occur. Anna's tight underwire bras were the source of the problem!

In Anna's case, as in many others, overreliance on medical science and underreliance on commonsense observations and deductive reasoning had led doctors down the wrong path.

The next case study is also musculoskeletal in nature, but it baffled physicians. If this retiree had known about the Eight Steps, she could have solved her mystery malady.

Case Study: Marjory

Marjory, a seventy-six-year-old retired reference librarian, was from the old school. She was always perfectly groomed and had manicured nails, wore stockings and short heels everywhere, and sat in a straight-backed chair. Her manners and politeness were her trademark. An avid bridge player since her retirement, Marjory sometimes sat for as long as eight hours a day playing bridge. Then one day she simply stopped. Although her friends at the bridge club were concerned and telephoned her almost daily urging her to return, she politely refused, declining to give a reason other than a "health problem." Marjory's tone of voice dictated that for her friends to inquire further would be impolite at best and an unforgivable intrusion at worst.

Marjory couldn't discuss her symptoms because they were embarrassing to admit. It hurt to sit down, she could no longer cross her legs, and even going to the bathroom was a task. When alone, she would simply stand up or lie down while taking her meals. When she could finally bear it no longer, she went to her internist, admitting that she was suffering from a painful "derriere."

Her internist referred her to a proctologist, and Marjory endured an exam that was uncomfortably contrary to her sense of propriety. When the proctologist's exam was negative, Marjory received a radiograph, a magnetic resonance imaging (MRI), a bone scan, and a computerized tomography (CT) scan, all of which also revealed nothing.

If Marjory had had a copy of this book—and given her sense of propriety along with her abilities as a librarian—she could have completed the Eight Steps to Self-Diagnosis and used the Internet to research her condition using the tips found in Chapter 5. Marjory would have discovered that what she had was once a very common condition called "weaver's bottom." It was so named because it was a recurring ailment among women in the seventeenth and eighteenth centuries who would sit on hard stools for hours at a time weaving at the loom. The pain in Marjory's gluteal bursae is easily treatable with cortisone injections and the use of proper cushioning when sitting for prolonged periods of time. She would have been back at the bridge club in no time, this time sitting on a softer chair and for shorter bridge-playing marathons. It took two years of suffering and multiple doctor visits before some young physician researched her condition. She could have helped herself very quickly without needless, continued suffering.

Finally, we share one of Dr. Rosenbaum's favorite neck pain mysteries.

Case Study: Jackie

Jackie was an extroverted fifty-one-year-old woman with a wide circle of friends. She especially loved talking on the phone while preparing her famous gourmet dinners. By the end of each day, she was in excruciating neck pain. So she called physical therapists, chiropractors, and orthopedic surgeons. She called to make appointments for x-rays, MRIs, and nerve conduction tests.

Jackie finally called Dr. Rosenbaum's office to make an appointment, called again to see if he was on her health plan, and then called again to see if he had received her records from all the other doctors. Later, she called a fourth time to determine if they had received her x-rays and MRI from the imaging center. On the day of her appointment, she called ahead to see if Dr. Rosenbaum was running on time. Then she sat in the waiting room complaining to her friends on her cell phone about how long she was having to wait. The nurses in Dr. Rosenbaum's office joked to him about Jackie's phone behavior.

So, Dr. Rosenbaum peered into the waiting room to observe for himself. He saw how tightly clenched the cell phone was between Jackie's ear and shoulder. It wasn't difficult for him to figure out an easy cure for her mysterious neck pain that no one had yet been able to diagnose!

Exploring Other Causes of Unexplained Pain

With musculoskeletal pain, one should never make an assumption that it is the result of an injury. Sometimes, it can be as complex as Brad's case. Other times, it can be simple biomechanical issue like a problem resulting from how you are exercising or even what you are carrying. How many women seem to carry their entire lives in their purses and then wonder why they have shoulder and neck pain? How many men sit all day on wallets tucked into their back pockets and then complain about lower back or hip pain?

Finally, when all other possible causes have been ruled out, tension myositis syndrome (TMS) as described by Dr. Sarno might be the culprit. In his book *Healing Back Pain: The Mind-Body Connection*, he describes TMS as a condition in which emotional stress is manifested as physical pain. It most often occurs in the back, neck, shoulders, or buttocks as a result of increased tension in the affected muscles, which decreases the flow of oxygen. This results in muscle pain similar to what an athlete might feel after a strenuous workout; the difference is that the athlete will feel relief when the workout is over, while the person with TMS feels the pain constantly.

Conclusion

As some of our cases have demonstrated, it's important to be sure to start with the obvious before you start searching out the exotic, especially when it comes to back, neck, or joint pain. Work through the Eight Steps to help you determine whether the answer is simply common sense or more complicated than that. Don't hesitate to consult a physical therapist on such issues, as they are often extremely knowledgeable and can treat these sorts of conditions very successfully.

In the meantime, while you continue your medical detective work and your quest for a cure, be sure to read Chapter 14 where we offer a number of useful tips on pain control.

12

Could Your Symptoms Be All (or Partly) in Your Mind?

Unfortunately, after a battery of medical tests have ruled out all possible conditions and no specialist has been able to assign a diagnosis, it is all too common for mystery malady patients to be told it's all in their head. Most of the time this is simply untrue. As we have said all along, your condition is most likely just a mystery in need of a solution.

Nevertheless, there are some disorders that, while not imaginary, are caused by underlying psychological problems. For example, there are patients who are suffer from hypochondriasis, which is a preoccupation with fears of having a serious disease (based on a misinterpretation of symptoms) that persists despite appropriate medical evaluation and reassurances. Hypochondriasis makes the patient think he has not yet received a proper diagnosis. There are also malingerers or those who suffer from fictitious illnesses where a disease is intentionally produced or feigned by a patient, usually for some secondary gain such as avoiding an uncomfortable situation or legal consequences or to gain desired attention.

It is very important for both you and your doctor to be able to make that distinction since it is all too easy to be labeled as someone with a psychological problem. It is just as easy for a patient to deny the fact that he or she has such a disorder. Being aware of these conditions may prevent a wrongful categorization by the medical community, or conversely, it may give you an answer to your unsolved problem.

Case Study: Gordon

At the age of thirty-nine, Gordon was a good-looking, personable, very successful real estate broker who was considered one of the most eligible bachelors in the Chicago area. But as is sometimes the case, looks can be deceiving. His tall, athletic physique belied his poor health. Gordon was afflicted with a number of medical problems beginning in childhood and continuing into the present that often disrupted what appeared to be an ideal life.

As a young boy, Gordon was considered a "worrier" who had persistent stomachaches and headaches that resulted in daily visits to the school nurse. She was very kind to Gordon since she knew he was the only child of a mother who was constantly in and out of the hospital with one medical problem or another. His father was sometimes given to bouts of "drinking and disappearing," according to Gordon, who often had to take care of himself. Indeed, the little boy had a lot to worry about.

In his teenaged years, Gordon suffered from asthma, which improved and disappeared when properly treated. That was important, because by then Gordon had become a real athlete and received pleasure and recognition for his talents both as a soccer player in middle school and as a football champion in high school and college. After graduation, he maintained his athletic physique, regularly playing tennis, jogging, and lifting weights in the gym.

As an adult, while he was outwardly a specimen of good health, he suffered quietly with serial illnesses, none of them of a truly serious nature, but all serious enough to adversely impact his life. He was very susceptible to whatever virus was going around the office. He rarely slept well and in his twenties was diagnosed with fibromyalgia.

Apart from that, from time to time, he suffered from numerous gastrointestinal issues, including peptic ulcers, irritable bowel syndrome, and continuous acid reflux (heartburn). Different doctors surmised different causes, such as food allergies, stress, and bacterial infections, for these medical phenomena.

Still, other ailments would come and go. In his thirties, he presented with swollen glands, fever, body aches and chronic fatigue that lasted more than six months. He was diagnosed with chronic fatigue syndrome (CFS) by his primary care physician, but another doctor declined to assign Gordon this diagnosis as he didn't meet all the documented criteria. Eventually, this condition dissipated, but he continued to suffer from occasional periods of chronic dizziness and light-headedness. This was later diagnosed as vertigo, but its origin was undetermined.

Although Gordon was functional, he often had to cancel appointments to meet clients and show them real estate, postpone vacations, or reschedule dates all because of his physical ailments. He was labeled a hypochondriac by some of his girlfriends, but the doctors would always find a real medical problem. This was complicated by the fact that Gordon would eventually get better. Mysteriously, though, as one malady would get resolved, another would take its place. Gordon did not take pleasure in any of this. He rarely discussed his ailments with anyone because he didn't want to lose clients or business, and most of all, he didn't want anyone's sympathy.

Gordon did, however, blame his drinking problem on his continuing struggles with his illnesses. The burden of his constant doctor visits and dealing with chronic, albeit not life-threatening illnesses was eased, at least for a little while, when he was drinking. At one point, though, after finding himself in bed with yet another strange woman and a sexually transmitted disease (which fortunately was treatable), Gordon became concerned enough to seek help. He contacted a former drinking buddy who had joined Alcoholics Anonymous (AA) and been clean and sober for three years.

With his friend's help and the support of AA, Gordon happily got sober. Within a year of what he called the "pink cloud of recovery," however, Gordon began having recurrent nightmares. Along with the nightmares, a great deal of emotional pain bubbled to the surface, and he desperately wanted to start drinking again. The nightmares began to reveal to Gordon how he had repressed the memory of repeated sexual abuse inflicted by his father.

Eventually, Gordon realized he needed professional help or he would relapse into drinking. He went into psychotherapy, and during this time, his variety of illnesses took a backseat.

With great courage and emotional effort, Gordon recovered from his past traumas. His physical illnesses abated to some degree. He had grown into a kinder, gentler man who had been "healed." In turn, he wanted to help heal others. He returned to school, learned to be a massage therapist, and consequently changed professions. As he was strong and skilled at massage, he quickly developed a following and became very successful.

Within a short period of time, he met and married a wonderful woman and they had a baby boy. Life was good for Gordon until, at forty-seven, he developed yet another chronic and painful ailment, which he attributed to his work as a massage therapist. His lower back gave out on him.

The intense low back pain and accompanying muscle spasms rendered him practically immobile. He had difficulty giving massages, began canceling many appointments, and consulted a physical therapist. The physical therapy helped, but the problem was not relieved. Finally, he consulted an orthopedic surgeon who, after x-rays and an MRI that revealed no physical impairment, suggested his patient look at what anxieties and repressed anger he might be experiencing that could be triggering his muscle spasms.

At first, Gordon was outraged at the suggestion that this was a psychological rather than a physical problem. This outrage quickly turned to depression because he truly believed he had "done his work" in therapy. After all, he no longer drank, he had healed from his traumatic childhood, he still attended AA meetings, and he was happy with his wife and child. He was convinced that this doctor was wrong; his symptoms had to be physical. He found a physician who was careful of Gordon's addictive history and refused to give him painkillers. He prescribed nonsteroidal anti-inflammatories and gave Gordon an exercise regimen, which Gordon followed tenaciously. He soon recovered, but then he began having sinus headaches.

Gordon returned to the allergist who had prescribed medication to clear up his previous sinus infections and congestion. The medication helped; his sinus headaches ended but his asthma returned. At that point, aware of her husband's history, Gordon's wife suggested that he return to therapy. Now Gordon was confused. Was the orthopedic doctor right? Were his physical symptoms a sign of repressed anger or some other deep-seated psychological need to cling to physical symptoms?

Gordon sheepishly returned to the orthopedic surgeon to explore this issue further. The doctor suggested that Gordon use a modified version of the Eight Steps to Self-Diagnosis to answer that question.

Using the Eight Steps

Gordon was told to do Steps One through Four and return to the office, at which time he would complete Step Seven only. He was told to take as much time as he needed to complete these tasks because the doctor knew this might be a painful process.

Step One: Record the Exact Nature of Your Symptoms. Gordon was told to modify this exercise to determine how many symptoms he had experienced during his lifetime and at what ages. He could get more specific, if necessary, once he and his doctor looked at the whole picture together. The list looked like this:

1. **Stomachaches:** Ages 6–11
2. **Headaches:** Ages 6–11
3. **Colds, viruses, and flu:** Age 4–present
4. **Asthma:** Ages 13–16
5. **Muscle strains and sprains:** Age 12–present
6. **Difficulty sleeping/insomnia:** Age 6–present
7. **Peptic ulcers:** Age 23
8. **Irritable bowel syndrome:** Ages 25–30 (alternating diarrhea, constipation, bloating, abdominal pain)
9. **Acid reflux:** Age 30 on
10. **Nausea/joint pains from food allergies:** Ages vary
11. **Short-term memory loss:** Ages 25–40 (alcohol-related)
12. **Occasional sexual dysfunction:** Probably alcohol-related
13. **Chronic fatigue, fever, swollen glands, body aches:** Ages 35–37
14. **Muscle and joint pains:** Ages 16–40
15. **Sinusitis and headaches (sometimes migraines):** Throughout adulthood
16. **Dizziness/vertigo:** Ages 40–41
17. **Alcoholism:** Ages 25–45
18. **Low back pain:** Age 47–present
19. **Depression:** Ages 15–45; again in present

Step Two: Think About the History of Your Mystery Malady. [Gordon was told to view his symptoms as an overall problem rather than individually and perform this exercise. Here is his observation.] When I look back on this list, I am amazed. All the while I was having these problems, I was so focused on the symptoms(s), I couldn't see the forest for the trees.

From doing Step One and now thinking about this step, I see that I've had one form of illness or another from childhood on just like my mother did. The symptoms were almost serial, although many overlapped. There was hardly a period in my life when I wasn't ill with one thing or another, and they affected different areas of my body from my chest to my head to my stomach to my muscles.

I see that some of my symptoms had a diagnosis, but others didn't. Still, many of the symptoms were the same, just in different combinations at different times.

Step Three: What Makes Your Symptoms Better (or Worse)? Overall, I think exercising has always helped me—in other words, my symptoms diminished—but my physical disabilities have not always allowed me to exercise. Also, whenever I sleep well, I feel better. Similarly, when I am with my wife and child, my symptoms don't feel as bad as they do when I am under stress or unhappy. Frankly, now I am not sure if I know which came first—my unhappiness or my symptoms.

Step Four: Do a Family Medical History and Determine If You Have or Had Any Blood Relatives with a Similar Problem. My mother had a number of illnesses that required hospitalizations, but she never had a diagnosis that I can remember. She is still alive at eighty-five and has chronic arthritis and depression, but she is not seriously ill otherwise. I guess I take after her. My father died of liver disease from drinking. I have a cousin who died of leukemia. My aunt had diabetes and died of complications of the disease. I don't know much more about my family's medical history.

Making the Diagnosis

Gordon returned to the orthopedic surgeon, who complimented him on his efforts. He gave Gordon some materials to read on somatization disorder and to compare them against his notes for Steps One through Four. The doctor explained that based on what he had read in Gordon's notebook, Gordon would be able to decide for himself whether he had found his diagnosis.

Gordon set aside a couple of hours to review the materials detailing somatization disorder. In a nutshell, he learned that this disorder was a chronic condition in which there are numerous physical complaints—many times lasting for years and involving many body systems—which often result in significant impairment in social, occupational, or various other areas of functioning.

People suffering with this disturbance will have a history of the following:

- Pain related to at least four different sites—such as head, abdomen, back, and chest—or functions such as lack of sleep
- Two gastrointestinal symptoms such as nausea, gas, or bloating
- One sexual symptom such as loss of libido, erectile dysfunction in men, or dyspareunia (pain on intercourse) in women
- One pseudoneurological symptom such as impaired coordination or balance, double vision, or amnesia

After appropriate investigation, these symptoms cannot be explained by any known general medical condition, or if they can, the symptoms seem excessive to the condition.

The features that indicate a diagnosis of somatization disorder rather than a general medical condition include the involvement of multiple organ systems, early onset (as in childhood), and a chronic course of illness in the absence of laboratory abnormalities that would characterize the suggested general medical condition. These symptoms are observed in approximately 20 percent of female first-degree relatives of women with the same disorder. While women are ten times more likely than men to have this disorder, male first-degree relatives of women with somatization disorder have an increased risk of antisocial personality, substance abuse disorders, and somatization disorder.

A patient who somatizes is having a real physical reaction to psychosocial and environmental stressors, and the disorder is *not* just psychological. The symptoms and the discomfort and pain they bring are very real; they are not faked. Nor are they voluntary or under the control of the patient. They may coexist with other proven medical and psychiatric disorders requiring diagnosis and treatment.

Gordon was absolutely stunned! Certainly he had enough symptoms judging from his replies in Step One. They were in different areas of his body with at least two being gastrointestinal and one pseudoneurological. He didn't think he had a sexual issue; although during his drinking days he occasionally had been impotent, he thought this was due to the alcohol.

He obviously had a mother who suffered from unknown illnesses her whole life (she was probably a somatizer herself). Assuming she was, then he, as a first-degree male relative, followed the pattern by the fact that he had a substance abuse problem. His problems had been lifelong, starting in childhood, and while he generally received a diagnosis for whatever complex of symptoms he was having at the time, no laboratory tests revealed objective findings. Most of the tests administered to him ruled out serious conditions more often than they actually confirmed whatever condition he had at the time.

The final paragraph he read on this disorder clinched it for Gordon. It said that recent studies linked childhood abuse, particularly physical and sexual abuse, with somatization disorder.

Gordon returned to the doctor, who was extremely sympathetic and explained that while this disorder is currently classified as psychological, it is clinically more complex than that. He explained that because studies on the effects of trauma on the human body are in their infancy, the medical community has not yet discovered specifically how trauma affects the immune system, digestive system, and brain functions that control pain, sleep, and depression.

He offered his own opinion that one day science might be able to prove that these conditions were a direct physical result, rather than just a psychological one, of trauma on the body. In any case, Gordon was assured that his condition was not under his control. In other words, he had not made up his symptoms in any deliberate or voluntary manner.

Research studies to date show that a somatizer's symptoms represent a coping strategy to deal with emotional discomfort at an unconscious level that results in the patient's diminished function. When a patient can identify the emotional conflicts that gave rise to symptoms, the disorder can be diminished even if it not entirely eliminated.

Gordon's doctor asked him to do one last step—Step Seven—in the hope that understanding his belief system might help his recovery. He suggested that Gordon take a close look at how he reacted or what happened to him when his symptoms arose. He asked him to look at how his day was modified by his current illness, how he coped with stress, whether he ever felt like the past affected his behavior, and whether he felt he was adequately taking care of himself.

Step Seven: Investigate Your Lifestyle and Belief System. These are Gordon's notes for this section:

> Every time I get sick, I get anxious. I wonder how I will keep going and fulfill my responsibilities. I just keep going even though I feel sick. Sometimes I feel like a racehorse that will run until it dies. Although I am often sick, I never give in to it. Why?
>
> Maybe I feel like I have to be perfect. When I was little, I was so ashamed of my family. My mother was always sick—like me, I guess—and my father was often drunk or gone. And since I was abused, I felt ashamed of myself even though I understand now that it was not my fault. My drinking used to help me escape from these feelings, but now I don't drink and even though I feel like I've worked through these feelings, perhaps there's still more work to do.
>
> Maybe I keep working at my job in spite of my illness as a way of escaping. The doctor asked if I get enough rest. The answer is no. Maybe this is also contributing to my getting sick.
>
> I feel angry when I get sick. Maybe I am angry all the time in the same way I feel ashamed, and it's easier to get angry at my illness than at those I really want to be angry at.
>
> *Maybe I am punishing myself by making myself sick.*

Gordon stopped right there. He called his doctor and said he thought it was time for him to return to psychotherapy. Working through Step Seven raised a lot of unanswered questions, and perhaps dealing with them would help resolve his somatization disorder. The doctor suggested that Gordon consult a psychiatrist to determine whether an antidepressant medication might be helpful. But he also concluded that he thought Gordon was well on his way to becoming truly healthy, perhaps for good.

Conclusion

Somatization disorder is a difficult diagnosis and one that should not be made without proper evaluation by an experienced psychiatric expert. Nor should this diagnosis be assigned simply because someone has a mystery ailment that has not yet been identified. In Gordon's case, his orthopedic surgeon had studied much about this illness after the pioneering work that had been done by John Sarno, M.D., on low back pain (see Chapter 11) and how it correlated with interpersonal and emotional conflicts. That, together with Gordon's lifelong pattern of illnesses, pointed the physician in the direction of a somatization disorder diagnosis.

Finally, Gordon's history of sexual abuse coupled with his high functioning in all areas made his doctor wonder what Gordon did and still does with the rage and emotional pain that would be a natural by-product of his history of sexual abuse. That rage needed an outlet, and based on Gordon's history, physical disorders may have been the only acceptable, albeit painful, way to release his rage.

Famed psychotherapist Alice Miller, in her book *Thou Shalt Not Be Aware: Society's Betrayal of the Child* summed it up this way: "The truth about our childhood is stored up in our body and although we can repress it, we can never alter it. Our intellect can be deceived, our feelings manipulated, our perceptions confused and our body tricked with medication. But someday the body will present its bill. For it is as incorruptible as a compromise . . . and will not stop tormenting us until we stop evading the truth."[1]

In Gordon's case, further psychological counseling and pharmaceutical intervention for depression and anxiety finally resolved his mystery illness. Of course, as we have said many times during the course of this book, it is easy for a doctor who does not have a diagnosis for your mystery malady to say it's "stress" or "in your mind," but *sometimes* it really is. If you suspect you might have somatization disorder, do the modified version of the Eight Steps for yourself. See if you find any patterns like Gordon did. Then consult your physician and a qualified psychotherapist.

If you are truly looking for wellness, you must be willing to go deep within and ask yourself the "hard questions." Perhaps your physical symptoms are easier to endure than something you want to avoid such as painful, underlying memories and feelings. It is certainly worth considering.

13

Does Your Child Have a
Mystery Malady?

ALTHOUGH THERE ARE countless books on them, childhood diseases are not always easily identifiable or diagnosable. Many children have mystery maladies, and the solutions to them must be sleuthed out in the same manner as for their adult counterparts. Some of these maladies have names; others don't. Some will require the participation of a pediatric pathologist to help you identify your child's illness. Others are simply a matter of tracking the origin of symptoms and creating a detailed enough picture of the mystery malady that any pediatrician—or even you, the parent—can identify.

Here's how the Eight Steps to Self-Diagnosis helped in four cases: eleven-year-old Jessica, eight-year-old David, four-year-old Lourdes, and nine-year-old Justin, each of whom had a different condition. Because their caring and diligent parents and doctors worked through the Eight Steps, each of these children is now a diagnostic success story.

Case Study: Jessica

Jessica was a red-haired, freckle-faced sixth grader who loved school and especially loved playing the flute in music class. Around Thanksgiving and quite out of the blue, Jessica began to complain of joint pains and stiffness. Her symptoms were worse in the mornings and on some of those mornings, she felt too sick to go to school. These days were random, but Jessica's mom, Marsha, knew just how sick her daughter was when it also happened on music-class mornings. On those days, Jessica would sometimes remain in bed until midday when she finally felt well enough to get up.

Of course, Jessica's mother took her to the pediatrician. There was just one problem: by the time she arrived at the doctor's office, Jessica appeared normal. She was in the ninetieth percentile for height and weight. Her musculoskeletal examination was entirely normal. Initial laboratory studies revealed a white blood cell count of 6.7. (A count higher than 6.7 would indicate an infection from bacteria. A count lower than 6.7 would indicate an infection from a virus). At that time, Jessica's blood also showed a normal sedimentary rate. (An elevated sedimentation rate would indicate an inflammatory process.) Thus, while her symptoms suggested some kind of inflammatory problem, her blood tests indicated the opposite.

Jessica must have visited her pediatrician six times over a two-month period, and each time her doctor could find no physical evidence of a problem. Finally, he suggested a referral for what he called "attention-seeking behavior." Jessica's mother was perplexed because she did not believe her daughter was faking her symptoms. Nevertheless, she followed the doctor's suggestion and took her daughter to a mental health counselor "just in case."

Because their health insurance limited the number of evaluation visits, after only two sessions, the counselor suggested that it was possible Jessica was suffering from conversion disorder—when a psychological condition is converted into a physical condition, resulting in actual physical symptoms. The other possible diagnosis he suggested was a "school phobia," where a child complains of pains on the morning of or night before school and consequently has a poor attendance record. In these cases, the pains usually resolve after the school bus has left. He reported that he didn't know the underlying reasons for this yet, which would require further sessions to determine. Marsha thought all of this was utter nonsense since her daughter loved school and wouldn't miss her flute classes unless she truly felt sick.

So Marsha took Jessica to a new pediatrician who couldn't find anything on physical examination either and suggested that perhaps the girl had growing pains—recurrent limb pains that occur during a growth spurt. When he explained these growing pains usually occurred at night, Jessica herself spoke up and told the doctor her pains were worse in the morning. The doctor commented that this would suggest an arthritic condition, but

Jessica had no objective signs that would confirm this. He repeated her blood tests and they were consistent with the earlier findings. The new pediatrician said he would like to continue to observe her.

Within weeks of this visit, Jessica developed two new symptoms. She began having spiking temperatures and joint swelling, different from the stiffness that was described earlier. These symptoms became very confusing: Jessica's temperature might spike as high as 103°F, but it would always quickly return to normal again.

The doctor found this to be extremely odd and suggested Marsha might not know how to take her daughter's temperature. This was highly offensive to the concerned and responsible mother of three. She went to the drugstore anyway and purchased three different types of thermometers, including an expensive deluxe digital thermometer and an ear thermometer. All this was to no avail—Jessica's temperature was indeed spiking and measured the same on all three thermometers. It then returned to normal.

The second new symptom was a salmon-colored rash that appeared mostly on her chest whenever her fever spiked. It would then disappear when her temperature returned to normal. At one point, Marsha marched her daughter into the doctor's office while she was experiencing one of her fever-and-rash episodes and insisted the doctor see these symptoms for himself. He found an exceptionally fatigued and sick little girl. He immediately performed blood tests again to determine if Jessica had an often difficult-to-diagnose autoimmune disease such as rheumatoid arthritis or systemic lupus erythematosus. These tests were negative. The pediatrician was perplexed, and once again said they would have to wait and see if any new symptoms developed.

Jessica was friends with my (Lynn's) daughter. When I heard about the problem, I shared our Eight Step method. Marsha knew she had to undertake her own investigation to get a correct diagnosis for Jessica because she couldn't get the doctors to do anything more. So Marsha began to work through the Eight Steps. I suggested that when her notebook was filled, she make an appointment to see Dr. Rosenbaum.

Using the Eight Steps

The following are Marsha's notebook entries for her daughter's mystery malady.

Step One: Record the Exact Nature of Your Symptoms.
  1. Spiking Fevers
     - **Quality and Character:** Sudden fevers to 103°F and then returns to normal.
     - **Quantity and Severity:** At least twice daily.
     - **Timing and Duration:** Late afternoon and evening.
     - **Setting and Environment:** Occurs anywhere and in any environment.
     - **Impact on Your Functioning:** She looks and acts sick with the fever. Jessica is extremely fatigued and stiff. At other times, she looks very healthy, is energetic, and can do everything.

  2. Rashes
     - **Quality and Character:** Light salmon-colored rash only appears when the fever spikes; it doesn't itch and looks like measles but not as uniform.
     - **Quantity and Severity:** Mostly on chest, but sometimes in different locations; very faint.
     - **Timing and Duration:** Afternoons and only for as long as the fever remains.
     - **Setting and Environment:** Daily at home with the fever.
     - **Impact on Your Functioning:** Jessica looks and feels poorly with the fever and rash; she appears very tired.
     - **Other Factors:** Does not seem related to eating, her activity level, or room temperature.

  3. Joint Stiffness and Swelling
     - **Quality and Character:** Painful like arthritis.
     - **Quantity and Severity:** Not all the time, but when it happens it is severe.
     - **Timing and Duration:** Worse in the mornings; gets better in the afternoons.
     - **Setting and Environment:** Anywhere.
     - **Impact on Your Functioning:** Jessica really looks and feels poorly; she has trouble doing anything she enjoys, such as playing her flute, when this happens.

Step Two: Think About the History of Your Mystery Malady. It started several weeks ago on a school day with some complaints of joint and muscle discomfort. Before that, it was two months when it happened and again lasted for several weeks. When it happens, it is worse in the mornings. Then there are fevers and the rash. Those two things happen in the afternoons. It is the opposite pattern from the joint and muscle aches. Did Jessica contract some contagious disease? If so, why did the blood tests reveal no infection?

Step Three: What Makes Your Symptoms Better (or Worse)? The symptoms seem related only to time of day. Joint and muscle pains get better in the afternoon, but the rashes and fever get worse. Whether the symptoms get better or worse does not seem to be related to food, room temperature, or any specific activity.

Step Four: Do a Family Medical History and Determine If You Have or Had Any Blood Relatives with a Similar Problem. The doctor indicated he thought Jessica's symptoms sounded like rheumatoid arthritis or a similar autoimmune disease, which is usually genetic, but she did not test positive for these conditions. The question was whether there were any other blood relatives with similar problems. Jessica's grandmother has had bad osteoarthritis for years. Jessica's great-aunt had rheumatic fever, which is an autoimmune condition. Maybe there is a genetic component to this.

Step Five: Search for Other Past or Present Mental or Physical Problems. Initially, the experts thought Jessica might be engaging in attention-seeking behavior or have a school phobia, but now there seems to be a real mystery. I am trying to see if there is anything else going on and doing a mental review of all her systems—digestive, respiratory, circulatory, and so on—but nothing stands out. Truthfully, Jessica has been completely normal for a child her age and healthy otherwise.

Step Six: Categorize Your Current and Prior Significant Medical Problems by Etiology.
- **Genetic:** No other family member with this problem, but her grandmother has severe osteoarthritis and her great-aunt had rheumatic fever when she was a child, if that's related.

- **Infectious (viral, bacterial, fungal, or parasitic):** Occasional cold or flu.
- **Structural or biomechanical:** Stiff and swollen joints, but her physical examinations don't show a structural or biomechanical problem. She doesn't do any physical activities regularly except volleyball whenever she can.
- **Environmental:** Maybe she is allergic to something at school. But she got worse while at home and even if I kept her home. Is there something in the house?
- **Metabolic:** She has no digestive problems, has normal energy except during a bout, and does not have her menstrual period yet.
- **Iatrogenic:** She is not taking medications; she does not appear to be doing this to herself. I have stood with her while taking her temperature so I've never seen her playing with the thermometer or hiding it.
- **Psychological:** This has been evaluated, and she seems well adjusted despite what were only suppositions or theories. How do you psychologically cause fevers?

Step Seven: Investigate Your Lifestyle and Belief System. Maybe I am overprotective, but she deserves our attention even if the doctors don't know what's wrong with her. Jessica is not a malingerer. As soon as she feels better, she is up and out of bed and into her regular activities with her usual enthusiasm. I simply can't imagine this is a lifestyle or belief issue.

Step Eight: Take Your Notebook to Your Physician and Get a Complete Physical Exam. Marsha took Jessica to be examined by Dr. Rosenbaum. With the prior lab work, review of the notebook created by Jessica's mother, and a physical exam, Dr. Rosenbaum was able to discern the answer immediately.

Making the Diagnosis

Jessica's mother turned in a wonderfully detailed notebook. It contained specific answers to the questions asked in the Eight Steps. She also gave very good descriptions, which was most helpful since the symptoms were not always present at the time of a doctor's examination. It turned out that these were the most revealing facts:

- The arthritic symptoms occurred in the morning and the spiking fevers accompanied by a salmon-colored rash occurred in the afternoons. The rash was evanescent (it disappeared), moved to different locations, didn't itch, and looked like measles.
- Jessica had a family history of arthritic and autoimmune disease.
- There was absolutely nothing else remarkable noted in the steps, ruling out other possible diagnoses.

The pattern of clinical symptoms, especially the timing and the detailed description of the rash described by Jessica's mother, the persistent arthritis lasting more than six weeks, then disappearing and reappearing months later for several weeks, and the prior lab work that ruled out infections, cancers, and other types of arthritis was specific enough information for Dr. Rosenbaum to correctly diagnose Jessica.

Jessica had a rare form of juvenile arthritis that has a systemic onset (bodywide illness besides simply joint inflammation). It is known as Still's disease. It is self-limited and usually runs a benign course over a period of weeks. It affects twenty-five thousand to fifty thousand children in the United States and accounts for 10–20 percent of all cases of juvenile arthritis. (If not for the careful notebook kept by Jessica's mother detailing the timing of symptoms, a doctor could have easily missed this diagnosis or confused it with another disease, namely fifth disease, which starts with fever but has a rash that occurs after the fever. That one detail made a huge difference in determining the correct diagnosis.)

With Still's disease, patients frequently have a high white cell count without infection as Jessica did. Also, the classic tests for rheumatoid arthritis are usually negative, as Jessica's were.

Treatment of Still's disease is directed toward the individual areas of inflammation. Many symptoms can be controlled with anti-inflammatory drugs, such as aspirin or other nonsteroidal drugs. Cortisone medications (steroids), such as prednisone, are used to treat more severe features of the illness. For those with persistent symptoms, medications that affect the inflammatory aspects of the immune system are used. Fortunately, Jessica's case was not the most persistent or severe.

Because of her mother's diligence in working through the Eight Steps, Jessica didn't have to suffer too long without the proper diagnosis or treatment.

Case Study: David

Eight-year-old David's tooth problems probably had their origins in infancy. David loved his bottle of milk and used it as a pacifier. He would fall asleep with the bottle in his mouth at naptime and at night. David's pediatrician surmised that the sugar in the milk lingered in David's mouth and caused his teeth to decay. As a result, the little boy had fillings in his teeth beginning at the age of three.

As his decaying baby teeth fell out one by one and began to be replaced by permanent ones, everyone rejoiced at the chance to be proactive and prevent any further tooth decay. He got his new teeth cleaned regularly and the dentist applied a protective coating to his teeth to prevent cavities. But after all he had been through, David was so nervous about getting any new cavities that he avoided most sweets and took his toothbrush wherever he went. As he grew older, his mother, Hilary, allowed him to have artificially sweetened drinks, desserts, and gum so he wouldn't have to feel so deprived next to the other kids.

Other than tooth decay, David was a healthy boy with only the usual array of common childhood diseases like colds, occasional ear infections, and a hefty case of whooping cough. Starting inexplicably at about age seven, he began having a constant runny nose, stomachaches, and diarrhea. On some days, the diarrhea was so bad he was afraid to go to school because he had once soiled his pants when he couldn't make it to the restroom on time.

The pediatrician, who at first thought he was looking at a stomach virus, soon became concerned with the chronicity of the symptoms. He referred David to a pediatric gastroenterologist. This specialist eliminated all the usual causes of diarrhea in children including *E. coli* and other forms of bacteria such as campylobacter, *Clostridium difficile*, and salmonella. He ruled out parasites like giardia and cryptosporidium and even rotavirus. He had David's blood tested for hemolytic-uremic syndrome, which was negative, and as a last resort ordered a series of upper and lower gastrointestinal tests to rule out anything more serious. When all of these tests turned out negative, he suggested David should see an allergist to determine if there were any food allergies.

The pediatric allergist guessed David might be allergic to the milk he so adored because his symptoms were a common indication of a milk allergy. She performed a number of tests that revealed that David had developed an allergy to milk and milk products. The allergist told Hilary that once she eliminated these products from her son's diet, his gastrointestinal symptoms would most probably disappear. Hilary followed the doctor's orders, and interestingly enough, while David's runny nose stopped, the stomachaches and diarrhea did not.

The allergist was then at a loss. She suggested psychological counseling for David's "nervous stomach." Hilary took her son to a psychologist, who after a battery of testing declared David to be a very normal little boy who was having a bad time with his medical problem. Now Hilary was at her wits' end. Her son had suffered enough; first with the tooth decay and now for almost a year with stomachaches and diarrhea. Fortunately for David, Hilary's cousin from Florida had been to see Dr. Rosenbaum and passed along a copy of the Eight Steps to Self-Diagnosis for Hilary to do on David's behalf. Using this model, Hilary was actually able to solve David's problem all on her own.

Hilary's sleuthing notebook began telling the story. She paid particular attention to the timing of his symptoms in Step One. Every time David complained of a stomachache or had a bout of diarrhea, she tried to determine what had happened immediately before and whether there was a relationship. A pattern soon emerged. She instructed David to do the same thing himself when he was at school. A pattern emerged there too.

Then she thought about the history, particularly the inception of these symptoms, in Step Two and recalled exactly what was happening in David's life at the time. All of it related to David's past medical problems, specifically his tooth decay and her reaction to his fear of developing more cavities. She also thought about Step Three and what made his symptoms worse.

Going through these steps showed a pattern of David chewing gum immediately before the onset of his symptoms. Because David had become so anxious about getting more cavities and was carrying his toothbrush around everywhere as if his life depended on it, Hilary thought she would ease her son's anxiety by allowing him to chew sugarless gum. She had explained to him that sugarless gum would not cause tooth decay. Frequently, instead of a sweet that was worrisome for him, David would chew a stick of sugarless gum, and his stomachaches appeared afterward.

Hilary looked at the ingredient labels on the sugarless products and found sorbitol listed. It is often added to processed foods such as chewing gum, diabetic candy, Popsicles, and even some children's medications like cough syrup to make them taste sweet. Using the Internet, Hilary researched that ingredient and found there was a documented condition known as sorbitol intolerance. Stomachaches, gas, and diarrhea are very common symptoms of this condition. (Indeed, besides the chewing gum stomachaches, Hilary recalled David having a bout of diarrhea after she had given him some cough syrup for a cold.)

Hilary removed the sugarless gum and all food products containing sorbitol from David's diet. Almost immediately his stomachaches and diarrhea were cured, and his mystery malady was solved! All the testing and doctor visits could have been avoided if David's mother had known about the Eight Steps earlier in the course of his illness.

Case Study: Lourdes

Lourdes was a bright, inquisitive, highly verbal (bilingual) and well-behaved four-year-old until she entered nursery school. Within three months of starting school, she suddenly developed problems. Even though by being in school with other children she had more stimulation than ever before, she seemed less inquisitive or interested in things than she had been. Slowly she stopped learning new words, her vocabulary became limited, and she seemed listless.

Things went from bad to worse when she began misbehaving, even to the point of throwing tamper tantrums. Lourdes stopped listening to her parents and teacher and even refused to look at the person speaking to her. Her mother, Elise, was beside herself. Her "dream child" had become unrecognizable. When Lourdes wasn't being difficult, she seemed to withdraw into herself.

Lourdes's teacher finally suggested that Lourdes might be autistic. Lourdes's mother immediately took her to the pediatrician who, after listening to her symptoms, reassured Elise that some children were just "wired that way." The pediatrician, having cared for Lourdes since she was an infant, felt it was just a phase and she would probably grow out of it.

Not only did Lourdes not grow out of it, she became progressively worse over the next three months. First, not feeling confident that her pediatrician was right in disregarding the teacher's suggestion that Lourdes might be autistic, Elise logged onto the Internet. She spent several hours surfing the most reliable sites on the subject. It became clear that her daughter did not have any of the significant symptoms or signs that one would expect with autism. This put her mind at ease. But what exactly *was* wrong with Lourdes?

Fortunately, Elise had heard about the Eight Steps to Self-Diagnosis from a friend, and before she began putting her child through all kinds of medical testing, she decided to work through them. In returning several times to Step Two, relating to the history of Lourdes's symptoms, she realized that her daughter had started exhibiting all her symptoms soon after she had caught a bad cold from the children at school. In fact, she had missed several days of school.

Then in considering Step Three relative to what made her daughter's symptoms worse, she noted that Lourdes was especially resistant and inattentive when they were driving in the car, with the little girl in the back in a child's car seat. Lourdes seemed best when her mother had her attention and was having a direct conversation with her. In other words, Elise had to have a face-to-face interaction to get her daughter's attention. This prompted a strong suspicion.

Instead of returning to the pediatrician, Elise took her daughter to an audiologist, who discovered that Lourdes had a significant hearing loss. This explained a lot, such as why she wasn't "listening" to the teacher or her parents and seemed inattentive, as well as why her vocabulary wasn't expanding in either Spanish or English. Her temper tantrums were a result of the little girl's frustration! Lourdes was worse in the backseat of the car because she couldn't read her mother's lips, whereas when she was engaged in direct eye contact and conversation, she became communicative again.

Since these symptoms started when Lourdes became sick, Elise took her daughter to an ear, nose, and throat doctor. He found that both of her middle ears were full of fluid—the remnants of the cold that Lourdes caught after beginning nursery school.

Once they placed drain tubes in Lourdes's eardrums (tympanic membranes), her hearing improved dramatically. Her vocabulary caught up to her age level, and Lourdes returned to being the bright, inquisitive, and well-behaved child she once was.

Without solid research on the Internet and a step-by-step analysis, Lourdes's mother would not have been able to get the help her daughter needed as quickly as she did.

Case Study: Justin

Justin was a nine-year-old who had just earned his first badge as a Cub Scout. After he attended scout camp that summer and achieved his second badge, he informed his parents he intended to work toward becoming an Eagle Scout. His parents were pleased and hoped his five-year-old brother would follow in his footsteps.

Around Christmastime though, Justin's whole demeanor changed. He began having trouble at school, often forgetting his homework. Sometimes he forgot to take out the trash and do his other chores. One morning, Justin's brother told his parents that Justin was not sleeping and was walking around the house during the night. Justin's folks began to worry that there was something going on at school that their son was not talking about. When they confronted him, he denied anything unusual was happening there.

One day Justin began to complain that he had tingling in his hands and feet. Sometimes he would complain that they burned. His mother immediately took him to the pediatrician, who could find nothing wrong. Before long, the boy developed bladder problems. Sometimes he wet his pants, and other times he went for long periods without urinating at all. He was miserable and cranky.

Again, his parents took him to the pediatrician, but the doctor could find nothing wrong. He referred Justin to both a urologist and a neurologist at the local children's hospital. Neither of these specialists could determine the cause of Justin's problems, although after numerous tests, the neurologist did find that he was indeed suffering from impaired short- and long-term memory, which accounted for his forgetfulness. She also documented evidence of numbness and decreased sensory perception. Still, the cause was undetermined.

Now Justin's parents were worried sick and begged the neurologist to do something. She put Justin on a regimen of multivitamins and screened him for diabetes and thyroid problems. Not only did the boy's symptoms not improve, but he was also in a foul mood all the time and becoming less and less motivated to do anything. He wouldn't even attend Boy Scout meetings, the one thing he'd always loved.

Fortunately for Justin, his mother and David's mother, Hilary, shared a carpool. Noting Justin's frequent absences, Hilary inquired about his health and his mother confided in her. Hilary told Justin's mother about how she'd solved David's mystery malady using the Eight Steps. Justin's mother decided it was time to take matters into her own hands.

She bought a notebook, listed Justin's symptoms in detail, and completed all the steps until she reached Step Five (past and present mental or physical problems). At that point, she decided to sit her son down and discuss it with him directly. She asked Justin to "play detective" and help solve this mystery. Justin perked up at the thought of playing the game. When his mother asked him if anything unusual had happened to him in the past—a symptom perhaps—that he'd forgotten to tell her about, Justin cheeks reddened. She assured him that he would not be in trouble and reminded him of what she had said consistently in the past: he would never be in trouble if he told the truth.

Reluctantly, Justin confided that while he was away at scout camp, he'd gotten a "rash." Because it was in his groin, he refused to show it to the camp counselors. He was too embarrassed to discuss it with anyone. Justin's mother did not know if this was relevant, but following the instructions of the Eight Step method, she made a note of it and asked him to describe it to her. He said it was weird because it looked like a bull's-eye, or an archery target.

Together they also recalled that three months prior to that Justin had had a case of the "flu," with fever, chills, achiness, fatigue, and a sore throat. It went away, but his mom thought it was odd that his brother hadn't caught it. This was especially surprising because she'd found the brothers spitting at each other and roughhousing in Justin's bed while he was sick.

When Justin's mom had completed all Eight Steps, she returned to the pediatrician. His first question after he heard about the targetlike rash that had occurred at camp was where the camp was located. When he heard it was in Connecticut, he ran some special blood tests and Justin's diagnosis was revealed.

Justin had contracted Lyme disease—a tick-transmitted illness where the symptoms often do not appear for several months after the initial infection. Lyme disease usually begins with the targetlike rash, but no one had observed it in Justin's case because he had been bitten in the groin and was too embarrassed to show it to anyone.

This disease is often difficult to diagnose because it mimics other diseases and may be asymptomatic until it reaches later stages. Then, if left untreated, chronic problems may develop like the ones Justin was experiencing. Although less common, chronic neurological involvement may become apparent months after the onset of infection, including bladder involvement, distal paresthesias (burning and tingling of the hands and feet), and sleep and mood disorders.

Fortunately, Justin's case was caught in time to be treated without permanent ramifications, thanks to the Eight Steps and his mother's diligence.

Conclusion

Children's mystery maladies are often a little more difficult to solve because of the difference between signs (an observable measurable indication of illness like a fever or rash) and symptoms (a sensation that is perceived by the patient and normally not measurable like pain) as we discussed in Chapter 3. You may be able to observe the "signs" of your child's malady but you will have to find a creative way to elicit all of his or her symptoms. Justin's mom was on the right track when she engaged Justin in the game of detective, and you may have to do the same. You know your child best and what will work to get him or her to help you. Still, children's mystery maladies are as solvable as those of adults using the Eight Steps to Self-Diagnosis.

Part 3

LIVING WITH YOUR MYSTERY MALADY

14

Mastering Your Pain

The whole is greater than the sum of its parts.

—ARISTOTLE

IT HAS BEEN documented that the most frequent reasons for doctor visits are colds and flu, followed by pain. Chronic pain is said to afflict an estimated fifty million Americans. Pain is also a symptom that accompanies a great many mystery maladies, and it can be more debilitating than any other single symptom. Dr. Rosenbaum and I live with chronic pain, and we would like to share some tips on how we've learned to master it. First, it's important to understand how pain works. Then it will be easier for you to see the "solutions" that can help you reduce the sensation. This chapter will also provide you with some concepts to consider in your efforts to achieve a sense of well-being even if you are forced to live with chronic pain.

How Pain Works

Pain is subjective in terms of the degree to which it is perceived. But it is also objective because it is measurable as a function of the nervous system. Pain interacts with the brain through a series of neurotransmitters. These neurotransmitters are essentially chemicals that send the message of pain. By applying what you have learned thus far about deductive reasoning, you have probably already concluded that if pain is a transmitted signal, then stopping or reducing pain would somehow involve interfering with that signal. Most pharmaceutical painkillers involve chemicals that act in this manner.*

But there are other options. In nature, generally every force has a counterforce, and the body has several of them for pain. One of those counterforces is endorphins, the "feel good" chemicals the body produces naturally when you exercise; sleep properly; fall in love; have acupuncture; or get very stimulated and excited in a positive way about some person, thing, or event. Just like any synthetically manufactured painkiller, endorphins interfere with the pain signals as well. So achieving a good night's sleep, exercising vigorously, and maintaining your passion and excitement for life is essential for pain management. The things you can do to ensure this will be addressed later in the chapter.

Another natural counterforce to pain is touch. Have you ever noticed when you hurt yourself that your automatic reaction is to put your hand where the pain is? Touch interferes with the pain signal because your nerve signals for touch are separate from those for pain and the transmission of those touch signals is faster than that of pain. It is instinct to "interfere" with the pain signal by sending another signal that can arrive at the brain first. So you instinctively rub, hold, massage, or otherwise touch the painful area of your body immediately on receiving a wound.

Another one of the body's counterforces to pain is the neurotransmitter serotonin. A serotonin deficit can create a lower threshold for pain tolerance. This is the reason certain antidepressants (such as Elavil) are often used to treat chronic pain, although there are other natural ways to influence serotonin levels as well.** Stress causes the release of another neurotransmitter called norepinephrine, which is a stimulating chemical that can worsen the sensation of pain and has the opposite effect to that of serotonin. Therefore, any stress-reducing technique that prevents the release of extra norepinephrine can also be effective in controlling pain.

---

*While this description is a vast oversimplification of a complicated process, it is valid and effective for our purposes.

**Antidepressants, when used to treat pain as opposed to depression, are often prescribed in lower doses but they are effective in slowing the release of the pain chemicals in nerves and stopping the pain signals from reaching the brain.

Regardless of what therapeutic method you choose to reduce your pain, it is important to respond to it as quickly as possible and hopefully before other natural body processes go into action that can cause even more pain. You may recall the one-to-ten pain scale we discussed in Chapter 3. You will achieve much more effective pain control if you treat pain when it's a three than if you wait until it's a ten. When the body feels it is under attack, such as when pain signals are transmitted repeatedly to and from the brain, the body can sometimes react with secondary inflammation or muscle spasms, which only worsen the pain.

Inflammation is a result of increased blood being sent to the injured area as the body tries to fight infection and heal itself. Muscle spasms are the body's way of making you stop moving the injured area so it can heal. However, if these defensive mechanisms are ignored for too long and the underlying pain is left untreated, that pain can become a chronic condition. When that happens, the nerves no longer recognize the original injury or trauma, and the pain signal begins to misfire and maintains the pain cycle long after healing has occurred. Nerves tend to recruit other nerves and rev up the whole nervous system. This is what is commonly believed to be the cause of chronic pain.* Under this theory, many pain clinics treat chronic pain with antiseizure medications which also act as nerve stabilizers that quiet misfiring nerves.

Let's take a moment to summarize the things you can do to help your pain levels (besides taking the narcotics or antiseizure medications administered by some physicians):

• Increase your endorphin (feel good chemicals) production through exercise, better sleep, or acupuncture.

• Take pharmaceutical antidepressants such as Elavil or Prozac that help boost brain levels of serotonin or other natural remedies such as *L*-5-hydroxyl trytophan (5-HTP) or St. John's wort.

---

*This is certainly what happened to me with my pelvic floor dysfunction. If I had received pain treatment earlier, I might have avoided having the pain turn into its own chronic disease of vulvodynia (see Chapter 8).

• Try treatments such as acupuncture (which, among other things, releases serotonin), massage, acupressure, shiatsu, and physical therapy as well as medications that act to inhibit inflammation and reduce muscle spasm and pain.

• Explore relaxation and stress-reduction techniques such as meditation, creative visualization, self-hypnosis, biofeedback, yoga, and psychotherapy to help you counteract any norepinephrine that is released due to stress. A new technique will be introduced in the next section.

All these interventions can help break the pain cycle on a physical level. Now let's look at what you can do on the emotional and mental levels to manage your pain.

How to Live Well Despite Your Pain

Have you ever noticed that the more you dwell on a problem, the worse it gets? Research by Dr. Susan Nolen-Hoeksema, M.D., and others demonstrates that women have a tendency to "overthink" and dwell on problems. Dr. Nolen-Hoeksema calls this negative thinking, and it can lead to depression. By contrast, men are less likely to get depressed, in part because they tend to distract themselves from a problem by going off and doing something else and not dwelling on it.

The same is true of pain. Focusing on your pain is like watering a plant—it will make it grow. I call it the watering plant analogy. So if negative thinking or obsessive concentration on the pain will make it worse, it is axiomatic that positive thinking and distraction from the pain will make it better.

But perhaps you are saying to yourself that when you are in pain, it's almost impossible to think of anything else! We know this is the way it feels, but feelings are not facts. Feelings relate to our mental and emotional processes, and we do have control over them. As I mentioned earlier, both Dr. Rosenbaum and I have lived with varying degrees of pain resulting from our mystery maladies. For part of the time that I (Lynn) was writing this book, I was practically debilitated by pain. Dr. Rosenbaum always has some pain associated with his mystery malady of many years (described in Chapter 16), yet he was still able to collaborate with me. In fact, during the time we were writing this book, both of us maintained full and active lives and professions. How did we do this? By recognizing that, except in certain instances, pain is never constant—there are always periods of more or lesser pain. We also developed some specific skills to help manage the sensation of pain so we could keep going. We'd like to share them so that you too can start living better despite your pain.

Recognize the Difference Between Pain and Suffering

Even though you may have the experience of pain, you don't have to suffer from it. There is a very real difference. Pain is a physical sensation, albeit not a pleasant one. Suffering is a mental and emotional reaction to that pain. My wise friend Twila said it best: "In life, pain is mandatory but suffering is optional." How you *react* to the pain sensation can actually affect how you experience it. When you place such a negative emotional reaction as suffering on top of the already unpleasant sensation of pain, it can only make the pain "feel" worse. Conversely, not suffering can lessen the sensation of pain. You have a choice.

Make a Decision Not to Suffer

Yes, you read it right—you have to make a conscious decision *not* to suffer. This is something that takes practice. Sometimes it means giving in to the pain and sometimes it will mean getting up and going on.

Dr. Rosenbaum and I have to make this decision every day. On days when our pain level is very high, the right decision is to not fight it because that would cause increased suffering. But after that kind of day, we always choose—as soon as we are able—to get up and get right back into life. This doesn't mean you deny your pain; it's there. But when it is not at its worst, you can choose not to focus on it or get overly anxious or depressed about it. You may have to modify your schedule or activities to accommodate the pain, but unless your doctor tells you otherwise, keep moving in the flow of your life. Do the things you like to do and try to focus on something positive instead.

Examine Your Beliefs

You may have to examine your beliefs about pain. As you learned in Step Seven, your beliefs can sometimes interfere with your ability to get a diagnosis; they can also interfere with your ability to stop suffering from your pain. Consider the case of Janna, a patient of Dr. Rosenbaum's, who was in a great deal of physical pain from a mystery malady. She suffered incessantly until she examined her belief system with the help of a therapist. She had been abused as a child, and as is the case with many abused children, her abuser made her believe that she had brought it on herself—that the abuse was somehow her fault. Unfortunately, she bought into that belief, and as a result, she also believed she deserved to suffer as punishment (like Gordon, whose story appeared in Chapter 12).

Sometimes suffering may be an attitude you've adopted to ward off potential disappointment. This would be like the old saying "He who expects nothing is rarely disappointed." So why expect not to suffer? If you do, you might be disappointed. Sometimes it may be a cultural belief such as "Well, I am Jewish/Catholic/a mother/[add your own category] and we are used to suffering." The point is that your personal history, experiences, and attitudes about pain should be examined and questioned. Once you do this, you can make a choice about whether to continue on with that attitude/belief or adopt a healthier one.

Sometimes we suffer because we have "catastrophized," as discussed in Chapter 3. In other words, we believe in something that is not a fact—something like "My pain will *never* go away, and it will only get worse." This kind of thinking creates enormous anxiety, and as we've already discussed, anxiety increases our perception of pain. We have to consciously decide to turn away from those thoughts. Unless the belief has a basis in fact such as this is what your doctor has told you, there is no reason to believe it or to even think it because doing so will cause more suffering.

Take Encouragement from Others

Besides examining your own attitudes, another thing that may help you choose not to suffer is to recognize how many folks out there are living with some degree of pain and are still functional. Statistics indicate that more than 25 percent of the U.S. population experiences some form of chronic pain each year, whether it is arthritis, back pain, migraines, or something else. This may explain why pain management clinics have popped up everywhere.

The fact that others share the experience of pain and have somehow learned to manage it can be a great source of encouragement. It can also reduce your anxiety since you'll know you're not alone in coping with pain.

Do the Butch

This is a physical stress management technique that can reduce your sensation of pain but that you are not likely to find anywhere else—and don't laugh, because it works! Here is the premise.

Researcher and author Peter A. Levine, in his book *Waking the Tiger*, examines how the body heals trauma.[1] There are many interesting and applicable concepts in this publication for mystery malady patients. In particular, the author describes how our nervous systems are not all that different from those of most animals. However, while animals and humans all immediately respond to fear and trauma with the classic "fight, flight, or freeze response," we differ in our long-term response to what we perceive as dangerous situations. Only humans routinely develop enduring aftereffects from the stress of trauma. Levine then goes on to speculate as to the reason for this.

According to his hypothesis, one important reason is that once the danger has passed, animals vibrate, shake, twitch, tremble, or do whatever each one does to physically release the muscles from their hypervigilant, tensed state. Humans, on the other hand, do not. This is not an instinctive human reaction, so we tend to hold stress in our bodies.

After reading this, I (Lynn) wondered about whether if we actually performed a similar ritual, it might be an effective stress reducer (and therefore a concomitant pain management technique). I began paying particular attention to my dog, Butch. Sure enough, every time Butch started to calm down after being excited or tense, he subsequently would shake himself vigorously—exactly as Levine described. Just as an experiment, I decided to follow suit. Whenever I began to feel stressed or tense, I would immediately try releasing that tension by physically shaking out my whole body and releasing any sound that I could emit at the same time. It worked like a charm. Both the stress and the pain level felt reduced. I now call it "doing the Butch." (Sometimes, when I feel the stress coming on, I will walk out of a meeting at work, lock myself in my office, and shake it off. So far I haven't been caught.)

If you want to try it, begin by paying close attention to your body. As you feel even a hint of stress creeping into your neck and shoulders, as your muscles begin to tighten, as your breathing becomes shallow or constricted: *stop*! Immediately change your position and location. Go to the restroom, into your bedroom, or anyplace where you can be alone. Take several deep breaths. Close your eyes if you need to. Then shake yourself all over. Do it until you feel your muscle tension release. Although there are no empirical studies to prove that this works as a pain management technique, Dr. Rosenbaum and I think you'll find it really does help. In any case, it certainly won't harm you, and at the very least, it will give you (and anyone watching you) a laugh. Laughter in and of itself can be good pain medicine.

If you can't avoid or release the stress from your body, please don't compound it and exacerbate your pain by stressing out about your stress. Sometimes—especially when you can't do the Butch or some other stress-management technique—it can be best just to let your stress be. Accept it. Allow yourself to feel whatever you are feeling at that moment and move on. At times, resisting stress can make it and your pain worse. In this case, refocus yourself as discussed in the next section.

Refocus on Something Other Than Your Pain

In addition to examining your beliefs about pain and suffering and knowing you are not alone with your pain, you can help yourself make a choice not to suffer if you can recognize that pain is not a deadly disease; it is simply a sensation. Like any sensation, you can chose to ignore it from time to time. You can experience hunger but refrain from eating by getting busy with something else. You can be exhausted but muster up the energy to do what needs to be done anyway. It simply requires that you turn your focus away from the sensation.

Try to refocus your consciousness for five minutes. Choose to do something that will absorb your attention—watch a TV program you enjoy, read an interesting article, feed the baby, play with your pets, do the grocery shopping, listen to a friend in need, or agree to do a telephone conference at work. Everyone in pain experiences times when they are so focused on something else that they forget their pain.

Once you can refocus your awareness on something besides your pain for five minutes, try extending it to ten minutes and so forth. In doing so, you will have achieved the power of mind over body, something most people have yet to learn. Remember the watering plant analogy—thinking about your pain is watering it and will only make it grow. Focusing on other things besides the sensation of pain will automatically reduce the sensation. How do we know you can do this? The mere fact that you are reading this book despite your pain tells us that you are capable of focusing on something else. You can still live your life despite your pain. Try refocusing on following the Eight Steps to find the correct diagnosis for your condition.

Let Go

Dr. Rosenbaum and I have great respect for you "fighters" out there who refuse to give up in your search for a diagnosis and cure for your mystery malady. But if you'll notice, we never use fighting words when dealing with pain. Pain is not your enemy; it is a sensation that accompanies the mystery malady you are in the process of trying to solve. Resisting it is a form of suffering. The key to any pain is to learn how to let go of it. That means accepting it or at least not resisting it when the level is too high. As soon as the sensation reduces enough that you are uncomfortable but not disabled from it, refocus and get on with your life.

Consider mystery malady patient Leticia, who has daily chronic pain. "When I finally accepted the fact that my pain was going to awaken with me every morning, I decided to say good morning to it—to greet it as if it were a constant companion. Then and only then did my pain miraculously reduce. I don't know how or why, but accepting it and letting go of my constant struggle with it made a difference in how I experienced it." Leticia continues on her search for answers using the Eight Steps, but she has learned to live well despite her pain.

Get on a Mental Diet

Since negative thinking can adversely impact your pain level, this leads us to the last but certainly not the least important skill in pain management: replacing negative thoughts (which are an understandable result of experiencing pain) with positive thoughts. Just think about it like you're going on a diet, a diet free of negative thinking. You will only nourish yourself with positive thoughts. These are the staples of your diet:

• Your thinking is a tool under your complete power and control. Most people think their mind controls them, but that is true only if you allow it to be. Your current thought—the one you are thinking right now—is totally within your power to change. Instead of thinking about how much you are hurting at this moment, say to yourself, "I am in the process of healing right now" or "My pain is decreasing with every positive thought I have" or "Every cell in my body is moving toward health and well-being." If your mind responds by screaming at you, "No, it isn't!" then allow that thought to pass. When it finally does, respond, "I believe it is." You may want to make up index cards with positive thoughts written on them and post them around your home and workplace. We all need positive reminders.

• Hope is a life force, and it is not unrealistic in any circumstance. Hope doesn't automatically mean your disease will go into remission or that you will find a cure. What it does mean is that you simply haven't discovered your correct diagnosis or treatment *yet*. And when your mind screams, "Right! So then why haven't I discovered the answer to my mystery malady?" remind your ornery mind that there is nothing that says you won't eventually find it. It simply hasn't happened yet. Yes, talking to yourself is not only okay, it's absolutely necessary on this mental diet.

• Like the unruly acts of rebellious children, your negative thoughts should bring specific consequences. Just as wild children need limits and consequences enforced for getting out of control, so does your negative thinking. A psychotherapist friend who had breast cancer used to wear a rubber band around her wrist. The minute she found herself sinking into negative thinking, she'd snap the rubber band against her wrist and say,

"Ow!" She was literally snapping herself out of her negative thoughts. (By the way, she beat her cancer too.)

• Appreciation is the final staple of your new mental diet. It is amazing how soon we lose appreciation for things. The pain stops and we appreciate it for a minute or a day, but before long we are right back to complaining about something else. I was once on a plane destined for England, and when we were halfway across the Atlantic Ocean, the plane turned around with the pilot announcing he had just received word there was a bomb aboard the flight and we had to land in Gander, Newfoundland. The plane was totally silent as we heard instructions about emergency landing, what to do if we didn't make it to land and ended up going into the ocean, and the like. Thank heavens we did land safely. At first, everyone was so grateful. That is, until we heard it would be twenty-four hours before we could take off again and there were fewer hotel rooms in Gander than there were passengers. Immediately everyone started moaning and complaining only minutes after surviving what might have been certain death.

On this diet, you will refrain from ingratitude. Instead, cultivate an "attitude of gratitude." How do you do that? It's all part of refocusing. Whatever parts of your body are in pain, don't mind them for a few minutes. Think about what parts function and aren't in pain. Try to feel total gratitude and appreciation for those healthier parts. You know what your mystery malady prevents you from doing in your life, but try instead to think about all the things you still can do. In fact, remind yourself of what you should be grateful for on a constant basis—perhaps, in the same way you used to think constantly about everything that was wrong with your body. Just reverse your thought process.

While all of this may seem like a lot of work, it is worth it. Controlled studies have found that when we get angry or upset, the sympathetic branch of our autonomic nervous system is activated and causes our heart rate to increase and our arteries to constrict, a pattern linked to death.[2] In contrast, when we think about something we really appreciate, the parasympathetic branch of the autonomic nervous system triggers a calming pattern believed to bestow a positive effect on the heart. The parasympathetic branch of the nervous system is also directly linked to the soothing of pain.

There is much research occurring in the area of pain, including gene technology that may be close to finding the key genes responsible for controlling pain. There are also many resources available on pain management. We've shared the ones we believe are most effective, but if these are not the ones for you, research until you find some that are. Remember, you are ultimately in control of your health and well-being.

Aristotle said, "The whole is greater than the sum of its parts." You are greater than your pain, which is only one part of your living experience right now. Once you make a positive shift in your thinking, you are already on your way to improved health even if you haven't yet found the diagnosis and cure for your mystery malady.

In the next chapter, we will address the most common feelings that derive from living with the uncertainty about your mystery malady and how to counteract those that can tax you just as pain can. Handling those feelings in an emotionally healthy way can even have a positive effect on your sense of pain.

15

Understanding Your Feelings About Being Sick

Everyone who is born holds dual citizenship in the kingdom of the well and in the kingdom of the sick and sooner or later each of us is obliged, at least for a spell, to identify ourselves as citizens of that other place.

—SUSAN SONTAG

WHEN FACED WITH a mystery malady, our emotions can start going haywire. Mystery malady patients often experience fear, anger, denial, confusion, and sometimes a sense of hopelessness. After all, having a mystery malady is not like having some other chronic, recognizable illness. There are no support groups, websites or chat rooms, periodicals, reference books, physician specialists, or research grants or studies for your illness because it has no name. Although we might need support as much, if not more, than patients with diagnosed illnesses, it may not be available. We feel alone and misunderstood, and worst of all, we fear some people don't even believe us. Without a diagnosis and a cure for our disease, we can feel stranded without direction or hope.

Emotional distress can cloud our minds and make it difficult to proceed with the important business of finding a diagnosis. This anguish also interferes with our intuition, that sensitive and often accurate inner perception of knowing what helps and what hinders us.

Try to take an objective look at yourself to determine whether you're sinking into a negative state of mind because of your mystery malady.

Checklist to Help Evaluate Your Emotional State
- Do you feel that you are the only one in the whole world with this problem?
- Do you feel hopeless and helpless?
- Do you sense that your physician has given up on you?
- Have you seen several physicians who have all failed to diagnose you?
- Do you feel that you know more than your physician does?
- Have you sought complementary or alternative health treatments solely because conventional medicine has offered no relief?
- Are you beginning to prefer your bedroom to life in the outside world?
- Is your family concerned and confused about how to deal with you?
- Have you begun to wonder if it is "all in your head" or "just stress"?
- Are you afraid that you may become permanently disabled?
- Are you losing your sense of humor?

If you answered yes to five or more of these questions, you will benefit greatly from examining your feelings about being sick. Your state of mind can be your strongest ally or your worst enemy in your efforts to cope with your illness. Getting in touch with your thoughts and feelings will help move you along the road to mastering your condition.

Know That Your Feelings Are Normal

Most people who are plagued by mystery illnesses often wonder if they'll get over them. You may well ask, "Will my pain ever end?" or "Will I ever feel good again?" Pessimistic thinking saps your courage. As Kurt Kroenke, M.D., wrote in *Annals of Internal Medicine*, "Symptoms are literally a fall from our usual state of functioning. Symptom-free, we can focus our full attention and energies on the world around us. But when we're symptomatic, we focus inward, distracted from what we know can and should be done."[1] Lewis Carroll put it in a more humorous way in *Through the Looking Glass*: "I'm very brave generally . . . Only today I happen to have a headache."

Self-doubt and paralysis can take over when vague symptoms continue unabated. It's normal to run the gamut of negative emotions, especially when those in whom you have placed your trust (your doctors and perhaps your friends and family) have abandoned you and your body has betrayed you. The stress can suck you into a downward spiral toward chronic anxiety, deep depression, or other serious emotional problems. Although you may have these feelings, the key is to not allow them to take over your life.

Acknowledge and Accept Your Illness

Janet was a very charismatic, take-charge kind of person. Her personality fit with her job as a television producer but it did not serve her well as a mystery malady patient. For the first six months of her mysterious illness, she convinced herself that if she simply pretended it wasn't there, she could keep control of the situation and maintain the long hours and fast pace of her stressful job. In fact, she ignored her condition until she became too weak and sick to work. She was forced to quit. Her self-esteem plummeted as she convinced herself that she had failed her boss, the TV station, and herself.

If Janet had only acknowledged her condition initially, she might have arranged a less strenuous schedule early on in her illness and made some other accommodations that would have allowed her to take care of herself so she could have continued working. Unfortunately, Janet is not atypical of those who are very motivated and successful because they know how to "make things happen." They often delude themselves into thinking that they are in charge of what happens at all times. Living with a mystery illness and the losses it may bring means we have to acknowledge that we have no control. And this unpleasant truth may be as difficult to acknowledge as the pain or other symptoms we suffer from.

But loss is simply part of life and like others who might lose a parent, a job, or a leg, we have to learn to accept our situation as part of life. We also need to do it in a way that is helpful rather than harmful to us and those around us. Thus, the first step toward receiving help is acknowledging and understanding the truth about your illness. You'll have to deal with the loss if you want to regain your health.

Finding and Maintaining Hope

While it's normal to feel discouraged about your ongoing symptoms and even angry that your doctors haven't helped you, sinking into hopelessness is the worst thing you can do. We cannot overemphasize how important it is to keep your hopes alive. Hope is your best friend and strongest supporter in the quest to find a diagnosis and cure.

The most important thing you can do to maintain your hope is to remember that very important three-letter word: *yet*. A diagnosis and cure for your condition is not known yet, but it may be found tomorrow, the day after, or perhaps a year from now. If your hope dwindles, it will be difficult for you to keep on searching for the answers.

Being powerless over having a mystery illness does not mean that you are powerless about your attitude toward it. Pessimism makes it difficult to do the work of looking for the cause of your mysterious symptoms and trying to live a satisfying life in the meantime. More information about your condition will surely become known with the passage of time if you are willing to keep working through the Eight Steps, find the right physician, and proactively seek answers. Until then, it is essential to work at sustaining your faith and hope.

Learning how to maintain a positive attitude, including a sense of trust that the answer that eludes you today will eventually come, can become one of the most important lessons you can learn from your illness. Initially, I (Lynn) struggled to maintain the hope that my mysterious pelvic condition would get resolved. After two years of unabated pain, I was feeling profoundly exhausted and discouraged. I was certain that a solution would never be found. It was during that time that a friend e-mailed me a message with a quote. It read:

> When you come to the edge of all the light you know, and are about to step off into the darkness of the unknown, faith is knowing one of two things will happen: There will be something solid to stand on or you will be taught to fly.

I was struck by these words, for I was very definitely standing on that ledge. The answer was right there, and my spirits began to buoy as I came to understand that if I were to have any hope of "flying," I had to release anything that was weighing me down. Sure, the pain was taking a toll, but it was really all those negative thoughts and attitudes that were my shackles. They were going to make me free-fall into the valley of hopelessness. And I wanted to fly instead.

Recognizing Self-Destructive Attitudes and What to Do About Them

The following common attitudes or responses to mystery maladies have the potential for being self-destructive and drowning us in pessimism. If you can learn to recognize and deal with these and other self-destructive attitudes before they get the upper hand, serious psychological distress can be avoided and progress toward your diagnostic solution can continue.

Self-Medicating to the Point of Addiction

Some of us self-medicate to the extent that we use drugs for more than our physical pain. Or we may do it to the point that we risk becoming addicted. Admittedly, it takes a great deal of honesty to face either possibility. If you are taking pain medication for more than just physical relief or your intake of pain medication keeps escalating, be willing to explore the possibility that you are using it to dull more than your physical pain or that you may be hooked. (For example, even the daily use of over-the-counter pain medications for headaches can create "rebound" reactions when used incorrectly.)

Be honest with yourself and your doctor by acknowledging exactly what you're taking, how much, and for what reason. Seek an opinion from those around you about this issue and then get help. Although he did not become addicted, Dr. Rosenbaum had to admit to himself that he had begun using his pain medication to numb his feelings of rage and shame. It was easier for him to make progress in coping with his mystery malady once he did. (His story is found in Chapter 16.)

Believing It's All in Your Mind

As a way of controlling anxiety or defending ourselves against it, we can sometimes discount our physical condition by deciding it's all in our mind. After all, most mystery malady patients have been told this more than once in the process of trying to find a diagnosis and cure. Unless you are suffering from somatization disorder (described in Chapter 12), this thought is dangerous for a whole host of reasons.

Believing our problem is psychological, we may ask for or be placed on antidepressants and antianxiety drugs when they are not necessarily what we need. In *A Dose of Sanity: Mind, Medicine, and Misdiagnosis* (John Wiley & Sons, 1996), psychiatrist Sydney Walker writes that one of the reasons patients with mysterious diseases like lupus don't always get diagnosed early on is because they often develop psychiatric problems before their physical symptoms appear. Dr. Walker states that many of these patients "are initially referred to psychiatrists. And a patient (particularly a woman) exhibiting 'psychiatric' symptoms and complaining of vague aches and pains that can't be substantiated by a superficial exam and less-than-comprehensive lab tests is all too likely to be labeled as having 'conversion disorder' (a fancy term for hysteria) and given psychotropic medications. These drugs—in addition to masking symptoms of a worsening disorder—can severely compromise a patient's already abnormal brain function."

Whether or not you are taking medication for depression or anxiety, deciding your mystery malady is imaginary can be a dangerous deception. You may decide, like overachiever Janet, to simply ignore the very symptoms that could otherwise lead you to a quick solution if only you paid attention to them.

Believing your condition is all in your mind can also give you a false sense that you can manage and control whether or not you have symptoms. Ultimately, this can lead to an emotional roller-coaster ride, from mistakenly believing that you have created your illness to being completely depressed when you fail to resolve it. Succumbing to this vicious cycle will leave you feeling even less able to cope than before.

There is no doubt that I (Lynn) was on this roller-coaster for the first two years of my pelvic pain mystery malady (see Chapter 8). I knew that because I couldn't get a diagnosis, and especially because of the nature of my problem, certain people were speculating that it was all in my head. When I would slip silently into allowing myself to believe they were right, I would try to overcome my condition. Telling myself it was simply a question of mind over matter, I would refuse to acknowledge or accept my physical limitations by wearing panty hose to work for a week, donning tight jeans on the weekends, and engaging in more sex or exercise than usual.

After a week or so, a ferocious flare-up of infection, inflammation, and pain would invariably erupt. This, in turn, would send me careening into that familiar wall of despair. Then I would become disconsolate for weeks until the symptoms quieted down. It was like the self-destructive cycle of addiction—getting that initial "high" from feeling that I possessed the power to make myself fine again, followed by the profound bottoming out borne of the crushing realization that I could not. As long as I bought into the "it's all in your mind" attitude, I could never come to any acceptance of my very real condition and put my energies where they needed to be—finding a solution instead of pretending there wasn't really a problem.

Feeling Guilty/Blaming Others

If you had a recognized diagnosis like arthritis, diabetes, or asthma, you might wonder "Why me?" but you probably wouldn't blame yourself for having it. When your physicians cannot diagnose your condition or help you, they become defensive, and this can feel as if they and others around you are blaming you. It's a very human reaction for doctors to want to avoid blame because they can't explain your problem. It's also easy for laypeople to assign responsibility for things because unexplained phenomena can be scary. Either way, they seem to be pointing the finger at you.

Tragically, some mystery malady patients actually start believing that their conditions are their own fault. "What did I do to cause this?" they ask. Often the sense of guilt is directly proportional to the length of time they have been ill and how severely their malady impacts their daily lives.

You may feel guilty because you cannot be the child, parent, spouse, or friend you feel you should be when you have a mystery malady. This is a way to punish yourself, but it only results in more pain and distress.

The other side of the coin is blaming others, especially doctors, for our health problems. We might dwell on their shortcomings so much that it becomes a destructive inner mantra: "They haven't helped me. They don't care, and if they did, they'd be able to fix me."

Rather than blaming yourself or others for the state of your health, which is essentially fruitless, try using some of the many techniques presented in Chapter 16 to find health in your mind and spirit.

Giving Up

Sometimes we believe it is easier to give up and give in than to persevere. Frustrated and fed up, we might even start believing it would be preferable to have a dreaded disease like cancer than to be stuck in diagnostic limbo. If we could at least name our disease, people might have more sympathy and at least we would feel more cared for and understood. Giving up sometimes feels like the best option.

And let's face it, sometimes self-pity feels good. After all, we're suffering, but no one seems to understand our frustrations, our pain, how our life has been ruined, and on and on. But while self-pity may feel good for a little while, wallowing in it will never get us where we need to be—healthy and well. So we need to remind ourselves that there is always another choice. We can choose to have faith and hope despite our physical distress. We can also choose to define health in ways besides how our bodies feel. (Chapter 16 talks more about this.)

Denying Your Condition

Denial is a defense mechanism against fear. It's a useful tool sometimes because it helps us allay our anxiety, at least initially. We might try to deny our fear and go into the "fight" mode, forcing ourselves beyond our limits—just like TV producer Janet or me (Lynn). Refusing to listen to your body and trying to deny your illness is often costly and never helpful. The only way to sleuth out your solutions is by being fully aware of your condition and working through the Eight Steps. This requires all your powers of observation and that means you cannot be in denial. You must open your eyes in order to help yourself.

Complaining and/or Withdrawing

Some of us, mainly women, release our frustration, fear, and anxiety by complaining to anyone who'll listen. Others, mostly men, cope by withdrawing. Friends and family don't know how to respond, and they can pull away in their frustration at not being able to help; the loss of their physical or emotional support leaves us feeling more alone than ever. The support of others can be very healing and valuable, so it is important to examine our own behavior to see if we are driving that support away.

Being Self-Absorbed

Many people who have undiagnosed illnesses sink into constant worry. If we're not careful, it can take over our lives and we can find ourselves doing nothing but "working on" or obsessing over our illness. We're left with limited energy for living, low self-esteem, and little sense of accomplishment. The quickest way to escape the undertow of self-absorption is to reach beyond our own problems and do something for others even in simple ways, as described in the next section.

Constructing Positive Attitudes

It is normal to falter on your path toward self-diagnosis, consumed with the idea that you'll never find answers. But in order to constructively cope with your mystery illness, try to turn your mind in a new direction, find new interests, or resume old ones (although it may be hard to do that at first). To get yourself in a more positive place so you can learn to take better care of yourself, we urge you to consider the following concepts.

Release the Compulsive Need to Control

When we are physically well and things go the way we expect, we believe it's because we're strong and in control of our lives. But the limit of our potency may be reached rather quickly when an illness strikes. As we've already discussed, the illusion of control shatters and we have to come to terms with being powerless. There are forces greater than we are, and we need to let go of the notion that if we simply try hard enough, are smart enough, or are good enough, we can overcome them. Although it may be possible to do so, relief may come in its own time rather than ours. This is especially true when we don't even know what our malady is and have great doubts about ever resolving it.

Like recovering alcoholics who, as a prelude to staying sober, must admit that they're powerless over alcohol, you can benefit greatly by acknowledging your lack of power over your medical condition. You didn't cause it, and as yet, you can't make it go away.

Letting go of the need to control is easier said than done. Your natural inclination will be to resist. Try to remember that control over your condition was only an illusion anyway, and the sooner you can accept this, the more peace of mind you will find. Letting go of the need to control can actually free up more energy for your diagnostic detective work and allow you to take more compassionate care of yourself.

Stop the Guilt and Blame

As we described earlier, one of our most self-destructive attitudes is feeling guilty or blaming ourselves or others. You certainly didn't choose to have this malady, and your family and friends would probably love nothing more for you than to see you healthy and well.

Feeling guilty takes too much time and energy—neither of which you can afford to waste. Here's how to look at it, and what you might do to avoid these feelings. Perhaps you can't cook dinner, do someone's laundry, chauffeur the kids around, go to work, play golf or tennis, or give a party. In fact, there may be many things you are unable to do, but no matter what shape you are in, you can always give someone your attention, a kind word, a loving look, a shoulder to cry on, or a sympathetic ear.

If you have a partner, you might feel guilty that you're too sick to have the "intimacy" you once enjoyed and presume that intimacy must mean sex. Not necessarily. The things I just mentioned are intimate and create intimacy. Touching and looking deeply into your loved one's eyes can be as intimate as sexual intercourse. Conversely, making love even when you might not be able to do much else for your loved one can be nurturing for both of you.

Paying attention to your children and listening to everything about their soccer game even when—or especially when—you couldn't drive them or be there for the game is nurturing for you and them. Telling them a story with your eyes closed, lying on your bed with them next to you, is certainly a means of loving them. Expressing your love in every way you are able can be enough, more than enough. In a world where everyone seems too busy, giving someone even just a little time and attention can be meaningful.

Calling friends or family to remember their birthdays or some event that may be happening in their lives can help you maintain those relationships even if you can't go to lunch, a shopping mall, a football game, or the weekly card game. E-mailing a joke and letting friends know you thought of them can be a means of loving them. You may not be able to make a holiday dinner or throw a birthday party, but that doesn't mean you can't participate in their lives in a joyful and meaningful way.

Finally, the best thing to do for everyone involved is to keep pursuing diagnostic answers without carrying the excess emotional baggage of guilt and blame.

Do Something for Others

Consider helping others as a cure for the blues. Try to find a creative way you can do so comfortably without increasing your pain or other symptoms. Not only does focusing on others take you out of your self-absorbed state, it will lift your self-esteem immediately. Perhaps you can help those who have the same condition by starting or attending a support group, creating a website, or publishing a newsletter. Taking part in constructive activities for and with those who suffer from similar undiagnosed conditions can bring you some wonderful companionship and support. (This is explored further in Chapter 16.)

Maintain Communication

We need to demonstrate how we value those who are trying to care for and support us by maintaining the lines of communication. Get help in explaining your mystery malady to your children so they can understand and not be afraid. Be honest; don't pretend to feel well if you don't. On the other hand, try not to dwell on your illness either. Although it may give you some relief from anxiety to talk about your problems, give your family and friends equal time to talk about the stresses and events of their lives.

Most important is communicating clearly about what you can and can't reasonably do based on your current condition and until you've found the solution to your malady. Don't be afraid to say, "I don't feel well enough to do this right now." It is better to set your limits clearly, calmly, and openly than to wind up angry at someone else because you didn't take care of yourself. Reassure the other person that when you feel better you will be happy to do what you can't do now. Just as you need their reassurance, those around you need yours too.

Love and Nurture Yourself

When your mystery malady is ongoing, you cannot reasonably expect even the ones who love you most to administer care on a constant basis. They have their lives and stresses to contend with as well. But there is no reason you can't love and nurture yourself. Listen to your body and what it needs, avoid stress and tension, do the things that you love as long as they're healthy indulgences—a warm bubble bath, a massage, listening to music, applying a scented lotion. None of these things take much energy, time, or expense, but they can recharge your batteries and help yourself feel loved and nurtured.

Maintain Trust and Keep Your Expectations Realistic

Trusting that you will find an answer (and facing down any fears that you won't) is probably the hardest task of all. From our personal experiences with mystery maladies, Dr. Rosenbaum and I have come to believe that there is only one answer. You have to build a solid base of trust: trust in the Eight Step process that we have given you, trust that you can and will find the right physician to work with (as we discussed in Chapter 4), and finally, trust that you will eventually find the correct treatment to restore your health.

In the Eight Steps and throughout this book, we have tried to let you know that you can trust yourself to be your own best healer. If you have a hard time with this concept, just know that this process has worked for many people, including ourselves. So if nothing else works, you can start with believing in that. As you experience little triumphs throughout the Eight Step process, you will come to trust more and more.

In the interim, be realistic about your expectations. Things sometimes take time. It took many years for me (Lynn) to find a diagnosis and then relief, but I did. Dr. Rosenbaum is still in the process of solving his mystery malady, but he has not lost his trust that he will. Patience and perseverance are a must! You are not alone. Simply live your life to the best of your ability until a correct diagnosis is found.

In the next chapter, we will explore how to find health in mind and spirit while you are working toward and waiting for the solution to your mystery malady. It includes Dr. Rosenbaum's story of his still-unresolved mystery malady, which we hope you will find inspirational in your quest to find wholeness despite illness.

16

Finding Health in Mind and Spirit

Meaning makes a great many things endurable—perhaps everything.
—CARL JUNG

BEING PHYSICALLY ILL with a mystery malady does not mean we cannot be healthy otherwise. Laura Hillenbrand, author of the acclaimed book *Seabiscuit: An American Legend* (later made into a movie of the same name), wrote her story lying in bed with her eyes closed as she suffered from a mystery illness, which began in 1987 and was only in recent years diagnosed as chronic fatigue syndrome. The author did not let her unknown illness define her.

Therein lies the key to managing and living well despite our illness—not having it define us. *A mystery malady is something we have; it is not who we are.* Illness in one's body does not preclude wellness in one's mind and spirit. In fact, it may be the catalyst to wellness. For many of us, not having the benefit of physical health makes us seek a broader sense of health and well-being beyond the physical. Rather than being limiting, having a mystery malady can make our lives deeper and richer if we choose to let it. But we must make that choice and use our illness as a gateway to wholeness and healing.

Those of you who are worn out from your pain and illness (like Dr. Rosenbaum and I have been from time to time) may ask, "How is it possible to feel well when I am so sick?" The answer is very simple. Illness in our body is not the entire experience of our lives. Our life experiences consist of what happens not just in our bodies but in our minds and hearts. In fact, a greater part of our lives occurs inside rather than outside ourselves. If we are well in spirit, if we have a sense of well-being on the inside, if we love and feel loved, if we feel connected to the outside world, our bodies become a mere container for all that other good stuff. This is a wider view of health. Our suffering can be transcended while we search for ways to cure it—and perhaps it is this very transcendence of our physical limitations that is a critical part of our healing.

The Meaning in Illness

Sickness and pain are a universal experience; some statistics show that on any given day, only 12 percent of the population reports having no pain or other symptoms. So the difference between a mystery malady patient and any other person is simply that we don't know the reason for our pain or illness or how long we'll have to live with it. The latter issue basically obliges us to find a way to cope for as long as we have to and still find a sense of greater wholeness and health; this in turn may bear directly on how soon and how well we recover physically.

So how do we find such meaning? Dr. Rosenbaum and I are not authorities on this subject; we can only tell you what has worked for us. Dr. Rosenbaum's story appears later in this chapter. I (Lynn) will share my personal conclusions about how to achieve this wider sense of health and well-being in the next few paragraphs. Believe us, it was not always easy.

Since an early age, I (Lynn) have always been the kind of person who has to know the reasons for things. When I found myself in the midst of the mystery malady I described in Chapter 8, the question that dogged me most was why this had happened to me. Of course, eventually I figured out what happened. But *why* it happened and why it happened to *me* were still unanswered. While I was estranged from my father (a Holocaust survivor) for some time, I reconnected with him when he was dying of mantle cell

lymphoma. Typical of him, he observed, "When other people on this cancer ward ask, 'Why me?' I laugh and say, 'Why not me?'"

While it was typical of him because he was a fatalist about much of life
(which may have been his attempt to gain acceptance of, and hence mas-
tery over, whatever was happening to him at any given time), there was still
truth in that statement. Acceptance is very important to gaining peace, but
to me, that is only half the solution. The other half is turning that acceptance into action.

Perhaps in reaction to my father's fatalistic attitudes, I'd spent much of
my life trying to find the "meaning." Even at a young age, when I didn't
understand why something was happening, I would spend hours reasoning
things out, analyzing all the facts in an attempt to gain answers. Years later,
with more humility and possibly the wisdom gained from experience, I have
softened. I accept that I may not always understand the reason for many
things. My father was half right; after all, why not me?

Still, there is the other half of the equation: finding the meaning in the
happenstance and turning it into action. I believe there is an ultimate purpose and a meaning to whatever happens, even if I don't see it or know it at
the time. And it often takes a while for the meaning to emerge.

My father might have argued that this entire discussion is ridiculous
and that life is simply about random chaos. He might have said that believing in "purpose" is simply another way of trying to have a sense of control
over things about which I am ultimately powerless. Perhaps my father was
right, but if I didn't believe my way, how else would Dr. Rosenbaum and I
have created this Eight Step self-diagnostic model?

Psychiatrist Victor Frankl was a survivor of the Nazi concentration
camps. He endured the unimaginable, but like so many others who turn
their tragedies into determination, Frankl developed an entire area of psy-
chology that teaches us that anything is bearable if you find meaning and
purpose in your experience. In his book *Man's Search for Meaning*, he writes,
". . . everything can be taken from a man but one thing: the last of the
human freedoms—to choose one's attitudes in any given circumstances, to
choose one's own way."[1]

Illness, like many other tragedies in life, can act as a catalyst and a challenge to find our spirit. Many times we hear of someone who survives a disaster and says, "It's turned out to be the best thing that ever happened to

me." Why? Generally, it's because the crisis caused them to get in touch with something else they really needed or wanted. It opened doorways to a new experience that otherwise wouldn't have occurred. The Chinese character for crisis is said to be the combination of two seemingly antithetical concepts: danger and opportunity.

If everything were going along just as we planned and life were seemingly within our control, we might find no need to challenge ourselves voluntarily. Why should we? It is only when things seem to spin out of control, when life isn't following our neat plan, and our lives are involuntarily changed in some significant way that we are forced to make a decision. We will either be angry, succumb to self-pity and fear, or use what is happening to not just survive but to thrive. Perhaps this is truly the reason *why* things happen. I believe the most powerful use of illness is to find our most authentic selves, our heart's desire, our true calling.

Courage First

Author and poet Maya Angelou says if we are not facing down demons, we are not really alive. But to face our demons and to find our own meaning takes courage, and this is sometimes very difficult to find when we're physically ill. It is easier to be brave when we feel good. Illness can take a lot out of us, and mysterious illnesses can fill us with fear.

Dr. Rosenbaum and I have discovered there is very little difference between fear and courage. Courage does not mean fearlessness. It means going on despite your fears. General Omar Bradley once said, "Bravery is the capacity to perform properly even when scared half to death." The very meaning of courage implies there must be something first to be afraid of.

Courage means finding faith when it seems all hope is lost. It means bouncing back after setbacks (flare-ups, a medication that doesn't work, another doctor who doesn't know what's wrong) and losses (a job opportunity, a relationship, the ability to do something with your child) and still believing that your physical ailment is intended to help you find your purpose. I will never forget a quotation from an unidentified author that often gave me the courage to try just one more thing in the darkest days of my mysterious pain: "Why not go out on a limb? Isn't that where the fruit is?"

Then Faith

Together with courage, faith is a prerequisite for going out on that limb. For some, faith is a religious and highly personal matter. Unfortunately for many, their faith has been shattered by their mystery malady. Some of you may ask, "If there is a God or some higher Being, why am I suffering?" Rabbi Harold Kushner explains that God didn't create your suffering but rather is there for your comfort.

But faith need not be religious. To me, faith is believing in what we cannot see, what we cannot prove, but what we somehow *know* at the deepest level of our being. Based on my own experience, it is a continuous knowing that once I have done all that I can do, some power greater than I—call it God, Christ, Buddha, the Light, or the Universe—will step in and carry me the rest of the way. Maybe it's not faith. Maybe it's optimism or hope. Maybe it is just the belief that tomorrow will be a better day. Maybe it is hearing a still, small voice from within that guides you. All I know is that it is essential to any state of wellness. And there must be something to it, because study after study reveals that patients with faith survive longer and better than those without.

If you think you don't have any faith, consider the ancient proverb: "When you breathe, you hope." So as you take that next breath, try on the notion that maybe you have more hope and faith than you are allowing yourself to consider. Frankly, if you are reading this book, I'd say you still have some faith, even if it is in tatters.

Finding Meaning and Purpose Through the Three Gs

Most people want to know their life has meaning and purpose. Those of us with mystery maladies are being given a unique opportunity to find ours. This may be the blessing in our illness. But how do we find this meaning?

There is clearly no single right way. And there is no one purpose that is greater than any other. Each person must find the sense of their own purpose. For mystery malady patients who are physically limited in some way, we need to focus on finding purpose in things that do not require large amounts of strength and physical energy. They do, however, require commitment and sincerity. Here are my three Gs for finding meaning and purpose:

Giving

It is so easy to become wrapped up in yourself when you are ill. Staying focused on only yourself will eventually deaden your spirit. To nourish your spirit, you must give of yourself. There are so many small ways to give that don't require much except to come out of your preoccupied self-focus and be aware of others. Pay a compliment, give a smile, utter words of encouragement, make someone a cup of tea, or laugh at someone's joke. It is not as altruistic as it seems, because giving usually recirculates. Someone smiles back at you, returns the favor, gives you a hug, expresses their admiration. The gift of caring is the greatest gift that can be offered, and if you decide to give it, you will boost your own spirit.

In so many ways, giving is putting our love into action, especially when the giving is done without expecting something in return. Somehow we find that when we give with loving intent, we actually gain self-esteem by doing something of value. Loving others becomes part of loving ourselves, and we can delight in ourselves and our relationships even though we are not feeling well physically. Even when our gifts are small because they are limited by our health, they are gifts nonetheless, and the return can be surprisingly big.

Gratitude

Sometimes it takes deprivation to really make you appreciate things—like the lyrics from an old Joni Mitchell song: "You don't know what you got 'til it's gone." But better late than never. How many people have so much and yet always have a sense of deprivation? We do not have to feel that way. I love how Albert Einstein put it: "There are only two ways to live your life. One is as though nothing is a miracle. The other is as if everything is." I choose the latter.

There is no doubt that gratitude made the difference in a study of concentration camp prisoners. Those who stayed the healthiest had a coping style the researchers termed "the differential focus on the good."

So practice appreciation. Make a list of the wonderful people, places, and things you are grateful for in your life—even your illness! I bet you never really appreciated your health until you got sick.

Even if you are completely bedridden, you can still feel the coolness of the air conditioning in your bedroom when it is hot outside or the warmth of the central heating or fireplace when it is freezing cold beyond your walls. You can appreciate the light that streams in through your window at midday, the nurturing you receive from a caregiver, the music that soothes your spirit, or the television show that makes you laugh and distracts you from your illness. Enjoy the silence and stillness of the room, the comfort of the clock ticking. Take a deep breath, fill your lungs, and appreciate the air that fills them.

As with giving, gratitude has a calming effect. Expressing your gratitude creates a sense of loving and being loved, which is also essential to the nurturance of the spirit. It has an energy all its own, and it creates an invisible thread that binds us to the universe around us. It connects us and makes our spirit soar.

Grace

Just like faith, grace means different things to different people. To me, grace is forgiveness and compassion given to others, if for no other reason than because it was given to me. Maybe we are born with grace, but sometimes we lose it until it is awakened in us—often by something like a mystery malady.

We've all heard the saying "by the grace of God." Usually we are referring to some divine reprieve we've been granted. Grace is the divine help I didn't deserve, which in turn makes me think that if I received it, the universe felt I was worthy. If I am worthy, then isn't everyone? If so, we are all the same. Then who am I to judge another person? Just as I may have had reasons for what I did that may have hurt others, so perhaps they had reasons for the things they did to hurt me. Part of compassion is the granting of forgiveness, and it is grace not only for them but for me. The ability to let go of my own past mistakes and allow others to do the same is grace.

Carrying around self-righteousness and resentments over being wronged is too big a burden, especially if we want to get well. When we forgive, we can practically feel the tension and weight lift from our body and soul. So in order to allow our spirit to soar, we must release that burden. And in so doing, we often find the very purpose and meaning we seek.

Grace also helps us find meaning. My father seemed to have found grace for both himself and others through his humor. He probably wouldn't have admitted it, since he would have wanted everyone to believe he died the cynic he always was. But at some point toward the end of his days, his cynicism seemed to have left him. Just when you would think his fear would have been greatest, he seemed to have let go of the fears that were always present in the earlier days of his life. In his last days in the cancer ward—a pretty grim place—as he lay in his bed, every nurse and doctor who visited him left his room laughing.

Somehow my father had received grace. By laughing in the face of death and sharing his laughter with others, it was almost as if he were lifting everyone else's burdens with his humor and thus lifting his own as well. He passed away soon afterward, but I would like to believe he went out of this world with grace and a sense of well-being in his spirit.

By exercising the three Gs—giving, gratitude, and grace—you will inevitably, inexplicably find your own purpose. Maybe not today or tomorrow but eventually. I don't know how it works; I just know it has in my life. The great mythologist Joseph Campbell used to say we are having experiences all the time that hint at our hungers, our callings, our meaning, and our purpose. He insists we must, however, listen for them and learn to recognize them. I think by exercising the three Gs, we can become more alert to our hungers and callings. We may find a meaning in our experience of having a mystery malady that will transcend all the pain and doubt. We will find a different kind of health whether or not our body regains total physical well-being.

Case Study: Dr. Rosenbaum

In the fall of 1987, I (Lynn) had a mystery malady and was referred by my family physician to Jerry Rosenbaum, a board-certified rheumatologist and internist. Dr. Rosenbaum had developed a reputation as the doctor who could figure out your diagnosis when nobody else could.

On the day of my appointment, I pulled into a sleek, angled building that bore his name and seemed to be architecturally designed to reflect his cutting-edge professional image. I took the elevator to the second story and entered the waiting room. Like its exterior, the interior offices had a clean, crisp, modern design. The art was modern, and the waiting room was packed with patients.

When the nurse called my name, I was directed to an inner office, which contained a contemporary, neatly organized desk and a glass cabinet filled with an antique camera collection that had been started by the doctor but was now growing from contributions made by grateful patients. Dr. Rosenbaum, it seemed, had an eye for things—architecture, photography, art, and, judging by the numbers in the waiting room—medicine.

As I waited in his office, I wondered what this doctor could do for me. I had already received several contradictory and unpalatable diagnoses for my condition. After a few minutes, in strode a gray-haired man in his late thirties with an air of supreme confidence that bordered on arrogance. Like his office building and interior furnishings, even his clothes seemed calculated to project a sharp image—a stark white coat over his starched shirt and expensive silk tie.

He smiled but was rather formal, and we got right down to business. He listened to my lengthy history, including my various diagnoses, taking notes all the while. He stared at me with intense, intelligent eyes and proceeded to ask me a few questions, which I answered to the best of my ability.

Quite suddenly and without warning, he rose from his chair, walked around the desk to the chair in which I was seated and proceeded to palpate certain points on my body. Within moments, he announced that he'd determined my diagnosis. I frowned. I had been to the best of the best who had run test after test, and this doctor claimed to know my diagnosis in a matter of minutes. Although I obviously wanted to be cured, part of me wished he'd be wrong, just because of his smugness.

He required a further check in the examining room, but once he was finished, he informed me of my diagnosis and prescribed medication to correct the condition. Lo and behold, he was right. I was truly amazed and over time, we became personal friends.

From my perspective, Dr. Rosenbaum had the perfect life. He was obviously a gifted physician. He had an adoring wife who also happened to be a practicing physical therapist. Working from the third floor of their office building, Barbara Rosenbaum received patient referrals from her husband and his partners. It was an ideal setup.

They had three bright and beautiful children, two girls and a boy. They had a custom-built, beautifully furnished home on two acres of land in an affluent suburb of Miami. They had lots of dogs, cats, and original artwork. In addition to being a doctor, Jerry was quite a weekend welder, designing and crafting many whimsical original sculptures that dotted the two-acre landscape of their home.

His smugness, it turned out, was merely superficial; underneath was a loving husband and father and a talented artist. His life simply could not have been better, and to me, he was a fortunate man. But as I have come to learn over the years, each of our journeys is unique, and appearances are often deceiving.

One weekend, at the age of forty-five, Jerry was welding one of his wonderful creations. Although he was wearing his goggles, he suddenly felt as if he had sandpaper in his eyes. He paid little attention, believing he might have had a chemical exposure from the materials he was working with. From that day forward, however, his eyes became more and more troublesome.

He found himself blinking frequently. He developed extreme light sensitivity and was having trouble reading his patients' charts. His eyes were also extremely dry. When he finally visited an eye doctor, he was diagnosed with dry eyes and treated in the conventional manner with lubricating eyedrops. He used them as directed, but the condition persisted. He noted, "At first, I was quite annoyed to be bothered with such a silly problem. I figured I would simply wait it out and eventually it would get better."

At the same time, because he and his partners had built up such a successful medical practice, Jerry was approached by a managed-care company that wished to buy their group as well as several other rheumatology practices around the state. Jerry and his partners entered into negotiations to sell with the agreement that they would continue, as employees of this new company, to treat their patients.

Jerry was far too busy with these negotiations to deal with his dry eyes. When they got worse, he self-medicated with cortisone drops, even trying oral cortisone. Once the sale of the practice was completed, Jerry made curing his eyes a priority. "After the first couple of months of no symptom abatement, I was confused. Dry eyes should not have caused this much pain and difficulty. At first, I tried to ignore it as I was not prepared at this busy juncture in my life to be ill. I remained hopeful I would simply find a solution."

After treating himself with no success, he went back to the eye doctor. Collagen plugs were placed in his tear ducts so that any tears that formed would not drain out. This helped, but when it didn't resolve the problem, he made an appointment with a specialist at a highly regarded eye clinic in Miami. There, after a two-hour wait, he was given the same cortisone drops with which he had already treated himself and a pair of specialized contact lenses that were ostensibly to act as "bandages." Neither remedy worked, but Jerry kept practicing medicine with what was now apparently becoming a chronic problem. As with most chronic medical conditions, it started to consume his thoughts.

"I was now seriously distracted by my eye problem. Even so, I tried hard to keep my mind on my patients and their problems. I desperately wanted to remain the sympathetic physician I'd always considered myself to be. I was extremely concerned that my patients would feel I wasn't listening to them because I was quite literally having difficulty looking them in the eye. By the end of each day, I was irritable from having to deal with my patients' problems as well as my own. My discomfort and pain were beginning to feel overwhelming."

At this point, Jerry was distrustful of the diagnosis he had been given. He called another highly regarded eye clinic for a second opinion and waited months to be seen, only to be given immunosuppressive eyedrops, which didn't work. The second suggestion he received was to try antibiotics for several months; this was of no help either. Jerry then put humidifiers in his office and constructed plastic side panels for his glasses to prevent the evaporation of tears. This offered some relief, but the new glasses now attracted the curiosity of his patients.

"Up until that point I was annoyed and irritated, but now I became alarmed—and only because my patients were expressing so much concern for me. Interestingly enough, my fear was less about their legitimate concern for me than that my patients, who were seeking answers from me, would begin to distrust my ability to help them because I couldn't fix my own problems. I tried to reassure them, but inside me was a rising anxiety."

Jerry began to seek out the best ophthalmologists in the country, no less than a dozen specialists in five different cities. Unfortunately, in each city he received a different diagnosis, ranging from genetic to infectious to neurological causes. Still, none proved correct, and there was no relief to be found. Worse, he began to lose his sight, especially in the dark. He continued to function but, try as he might to deny it, the reality of his medical crisis began to settle in. He was in pain much of the time, and he could no longer drive himself anywhere after sunset. Apart from reporting to work each day, his life was becoming more limited, and he was becoming reclusive.

"Upon reflection, at this point, I was definitely beginning to exhibit some signs of depression. All I could think was how this could be happening to me. I tried to maintain hope. After all, hadn't I been the one who found answers for most of my patients when no else could?"

Jerry continued his search for answers and prescribed a new medication for himself which was designed to promote sweating and salivation and which he reasoned might promote tearing as well. It helped somewhat. In the meantime, he continued treating patients and functioning as a physician, but his condition continued to deteriorate, and he eventually developed an ulcer in his eye.

The doctors at the local eye clinic referred Jerry to another clinic in Boston. There, he spent two weeks being fitted with special plastic lenses that contained a tear solution. They felt like satellite dishes. Unfortunately, as sometimes happens when searching for the answer to a mystery illness, this "solution" only led to a much worse problem. He developed blisters on the surface of his eye, a condition his doctors had never seen.

"I always believed in science, not God, but since science was clearly not working, in desperation, I turned to a higher source. So I began my bargaining with God. I gave up my one vice—an occasional cigarette—and started attending temple regularly. I reasoned that if I met God halfway, He would return the favor by restoring my vision to normal. This got me nowhere."

The physicians in Boston sent Jerry for surgery to remove the outer layer of his cornea. This procedure, performed with a scalpel, was incredibly painful and turned out to be unsuccessful. Jerry was now missing substantial amounts of time from work due to his travels. He still refused to believe he was becoming too disabled to practice rheumatology. However, the managed-care company that had bought his practice and now employed him did. They fired him and sued him for misrepresenting that he was in good health at the time of the sale of the practice.

"I was in what you call true denial. I didn't want to believe I had become disabled to this degree. I worked until the company not only fired me but also sued me. I continued to drive my car until my wife finally restrained me. Only now can I admit being startled when I remember trying to perform a small joint injection on a patient only to later realize that I never came close to the joint! It seemed the worse my affliction became, the more I denied it. The more disabled I became, the busier I made myself to avoid facing it. I entered other business ventures just to distract myself from the knowledge that I was not okay. I slept less and did more. Worst of all, after the company fired me and I was at the lowest point in this process, I realized I was using my prescribed painkillers not just to numb the eye pain but also to numb my feelings of anger, despair, and anxiety. I stopped the pain medication immediately and became more determined than ever to fight back."

Jerry spent the next several years searching out a diagnosis and devising creative solutions. Based on different hypotheses, he tried alternative treatments. He located a physical therapist in Melbourne, Florida, who—at four-week intervals—placed Jerry under anesthesia and forced the glands of his eyes to express their fatty layer over the tears. Jerry attempted to modify his own hormonal balance to improve his own condition by using dehydroepiandrosterone (DHEA) and testosterone in correct amounts and even estrogen. He used Botox in his eyelids to relieve the incessant, involuntary blinking that was continuously scratching his corneas because the eyelids rubbed against his eyes with no tears to act as a buffer.

He developed different kinds of drops and ointments and ordered many others from around the world. He even had a piece of amniotic membrane sewn onto the surface of his eye to see if that would help. It didn't. He attended medical conferences and conventions and talked to everyone he could find who had some knowledge on this subject. He was having some positive results with his creative solutions, but as long as he couldn't define the root problem, he couldn't solve it.

In the meantime, his insurance wouldn't cover many of his experiments. His former medical partners were now testifying against him in the lawsuit brought by the managed-care company. His patients began seeing his partners for their medical care. The profession he'd so believed in and to which he had devoted his entire life was failing to come up with real solutions to his suffering. He felt deeply and profoundly betrayed.

Worse still, this betrayal was bringing back terrible memories from childhood. Jerry sank into a deep depression as he recalled being eleven years old and climbing a tree from which he fell, crushing his left leg. The family doctor set the leg improperly, and for five years, Jerry was in and out of body casts and wheelchairs and on crutches.

The first doctor's mistake was compounded by that of another who pinned a portion of Jerry's bone in such a way that the leg could not grow. As a direct result, while the rest of Jerry's body continued to develop into his teen years, the pinned leg did not. One leg became longer than the other. While it was the doctors who created the problems, Jerry's father blamed his son.

"I remember my father was so angry about the amount of time and money my problem was costing. He totally blamed me for this, and like most kids, I believed what my father told me. I genuinely felt that everything that was happening was my own fault. All I could do was try very hard not to make things any worse than they were. I learned early on not to complain. I tried not to be a bother and tried my utmost to never make my father angry or my mother hysterical. It became my job to take care of them, even though ironically, it was I who was suffering the physical and psychological damage. And that damage went on for years.

"As a teenager, I suffered shame and embarrassment when nurses bathed me while I was in body casts. I remember the kids at school making fun of me during my early adolescence—at the very time, like other kids, that I wanted desperately to fit in and be accepted. They called me a cripple and a freak.

"My only recourse, it seemed at the time, was to wait it out (the same as I was going to wait out my eye problem), read everything I could about medicine, and resolve to become a smarter doctor that the ones who had treated me. I wanted to try to help avoid for others that which I had to endure."

The events surrounding Dr. Rosenbaum's mystery eye malady were evoking the despair he thought he had long since buried. Old feelings of fear, powerlessness, and hurt resurfaced from an event in his life that had created such a similar hell.

"Here I was, some thirty years later, back in the same situation. My medical partners, the company I signed my practice away to, my patients, and my profession were not only unable to help me, they were betraying me. My partners and the company were blaming me just like my father had so many years ago. Once again, I was encountering one doctor after another who were not only unable to help me but, in some cases, were exacerbating my problem.

"Feelings of rage, guilt, and hopelessness that I must have repressed since childhood came rushing forward, welling up like a flooding river whose dam had broken. Worst of all, now I didn't even have the tears to cry with!"

Dr. Rosenbaum's feelings were boomeranging like billiard balls on a pool table. Sometimes he was furious; at other times, he sank into the depths of despair. But mostly he felt irrational guilt that somehow he must have caused this and was now ruining his family's lives as his medical problem replaced his children as the focus of his attention. He would then start the cycle all over again. It was a hopeless merry-go-round until he finally went into psychotherapy to deal with his complicated morass of feelings.

"With the help of a therapist, I came to understand that I was suffering from a form of post-traumatic stress disorder. I began a grieving process that accompanied the many losses I had suffered as a child and was now suffering as an adult as a result of my mystery illness. I had to let go of the one thing that made me feel good in life—being a doctor and solving my patients' problems. In fact, I had to face the possibility that I might never practice medicine again. I lost my professional relationships. I lost money. I lost my independence due to my vision impairment. The losses felt great enough that, from time to time, I questioned the very meaning of life itself."

Rarely does a mystery illness not trigger a psychological and spiritual crisis for people. Jerry was beginning to understand that he may have become a renowned doctor in part to overcome the rage, anger, shame, and feelings of powerlessness he'd experienced as a child. Being a doctor gave him the power instead of others, and with that power, he felt better about himself. So when his mystery illness took away his white coat—the very thing he needed to feel good about himself and give him purpose—he was confronted with a crisis.

Fortunately, Jerry had the courage and faith to take the opportunity to heal in the larger sense of the word. "When Lynn told me about the three Gs (giving, gratitude, and grace), it struck a chord. I figured I would try it. I started conferring with Lynn and others about their mystery maladies. I couldn't practice medicine like I used to, but I still had a great deal of experience and knowledge to give others. I even opened a tissue bank to help others like me. And even with my difficulties with my eyes, I opened them to see how much I still have in my life.

"As a result of these things, I started feeling better about myself again. Lynn always told me how grateful she was to me for my help with her mystery maladies, and I realized there were many people who had helped me as well. As I helped her with my medical knowledge, she helped me with her experience and understanding of how to get through my own crisis. Of course, I could hardly begin to express my profound gratitude to my family—my wife, my children, and my sister (who is a dentist and replaced every silver filling in my mouth in case those fillings were the cause of my problems). All of them have been right by my side through everything, and we are an extremely close family.

"And when I feel sorry for myself, I think about the therapist the doctors referred me to who was supposed to help me with my low-vision problem. I remember walking into his office 'loaded for bear'; I was angry and wanted to know what the heck he was going to do for me. When I entered his office, I found a man with no arms who was taking notes on my case with his feet. It humbled and reminded me that even with my mystery malady, I had a lot to be grateful for!

"As to grace, I know I have received grace through forgiveness and humor. I am still quick to anger, but I am also quick to forgive. I don't want to waste my time fighting with people. And I have learned to laugh at my situation. There were many times during the writing of this book when Lynn and I would howl with laughter about what cripples we were—she couldn't sit and I couldn't see. How do you write a book standing up and blind? But we did it.

"Finally, as others have become so dear to me, I know I am dear to them—with or without being a practicing doctor and with or without my physical health."

Sometimes things have a way of working out but not always in the way we think. To date, Jerry has not been able to get the correct diagnosis, but he has gained some symptomatic relief. His armor was shattered, but in its place, he has emerged a more whole human being. He is much more in touch with who he is and his value as a human being without the need for the white coat.

And as for his wanting to help people as a doctor so they didn't have to suffer as he did, he is doing just that. Because of his mystery malady, Jerry has been willing to devote his considerable talent and time to assist me in perfecting the Eight Step Method to Self-Diagnosis. By joining me in the writing of this book, he may actually help many more patients than he ever would have as a practicing physician.

"I know it may be hard to believe, but as Lynn has said many times to me and in this book, my mystery illness has actually been a gift. From it, I may have lost my practice, my profession, my wealth, and (partially) my sight. But now I 'see' clearer than ever, and I will certainly not allow my mystery malady to prevent me from living as rich and full a life as I am able to until I find a diagnosis."

Final Thoughts

Mastering others requires force; mastering self needs strength.
—CHINESE SAYING

MYSTERY MALADY PATIENTS may not be free of their condition, but they are free to take control of their health and move into action to help themselves. We hope that we have given you some positive and clear direction both in teaching you how to become your own medical detective and in sharing how to master your mystery malady and live well while you are searching for your solutions.

We hope by our candor, self-revelation, and experience you can believe that the same is possible for you. Follow the Eight Steps, create a partnership with your physician, try alternatives, and know you are not alone. Take care of yourself, take control of your attitudes, seek health in your mind and spirit even when your body is not well, and we guarantee you will find a greater wholeness. You now have all the tools you need, including—not the least important of these—hope.

If you feel like you are stumbling as you proceed along this path, refer back to specific sections of this book. It's not easy, but it's all here for you. And if, for any reason, you start to feel like you are losing hope because you haven't found your answers yet, know that this program has worked for us and many others. It can work for you!

APPENDIX A

Quick Reference Guide to the Eight Steps

Step One: Record the exact nature of your symptoms.

Step Two: Think about the history of your mystery malady.

Step Three: What makes your symptoms better (or worse)?

Step Four: Do a family medical history and determine if you have or had any blood relatives with a similar problem.

Step Five: Search for other past or present mental or physical problems.

Step Six: Categorize your current (and prior) significant medical problems by etiology.

Step Seven: Investigate your lifestyle and belief system.

Step Eight: Take your notebook to your physician and get a complete physical exam.

Tips for Doing the Eight Steps

Some of the questions that you'll be asking yourself in different steps may seem to overlap or duplicate one another. This is deliberate, so answer them carefully and completely anyway. The overlap is designed to pick up things you might have overlooked along the way.

Take your time in working through each step. If you don't know the answers immediately, start paying more attention to your body and see if you can make the determination over time.

If you are not certain at first whether a "symptom" is really a symptom, record it anyway with a question mark. By the time you are done, you will be able to either remove the question mark or eliminate that symptom altogether. Pay close attention to the things you want to dismiss immediately as having no bearing on your symptoms, for these may be the very things that can give rise to an important clue.

Step One: Record the Exact Nature of Your Symptoms

Symptoms Versus Signs

Medical textbooks describe *symptoms* as any perceptible change in the body or its functions that signals disease or phases of disease. A symptom is a sensation that only you can perceive and normally is not measurable (like pain or fatigue). A *sign* is an indication of illness that's actually observable and measurable (like a rash or a fever). For our purposes, we will refer to both generally as symptoms.

- Quality and character
- Quantity and severity
- Timing and duration
- Setting and environment
- Impact on your functioning
- Other factors

We urge you not to overlook any bodily change, no matter how insignificant it may seem to you.

Step Two: Think About the History of Your Mystery Malady

How long you have been having symptoms and when you first began having them are very important clues.

Step Three: What Makes Your Symptoms Better (or Worse)?

- Time-of-day factors
- Associated life events

Step Four: Do a Family Medical History and Determine If You Have or Had Any Blood Relatives with a Similar Problem

- It is often important to consider degrees of consanguinity (connectedness).
- Although unrelated, people of similar backgrounds often have similar conditions.

Step Five: Search for Other Past or Present Mental or Physical Problems

- Has anything else been bothering you? What about during the time previous to the "onset" of your current mystery malady?
- Have you had any emotional or psychiatric problems in the past? What about currently? Sometimes it is difficult to separate your distress about your medical condition from other stressors, but try to be objective.
- Do a systematic review of your systems: digestive, respiratory, circulatory, skeletal, cardiovascular, lymphatic, endocrine, nervous, muscu-

lar, reproductive, and urinary. Are you having difficulties within any of them?
- Try to obtain all of your medical records, past and present.

Step Six: Categorize Your Current (and Prior) Significant Medical Problems by Etiology

Etiology is the cause or causes of disease.

- Genetic
- Infectious (viral, bacterial, fungal, or parasitic)
- Structural or biomechanical
- Environmental
- Metabolic
- Traumatic
- Iatrogenic (medically induced)
- Psychological

Step Seven: Investigate Your Lifestyle and Belief System

- What does an ordinary day entail for you, and has it been modified by your illness?
- In general, how do you cope with your illness?
- Have you coped with other illnesses in the same way?
- Are there financial problems related to your job or lack of a job?
- How do you unwind from the stress of daily living?
- How are you coping with difficult issues? Do you eat more or differently than normal? Do you drink, smoke a joint, pop a pill? Meet and go home with people from bars, clubs, or parties? Or do you prefer to be alone, avoid social contact, not eat, watch TV all night, surf the Net for hours, or exercise excessively? Do you overspend or collect things and then refuse to return or discard them? How do you unwind from stress?

- Does it ever feel like your past sometimes affects your behavior in the present? For example, do you repress your anger? Do you avoid social contact because you are afraid of getting hurt like you were in the past?
- Are you getting enough rest and relaxation? How do you feel about sleeping more than seven hours, napping in the afternoon, sleeping late, relaxing in general, and leaving chores undone in order to have time for fun or relaxation?
- Do you feel you have to be perfect?

Step Eight: Take Your Notebook to Your Physician and Get a Complete Physical Exam

Refer to Chapter 4 on this step.

Appendix B

Useful Websites

For our official website, visit diagnosishelp.org.

Government Sites

• The Centers for Disease Control and Prevention (CDC) maintains a site with a long list of health topics (www.cdc.gov). Both infectious diseases and noninfectious diseases are covered. Links to other sites regarding public health issues are provided. For the diseases covered, the site gives a quick and understandable explanation or definition and then lists further resources, both on and off the Web.

• Healthfinder (healthfinder.gov) is a site put up by the U.S. Department of Health and Human Services as a gateway to reliable health information for consumers. Topics include AIDS, heart disease, and fibromyalgia. There is a list of national support groups for various conditions. A Spanish version is also available. A master list of health information from federal government agencies can be found here.

• Consumer Drug Information (www.fda.gov) is run by the Food and Drug Administration (FDA) to educate the public on new medications. Also covered are drug recalls, safety issues, and hot topics. Here you can learn what is regulated by the FDA, including radiation-emitting products (cell phones) and foodborne illnesses.

• The Drug and Herbal Database (http://my.webmd.com/medical _information/drug_and_herb/default.htm) is an evidence-based, alphabetized database of drugs and herbs designed for consumer use.

• Supplement Watch (www.supplementwatch.com) This website offers (for a charge of $25) in-depth, documented reviews of various herbs and supplements.

Pediatric Sites

• The American Academy of Pediatrics (aap.org) provides information on children's health.

• Children's Health Environmental Coalition (checnet.org) has a website devoted to preventable health and development problems caused by exposure to toxic substances in homes, schools, and communities.

• The National Institute of Mental Health (nimh.nih.gov) provides information and publications at no charge on a variety of issues such as eating disorders, attention deficit/hyperactivity disorder, autism, and learning disabilities.

Organization Sites

• Medem (medem.com) is a for-profit site that is owned by the American Medical Association (AMA) along with several other medical societies. Its mission is to provide the most comprehensive information in the world: "Together with leading health care partners, Medem has established the premier physician-patient communications network, designed to facilitate online access to information and care for more than 90,000 physicians, their practices and their patients, while saving patients time and money and helping physicians generate revenue."

• The AMA has a Health Information page (ama-assn.org/ama/pub/cat egory/3158.html) with links to Medem and a physician locator. The physician locator has information about doctors in your area. It allows you to research U.S. doctors (almost seven hundred thousand of them) by name, specialty, and location. You can consult the site's medical library or read information supplied by the doctors about their practices.

• AAFP Health Information for Patients (http://familydoctor.org) has a good collection of patient handouts and is sponsored by the American Academy of Family Physicians.

• The American Heart Association's website (americanheart.org) provides rather extensive information on topics related to cardiovascular health.

• The American Cancer Society (cancer.org) gives a complete listing and discussion of cancer-related medications and a section devoted to alternative therapies.

Search/Index Sites

• Yahoo Health (yahoo.com/health) is generally a bad place to start looking for information.

• HealthlinkUSA (healthlinkusa.com) has comprehensive listings of diseases and conditions with links to pertinent sites on the Web. Their site describes itself as having "excellent health information concerning treatment, cures, prevention, diagnosis, risk factor, research, support groups, email lists, personal stories, and much more."

• MedExplorer (medexplorer.com) had an extensive collection of medically related sites that do not work as of this writing. It was originally a good search engine but is now a good example of what happens when a website changes over time and completely focuses on selling prescription items for a profit.

• eMedicine.com (emedicine.com) has evidence-based, peer-reviewed articles that subscribe to honor code principles on over seven thousand diseases and disorders. Registration is required, but there is no fee. It is regularly updated.

• Health on the Net (www.hon.ch) is a nonprofit project based in Switzerland (see Chapter 5).

• Knowledge Finder (www.kfinder.com), part of Aries Systems' website, allows you to enter your search query in natural language and then automatically maps it to the underlying terms in the database. For example, if you type in *use of Ritalin to treat ADHD*, your search will be mapped automatically as follows: *Ritalin* will be changed to the generic drug name *methylphenidate*; *ADHD* will be expanded to *attention deficit/hyperactivity disorder*; and synonyms for *treat*, such as *therapeutics*, will be retrieved. The site claims faster results and draws information from MEDLINE and Pre-MEDLINE (updated weekly). There is a fee for using Knowledge Finder, but the site does offer a thirty-day free access trial after registration.

• PDRhealth (pdrhealth.com) includes the Physician's Desk Reference for prescription and herbal medicines and information on numerous drug interactions. Registration is required, but no fee.

• Medline Plus (medlineplus.gov) has the excellent ability to research topics from AIDS to toxicology. Once the preserve of physicians, this version of MEDLINE's formidable database is easier for laypeople to use and is open to everyone. You can easily search for a symptom, condition, or disease and get quick links to studies, definitions, news about clinical trials, a dictionary of strong drugs, and an illustrated medical encyclopedia. For heavy-duty medical information, go to nlm.nih.gov for tools from the U.S. National Library of Medicine and the core MEDLINE database.

• The Merck Manual (merck.com/mrkshared/mmanual_home2/home .jsp) is a service of the pharmaceutical giant for all things medicinal.

• The Food and Drug Administration Center for Drug Evaluation and Research (www.fda.gov/cder/orange/default.htm) enables you to compare prescription, over-the-counter, and even discontinued drugs by name and ingredient.

• For information on complementary and alternative medicine, try www.nccam.nci.nih.gov and www.ahrq.gov, which offer excellent, comprehensive information about all available therapies and how to find the best practitioners.

Medical Center Sites

• The Mayo Clinic Health Oasis (mayohealth.org) is one of the better-known and -run sites for consumer health information. There is a complete drug reference guide for consumers, an extensive list of articles, and an "Ask the Mayo Physician" area where fairly extensive answers and links are given for commonly asked questions.

• Oncolink (oncolink.org) is a site from the University of Pennsylvania Cancer Center that has explanations about chemotherapy drugs and treatments.

• InteliHealth (www.intelihealth.com) is a joint venture between Aetna US Healthcare and Harvard Medical School's Consumer Health Information. It has sections for consumers and professionals. You can also exchange information with others who have the same health problem you do and learn about treatment options they may have tried or heard about. Visitors can find drug information, including recent approvals and recalls as well as discussion boards and chat rooms organized by topic. "Ask the Expert" has some well-thought-out answers.

• Net Wellness (netwellness.org) is the collaborative effort of three university medical centers and includes an "Ask an Expert" section.

• Duke University (dukehealth.org) has a site with the ability to look up symptoms. Go to the health library and the "A-Z Health Encyclopedia." Enter the symptom you want to look up on the "health library" line.

Notes

Chapter 1

1. *New York Times*, "Errors that kill medical patients," December 18, 2002.
2. John D. Lantos, *Do We Still Need Doctors?* (New York: Routledge, 1997).
3. Geoffrey Cowley, "How progress makes us sick." *Newsweek*, May 5, 2003.
4. Natalie Angier, *New York Times*, May 6, 2001, p. 67.

Chapter 2

1. *Harrison's Principles of Internal Medicine, 15th Edition.* New York: McGraw-Hill Professional, 2001; p. 2540.
2. Mary Shoman, *Living Well with CFS and Fibromyalgia.* New York: HarperResource, 2004.
3. Katrina Berne, Ph.D., *Chronic Fatigue Syndrome, Fibromyalgia, and Other Invisible Illnesses.* Hunter House Publishers, 2002.
4. *Harrison's Principles of Internal Medicine, 15th Edition.* New York: McGraw-Hill Professional, 2001; p. 2010.
5. *Harrison's Principles of Internal Medicine, 15th Edition.* New York: McGraw-Hill Professional, 2001; p. 1922.
6. Bell, Baldwin et al. "Illness from low levels of environmental chemicals: relevance to chronic fatigue syndrome and fibromyalgia." *American Journal of Medicine*, 1998: 105. California Department of Health Services, Am J Public Health, 2004.

7. *Harrison's Principles of Internal Medicine, 15th Edition*. New York: McGraw-Hill Professional, 2001; pp. 2493, 2412.

8. *Miami Herald*, "Understanding autoimmune disease," March 20, 2003.

9. Randolf Evans, M.D. WebMD.com, "What causes headaches?"

10. P. Sandroni et al., "Complex regional pain syndrome, incidence and prevalence," *Pain*, 2003 May–Nov. 106 (1-2): 209-210.

11. M. D. Hord et al., "Reflex sympathetic dystrophy," emedicine.com, viewed February 19, 2004.

12. Manish K. Singh, M.D., "Chronic pelvic pain," emedicine.com, citing several authors under the topic of chronic pelvic pain.

13. Fred Ferri, *Ferri's Clinical Advisor*. C. V. Mosby, 2005.

14. Paul J. Donohue, Ph.D., and Mary E. Seigel, Ph.D., *Sick and Tired of Being Sick and Tired: Living with Invisible Chronic Illness*. W. W. Norton & Company, 1992.

15. Howard Glazer, Ph.D., and Gae Rodke, M.D., *The Vulvodynia Survival Guide*. New Harbinger Publications, 2002.

16. National Institute of Occupational Safety and Health, NY Committee for Occupational Safety and Health.

17. *Harrison's Principles of Internal Medicine, 15th Edition*. New York: McGraw-Hill Professional, 2001; p. 2067.

18. R. A. Aronowitz, "When do symptoms become a disease?" *Annals of Internal Medicine* 2001; 134: 803–8.

19. K. Kroenke and L. Harris, "Symptoms research: a fertile field," *Annals of Internal Medicine* 2001; 134: 801–2.

20. E. A. Walker, and others, "Understanding and caring for the distressed patient with multiple medically unexplained symptoms," *Journal of the American Board of Family Practitioners* 1999 Mar–Apr; 12(2): 182–83.

21. Centers for Disease Control and Prevention, Special Pathogens Branch, "Tracking a mystery disease: the detailed story of hantavirus pulmonary syndrome." See Case Information, National Center for Infectious Diseases, Special Pathogens Branch, www.cdc.gov.

Chapter 5

1. G. Eysenbach and C. Kohler, "How do consumers search for and appraise health information on the world wide web? Qualitative study using focus groups, usability tests, and in-depth interviews," *British Medical Journal* 2002 Mar 9; 324(7337): 573–7.
2. H. W. W. Potts and J. C. Wyatt, "Survey of doctors' experience of patients using the Internet," *Journal of Medical Internet Research* 2002; 4(1):e5.
3. R. Styra, "The Internet's impact on the practice of psychiatry," *Canadian Journal of Psychiatry* 2004 Jan; 49(1):5–11.
4. A. G. Crocco, and others, "Analysis of cases of harm associated with use of health information on the Internet," *Journal of the American Medical Association* 2002 Jun 5; 287(21): 2869–71.
5. M. Martin-Facklam, and others, "Quality of drug information on the World Wide Web and strategies to improve pages with poor information quality. An intervention study on pages about sildenafil," *British Journal of Clinical Pharmacology* 2004 Jan; 57(1): 80–85.
6. S. Adams, "Assessment strategies: How patients cope with the diverse quality levels of websites when searching for health information," *Proceedings of the American Medical Informatics Association Symposium* 2003: 774.
7. S. J. Darmoni, and others, "Level of evidence as a future gold standard for the content quality of health resources on the Internet," *Methods of Information in Medicine* 2003; 42(3): 220–25.
8. G. Eysenbach, and others, "A framework for improving the quality of health information on the world-wide-web and bettering public health: The MedCERTAIN approach," *Medinfo* 2001; 10(Pt 2): 1450–54.
9. A. Gagliardi and A. R. Jadad, "Examination of instruments used to rate quality of health information on the internet: Chronicle of a voyage with an unclear destination," *British Medical Journal* 2002 Mar 9; 324(7337): 569–73.
10. G. Eysenbach and C. Kohler, "How do consumers search for and appraise health information on the world wide web? Qualitative

study using focus groups, usability tests, and in-depth interviews,"
British Medical Journal 2002 Mar 9; 324(7337): 573–77.

11. S. Sagaram, and others, "Evaluating the prevalence, content and read-
    ability of complementary and alternative medicine (CAM) web pages
    on the Internet," *Proceedings of the American Medical Informatics Asso-
    ciation Symposium* 2002: 672–6.

12. M. A. Graber and M. Weckmann, "Pharmaceutical company internet
    sites as sources of information about antidepressant medications,"
    CNS Drugs 2002; 16(6): 419–23.

13. M. A. Veronin and G. Ramirez, "The validity of health claims on the
    World Wide Web: a systematic survey of the herbal remedy Opun-
    tia," *American Journal of Health Promotion* 2000 Sep-Oct; 15(1):
    21–28.

Chapter 9

1. Denise Grady, "Fat: The secret life of a potent cell," *New York Times*,
   July 6, 2004.
2. Ibid.

Chapter 11

1. John E. Sarno, *Healing Back Pain: The Mind-Body Connection*. New
   York: Warner Books, 1991.

Chapter 12

1. Alice Miller, *Thou Shalt Not Be Aware: Society's Betrayal of the Child*.
   New York: Farrar, Straus and Giroux, 1984.

Chapter 14

1. Peter A. Levine, *Waking the Tiger: Healing Trauma: The Innate Capacity to Transform Overwhelming Experiences*. Berkeley, CA: North
   Atlantic Books, 1977.

2. McCraty, Atkinson, and others, *BrainMind Bulletin*, November 1995, p. 1.

Chapter 15

1. Kurt Kroenke, M.D., "Symptoms research: a fertile field." *Annals of Internal Medicine*, May 1, 2001. 134; 9: 801–802.

Chapter 16

1. Victor Frankl, *Man's Search for Meaning*. Beacon Press, 2000.

Index